TIMES SQUARE

THE WORK IS LOCATED ON A PEDESTRIAN ISLAND: A TRIANGLE FORMED BY THE INTERSECTION OF BROADWAY AND SEVENTH AVENUE, BETWEEN FORTY-SIXTH AND FORTY-FIFTH STREETS, IN NEW YORK CITY'S TIMES SQUARE.

THE AURAL AND VISUAL ENVIRONMENT IS RICH AND COMPLEX. IT INCLUDES LARGE BILLBOARDS, MOVING NEON SIGNS, OFFICE BUILDINGS, HOTELS, THEATERS PORNO CENTERS AND ELECTRONIC GAME EMPORIUMS. ITS POPULATION IS EQUALLY DIVERSE, INCLUDING TOURISTS, THEATREGOERS, COMMUTERS, PIMPS, SHOPPERS, HUCKSTERS AND OFFICE WORKERS. MOST PEOPLE ARE IN MOTION, PASSING THROUGH THE SQUARE. THE ISLAND, AS IT IS THE JUNCTION OF SEVERAL OF THE SQUARE'S PATHWAYS, IS SOMETIMES CROSSED BY A THOUSAND OR MORE PEOPLE IN AN HOUR.

THE WORK IS AN INVISIBLE UNMARKED BLOCK OF SOUND ON THE NORTH END OF THE ISLAND. ITS SONORITY, A RICH HARMONIC SOUND TEXTURE RESEMBLING THE AFTER RING OF LARGE BELLS, IS AN IMPOSSIBILITY WITHIN ITS CONTEXT. MANY WHO PASS THROUGH IT, HOWEVER, CAN DISMISS IT AS AN UNUSUAL MACHINERY SOUND FROM BELOW GROUND.

FOR THOSE WHO FIND AND ACCEPT THE SOUND'S IMPOSSIBILITY THOUGH, THE ISLAND BECOMES A DIFFERENT PLACE, SEPARATE, BUT INCLUDING ITS SURROUNDINGS. THESE PEOPLE, HAVING NO WAY OF KNOWING THAT IT HAS BEEN DELIBERATELY MADE, USUALLY CLAIM THE WORK AS A PLACE OF THEIR OWN DISCOVERING.

MAX NEUHAUS

Times Square

Extant: 1977–92 and 2002–present
Location: Pedestrian island in Times Square
between 45th and 46th streets, New York City
Collection Dia Art Foundation, New York

Max Neuhaus's *Times Square* is an unmarked sound installation sited at the north end of a triangular pedestrian island in midtown Manhattan. Its rich harmonic soundscape emerges from a subway ventilator shaft beneath a sidewalk grating.

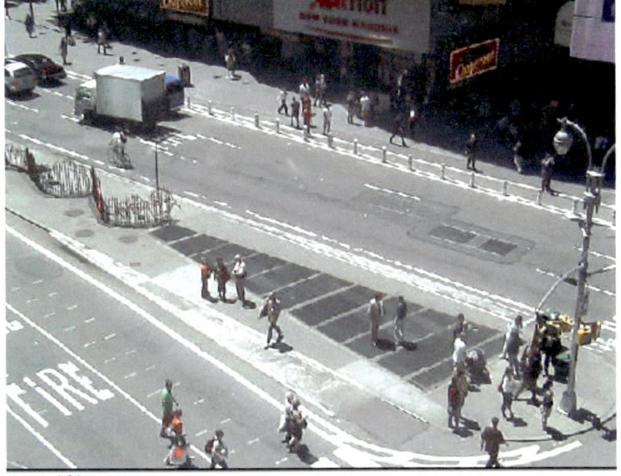
Live 1:24 pm

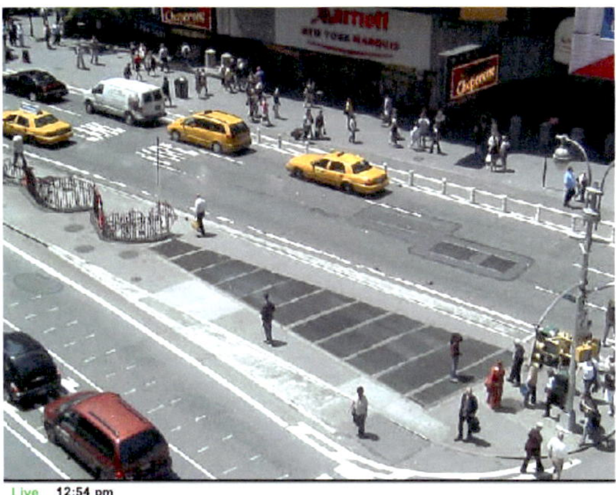
Live 12:54 pm

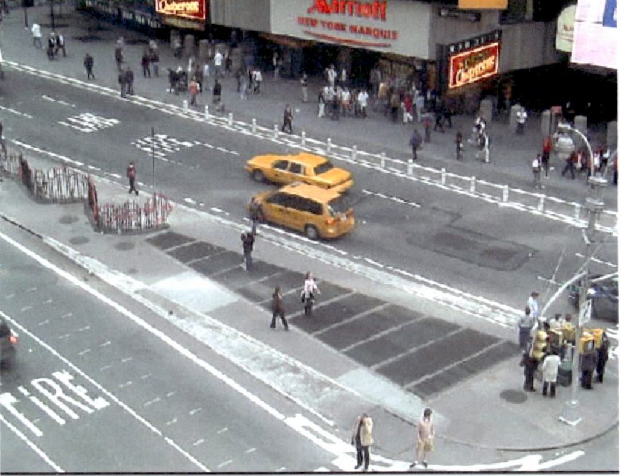
Live 3:49 pm

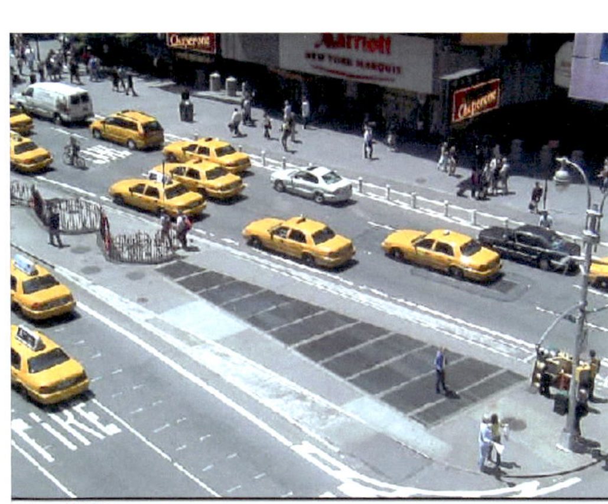
Live 12:55 pm

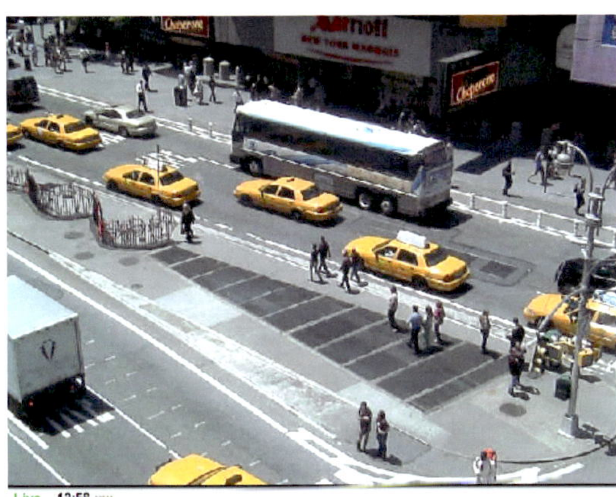
Live 12:52 pm

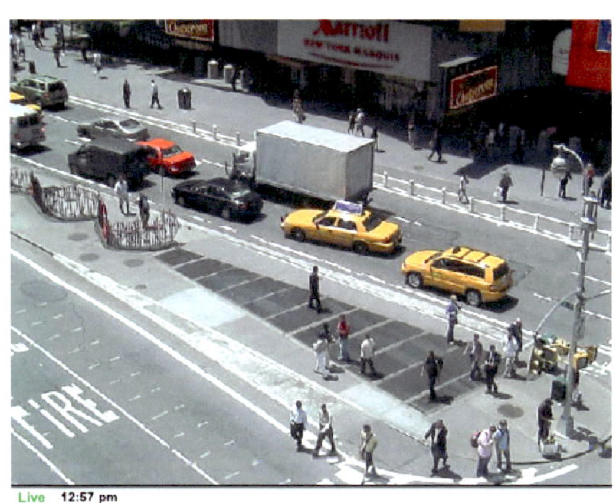
Live 12:57 pm

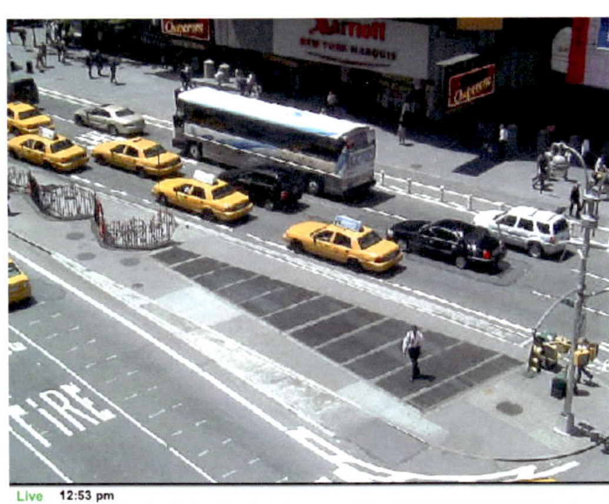
Live 12:53 pm

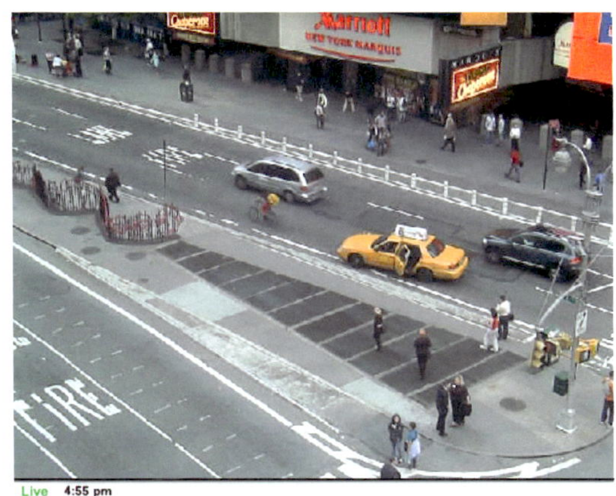
Live 4:55 pm

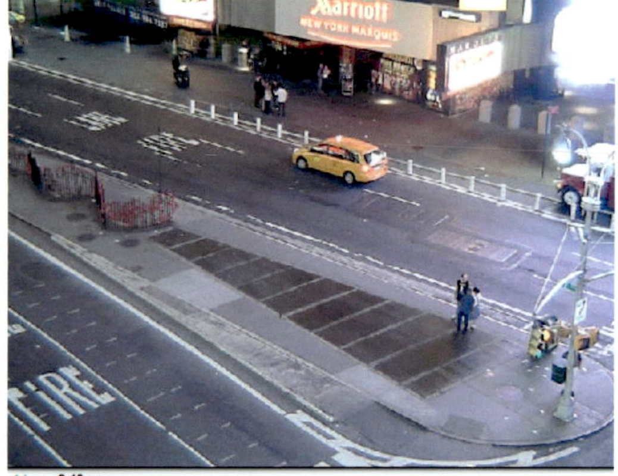

Live 2:43 am

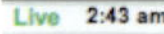

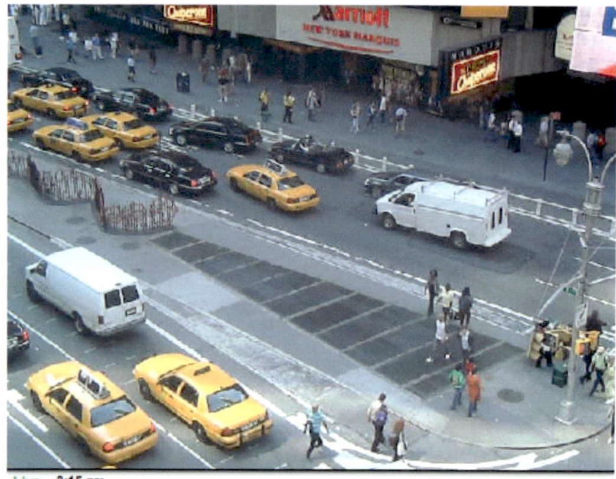

Live 3:15 pm

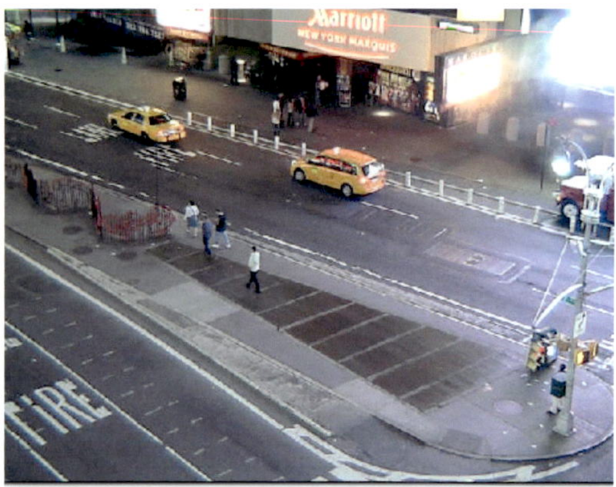

Live 2:43 am

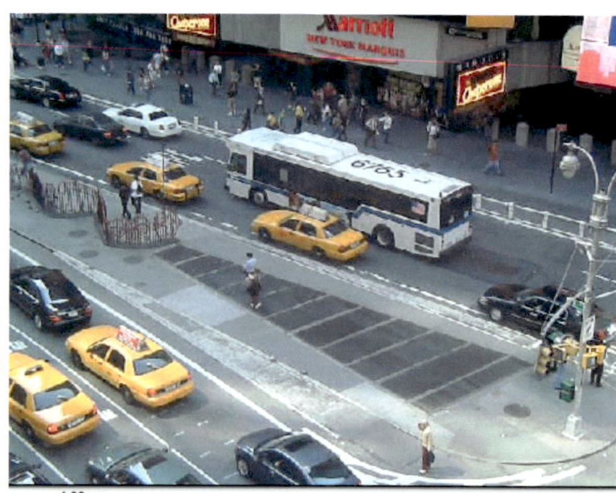

4:00 pm

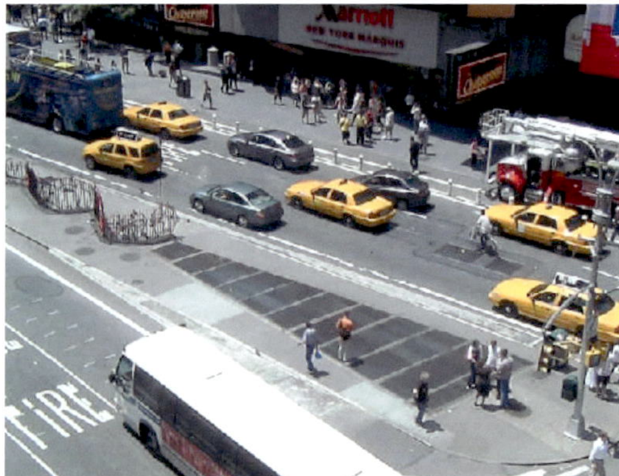

Live 12:54 pm

Live 12:53 pm

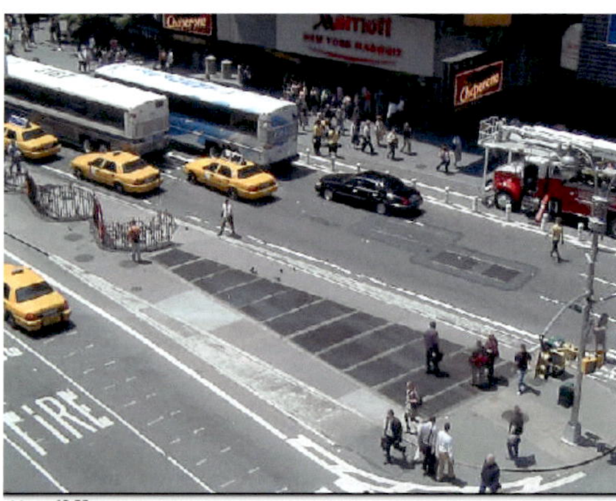

Live 12:55 pm

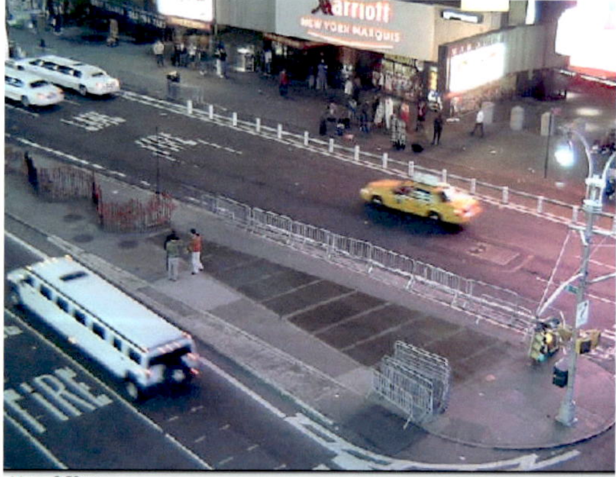

Live 2:52 am

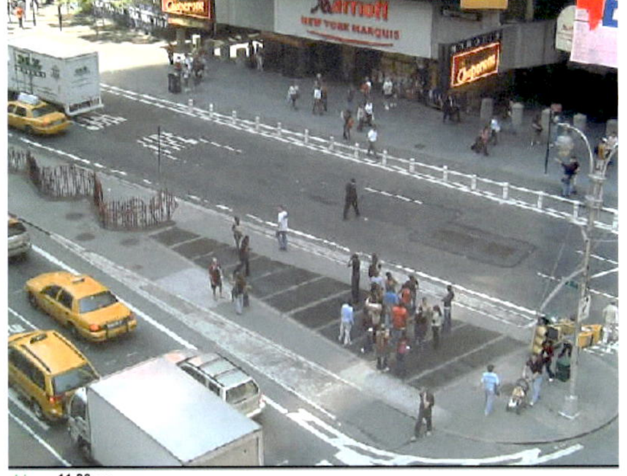

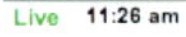
Live 11:26 am

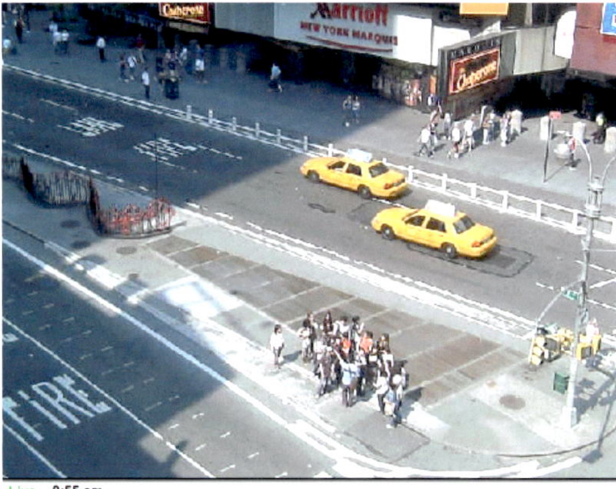

Live 9:55 am

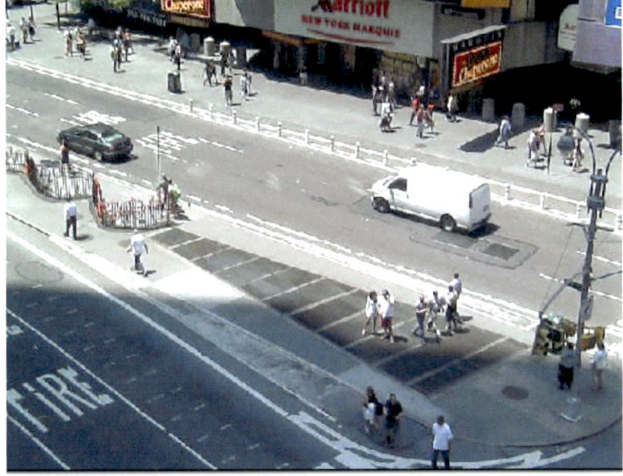

Live 12:29 pm

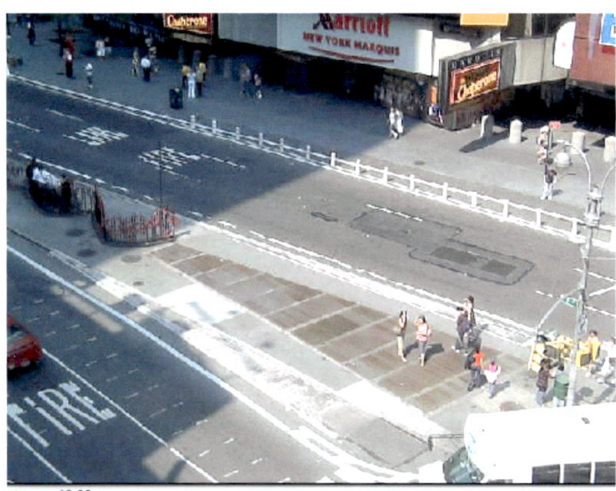

Live 10:00 am

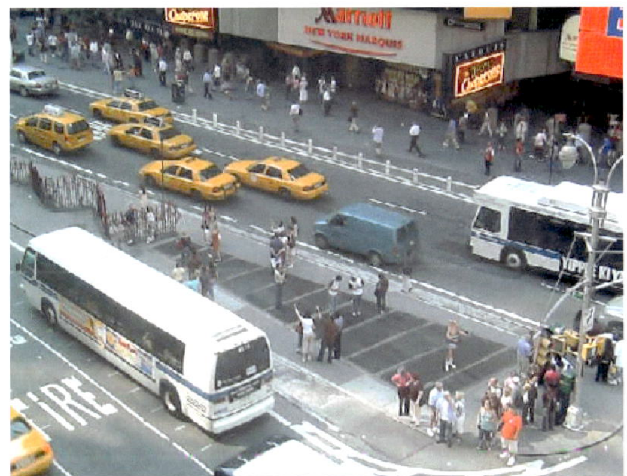

Live 3:15 pm

Live 10:08 am

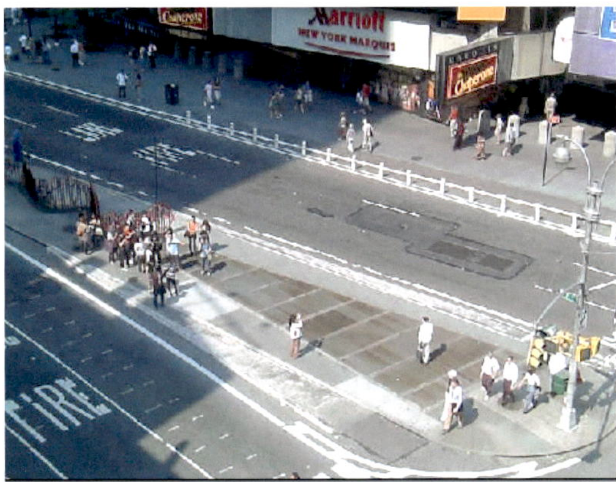

Live 9:54 am

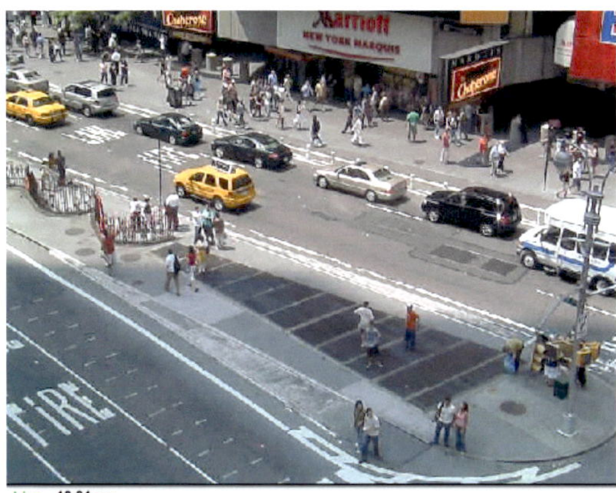

Live 12:24 pm

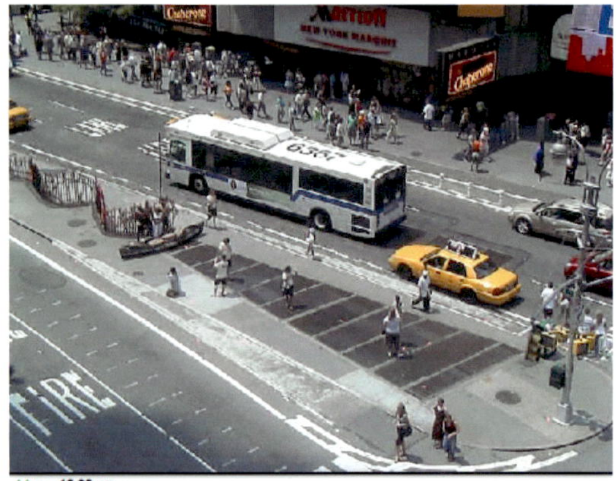

Live 12:38 pm

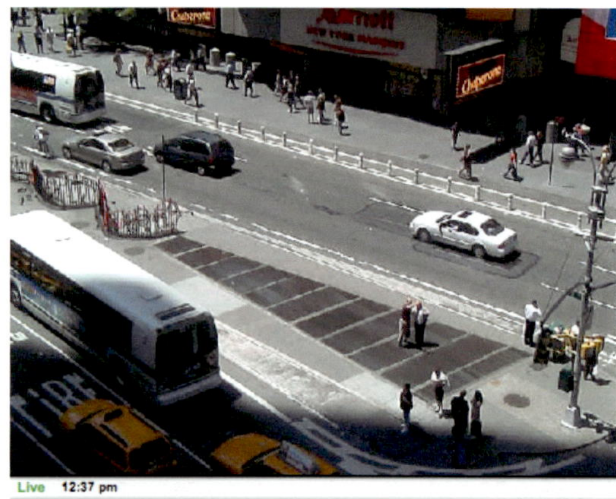

Live 12:37 pm

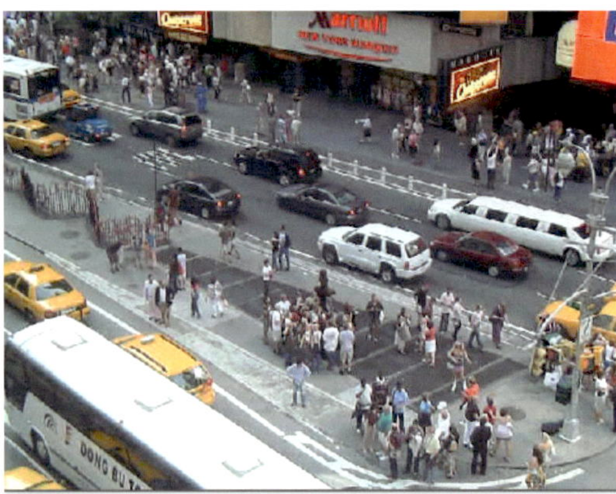

Live 4:55 pm

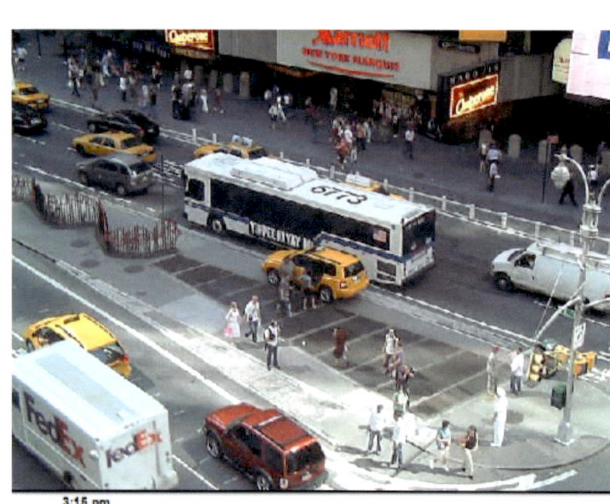

3:15 pm

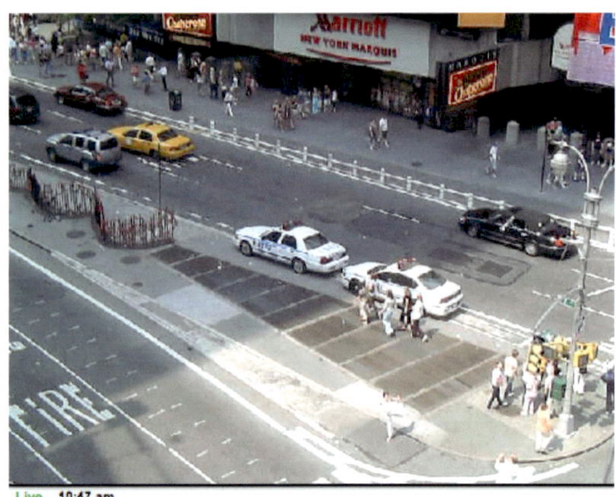

Live 10:47 am

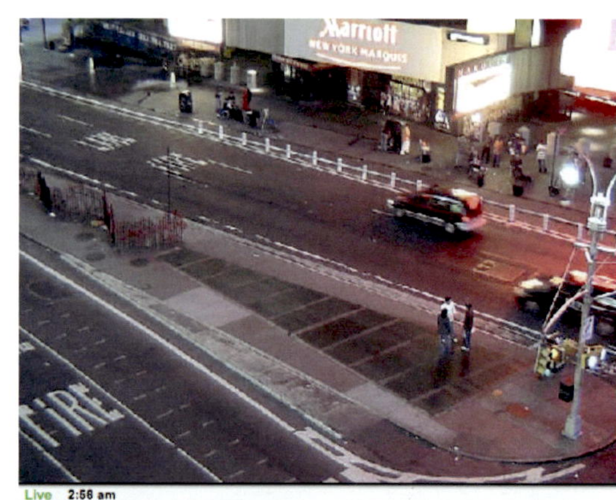

Live 2:56 am

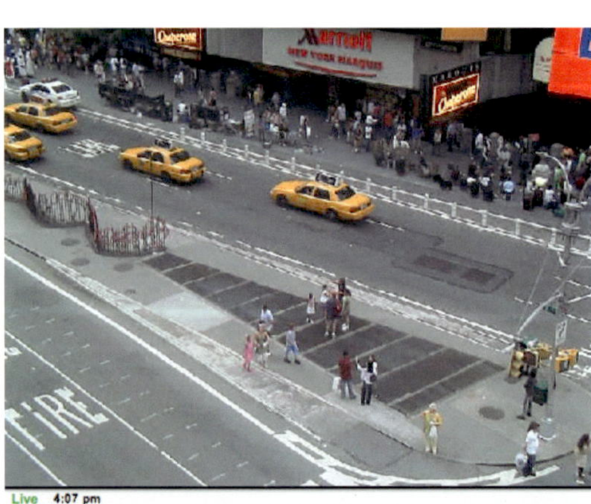

Live 4:07 pm

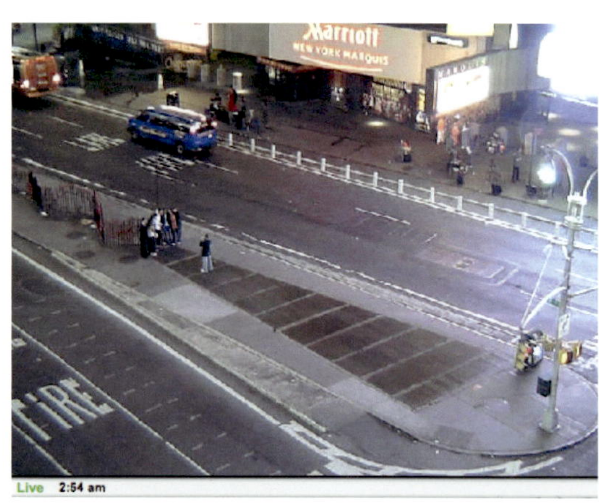

Live 2:54 am

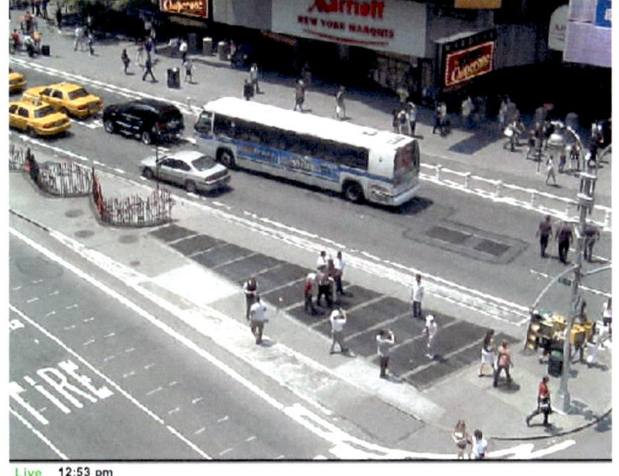

Live 12:53 pm

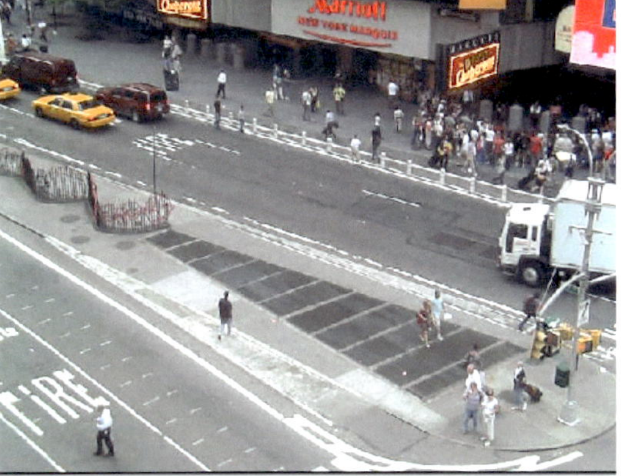

Live 3:02 pm

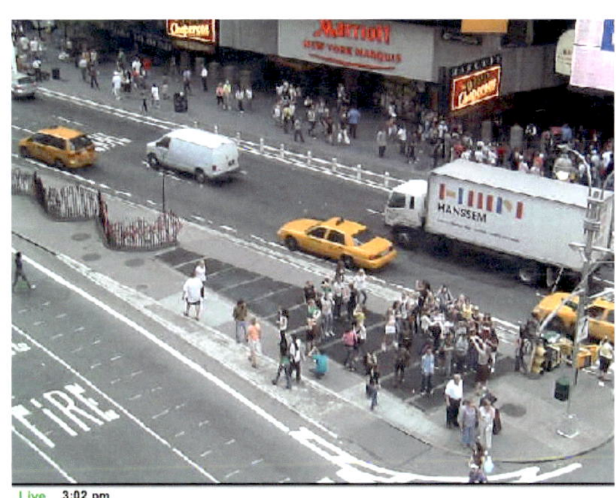

Live 3:02 pm

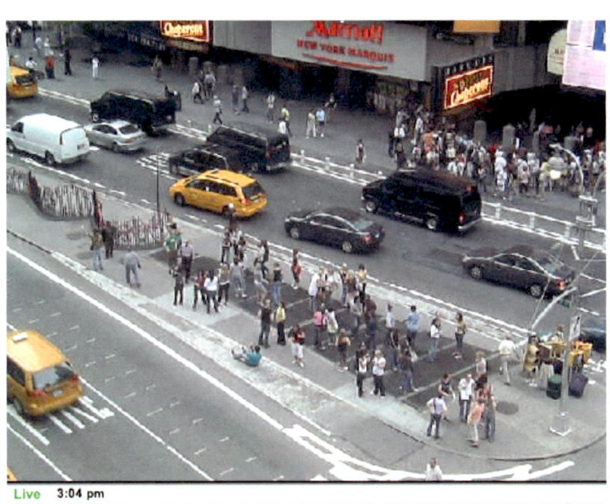

Live 3:04 pm

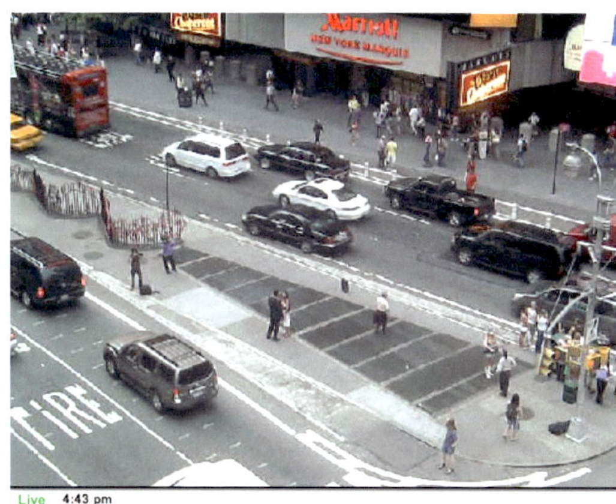

Live 4:43 pm

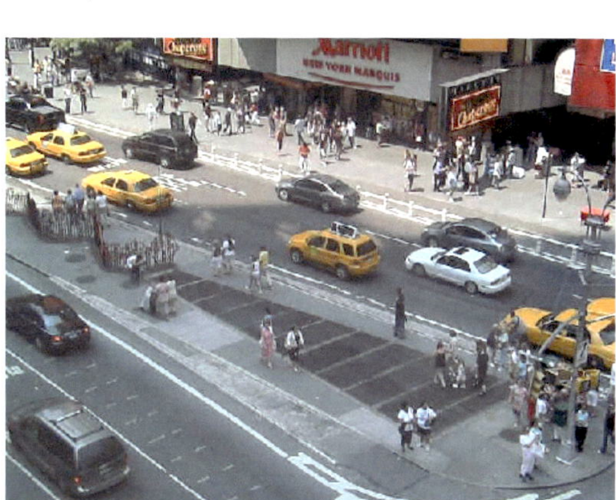

Live 12:10 pm

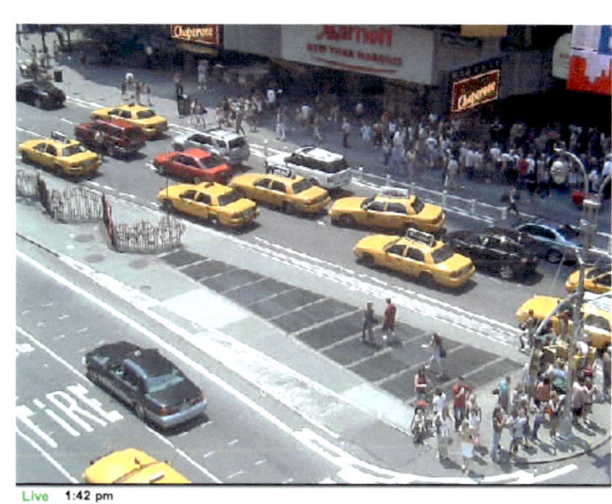

Live 1:42 pm

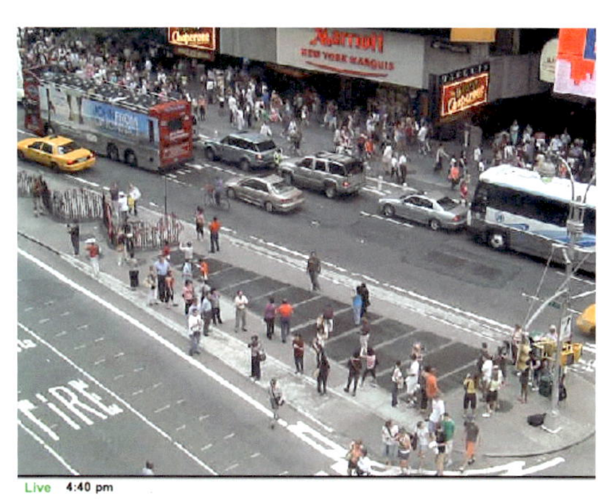

Live 4:40 pm

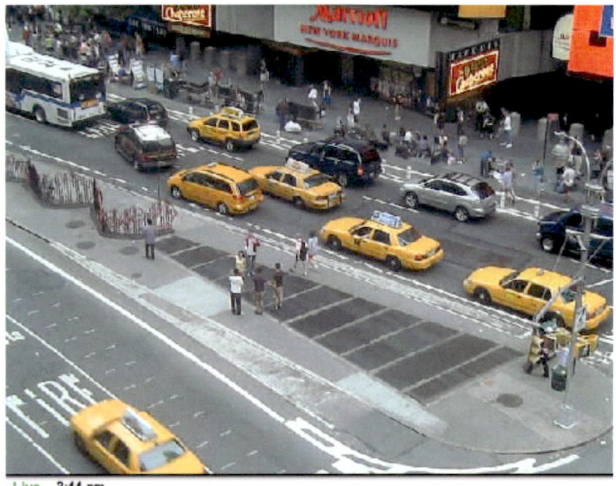

Live 2:44 pm

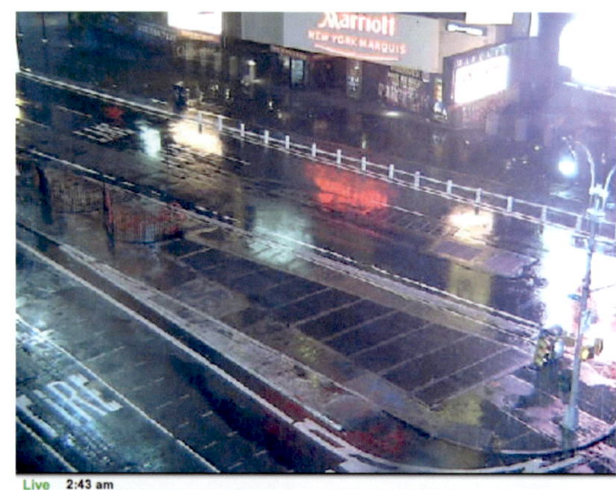

Live 2:43 am

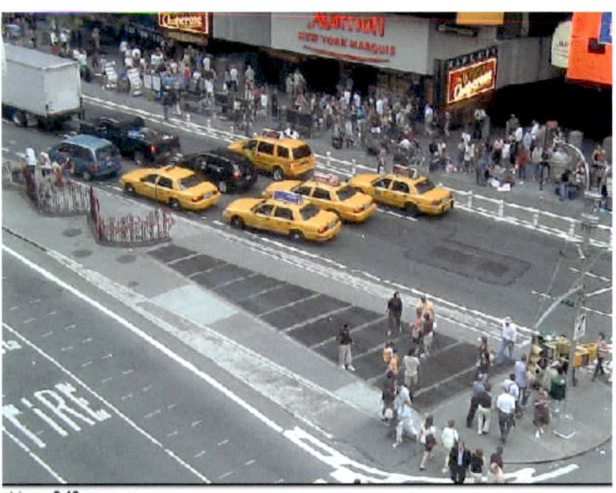

Live 2:46 pm

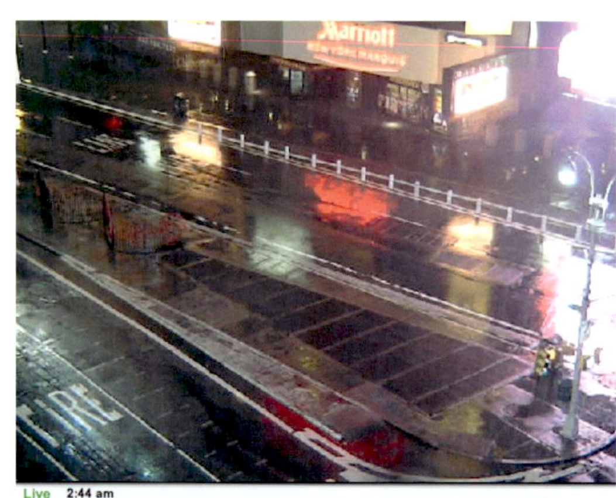

Live 2:44 am

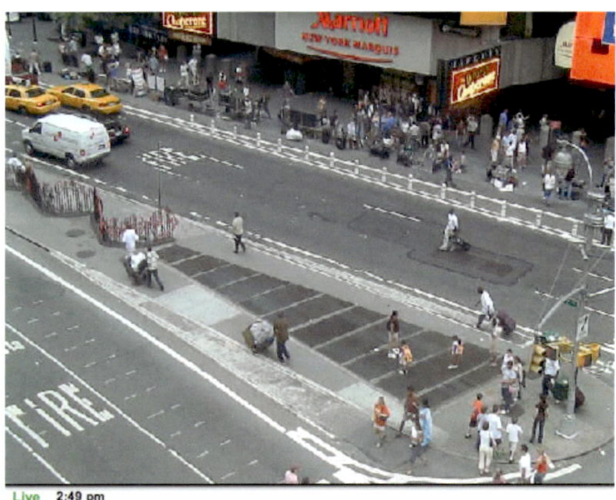

Live 2:49 pm

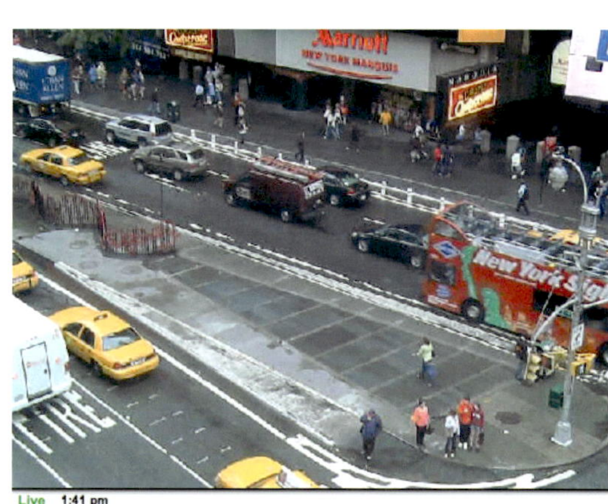

Live 1:41 pm

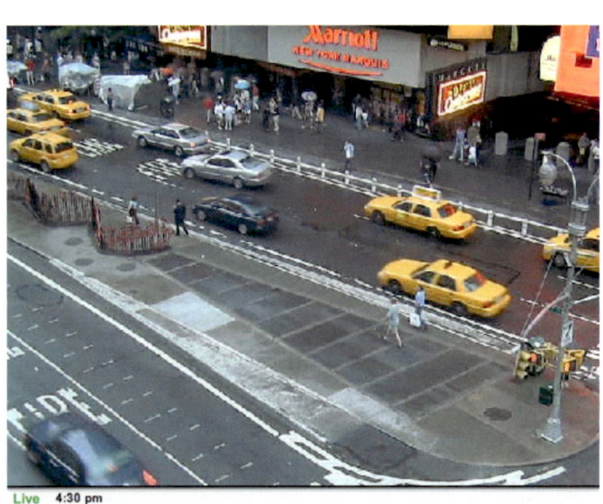

Live 4:30 pm

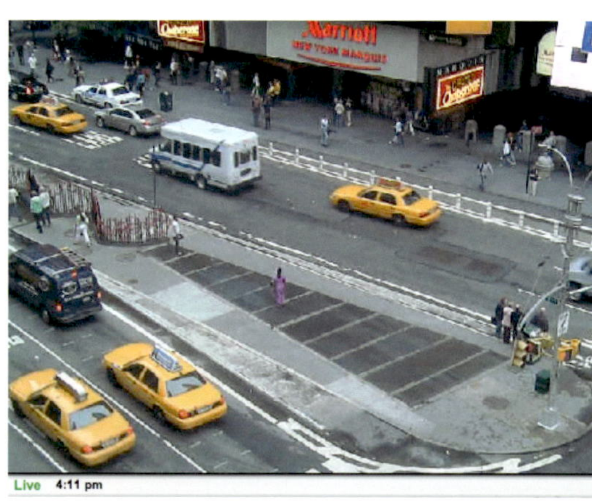

Live 4:11 pm

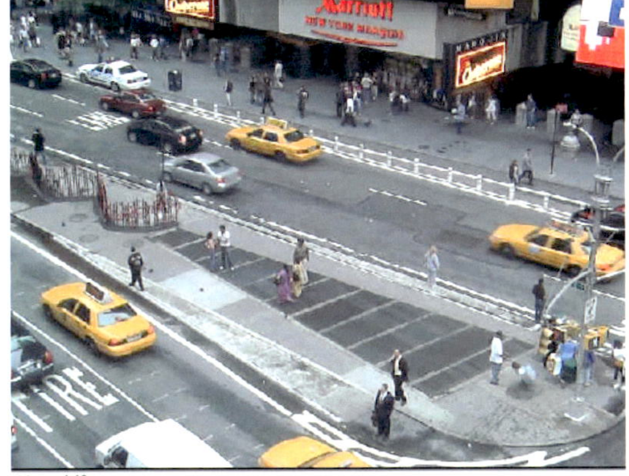
Live 4:13 pm

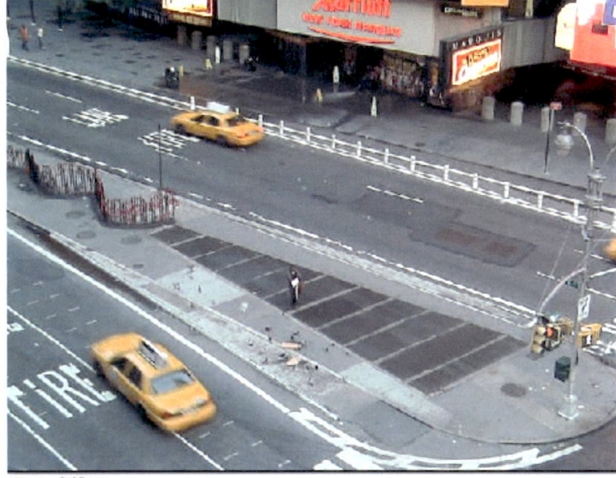
Live 6:15 am

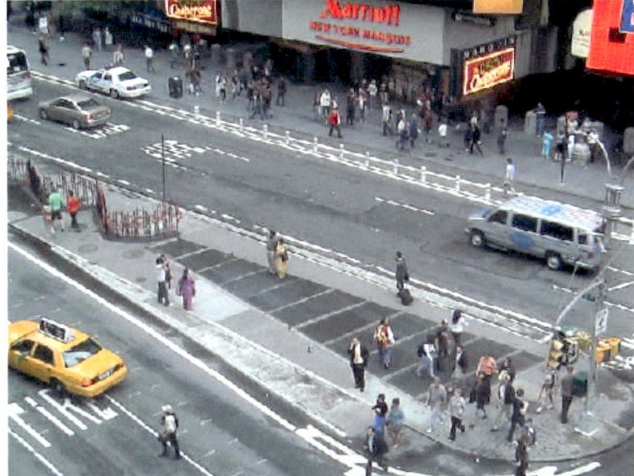
Live 4:13 pm

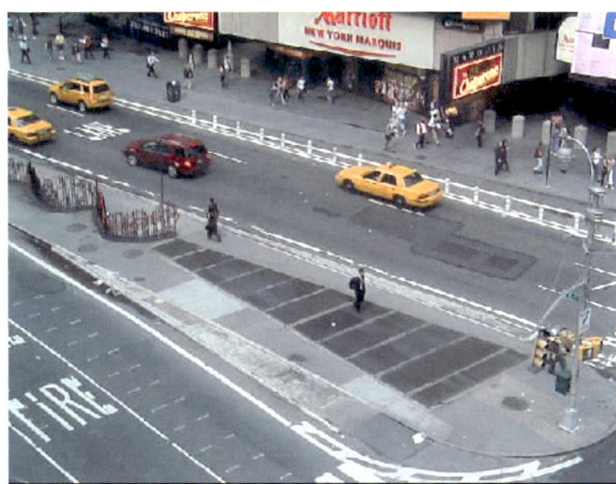
Live 8:37 am

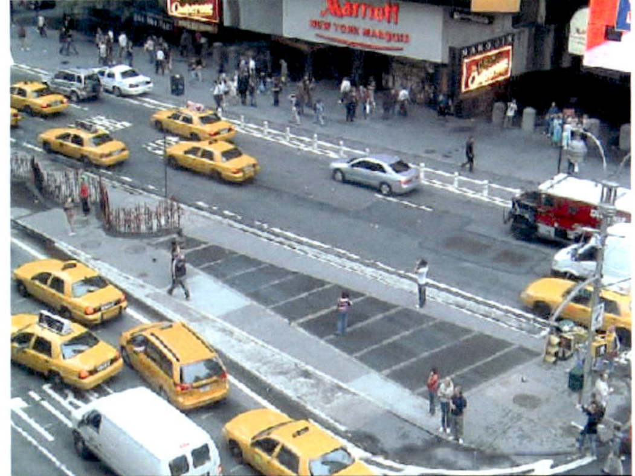
Live 4:14 pm

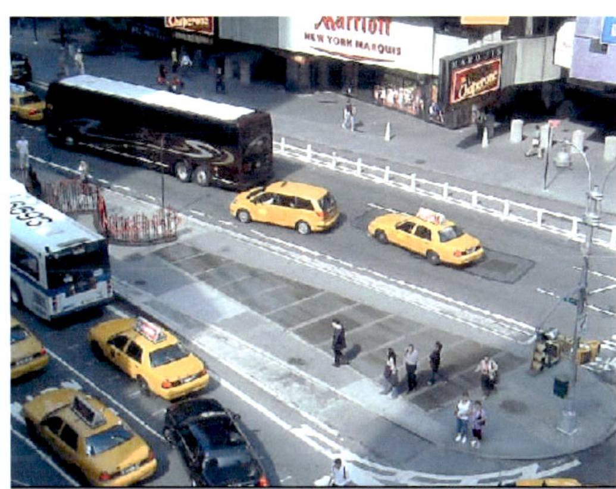
Live 9:35 am

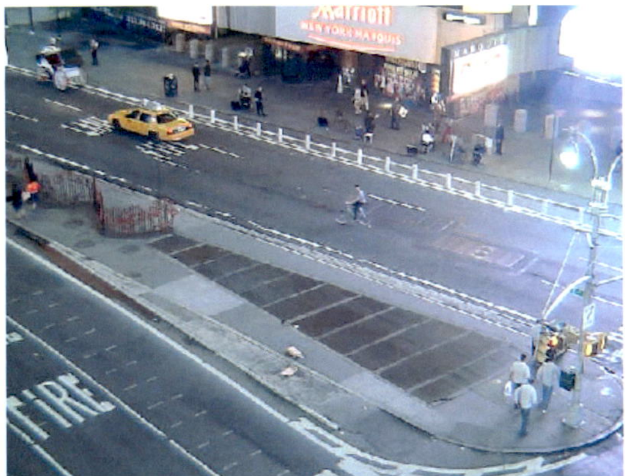
Live 2:18 am

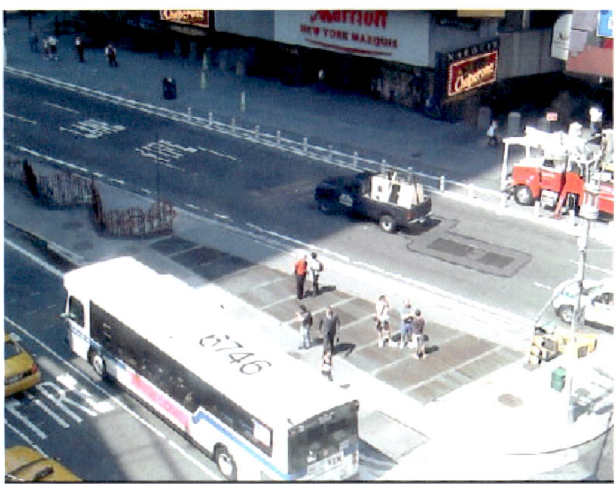
Live 10:38 am

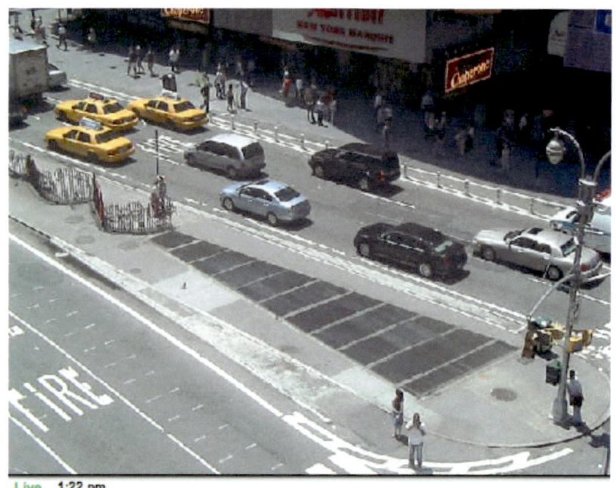
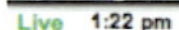
Live 1:22 pm

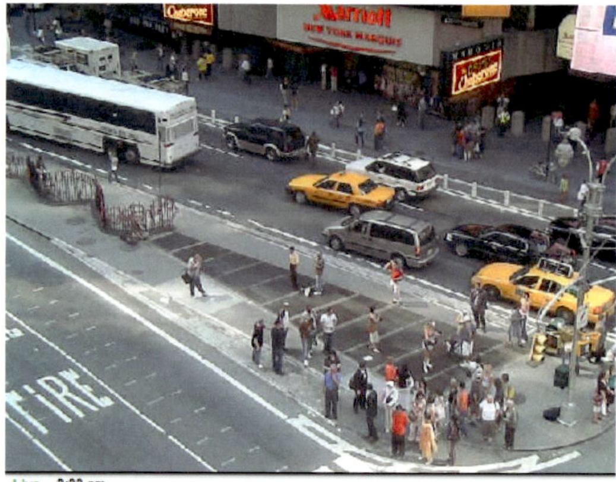
Live 3:33 pm

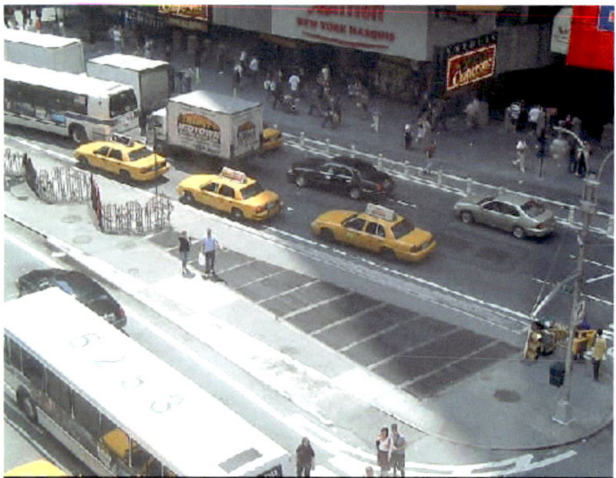
Live 2:16 pm

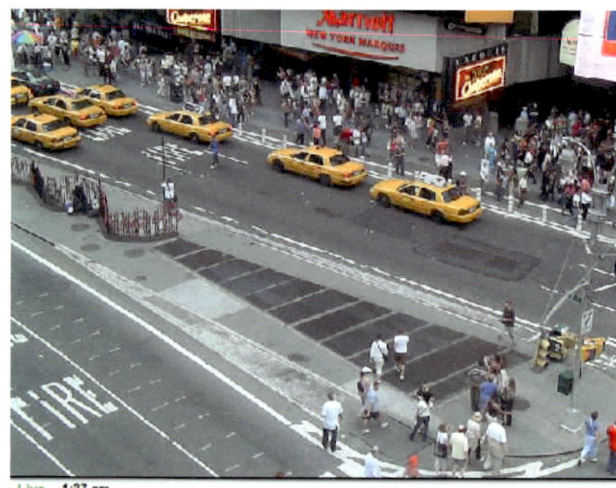
Live 1:27 pm

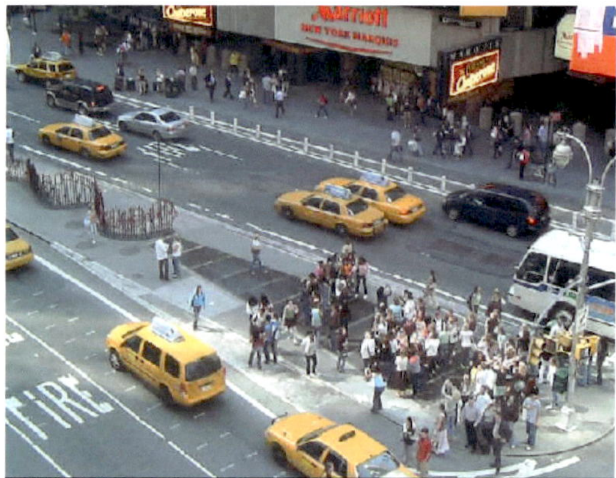
Live 3:23 pm

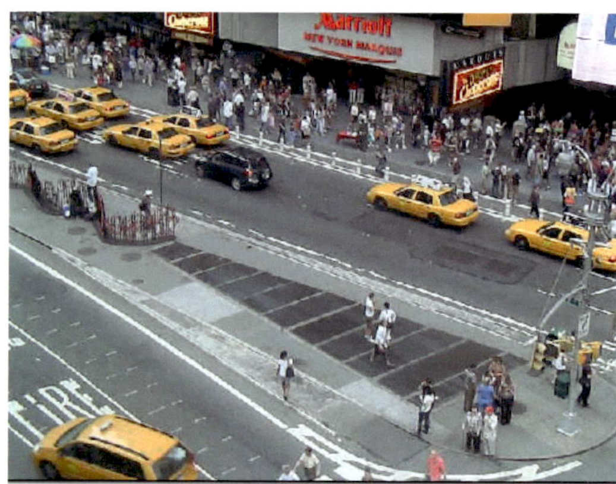
Live 1:27 pm

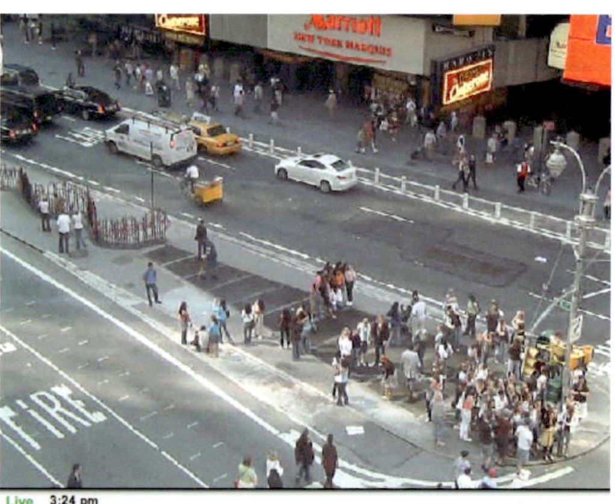
Live 3:24 pm

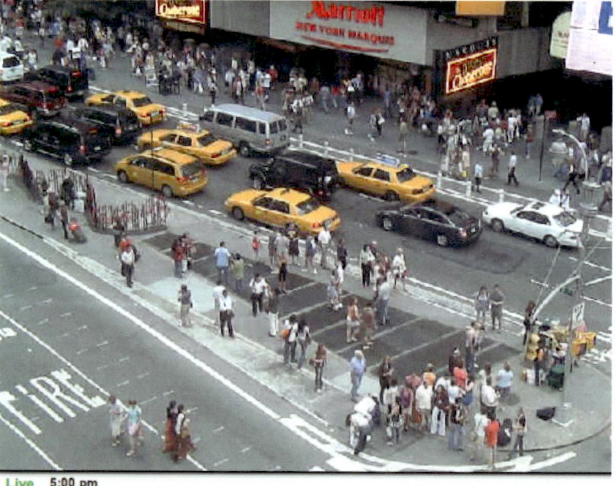
Live 5:00 pm

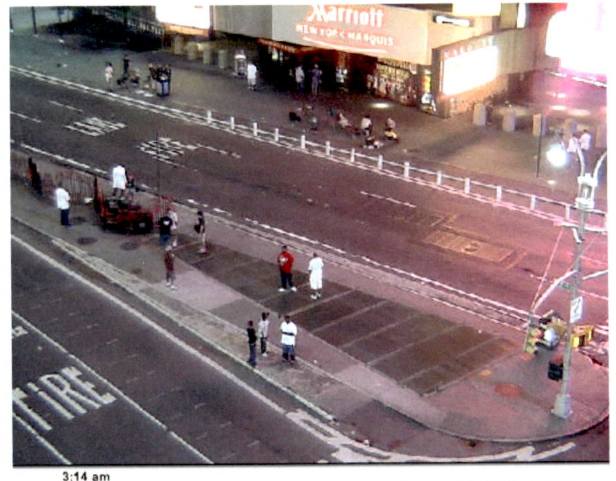

3:14 am

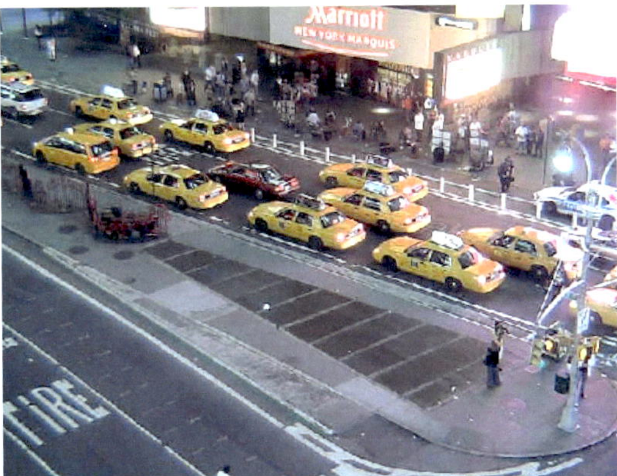

Live 2:07 am

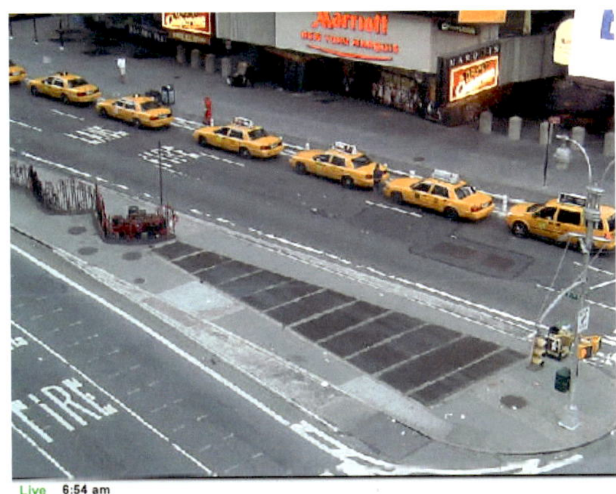

Live 6:54 am

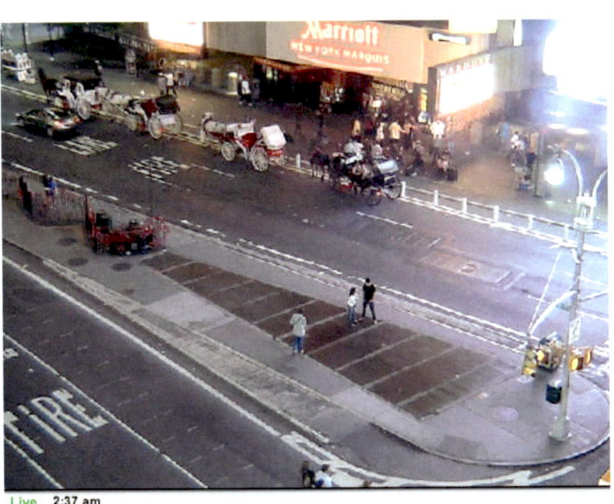

Live 2:37 am

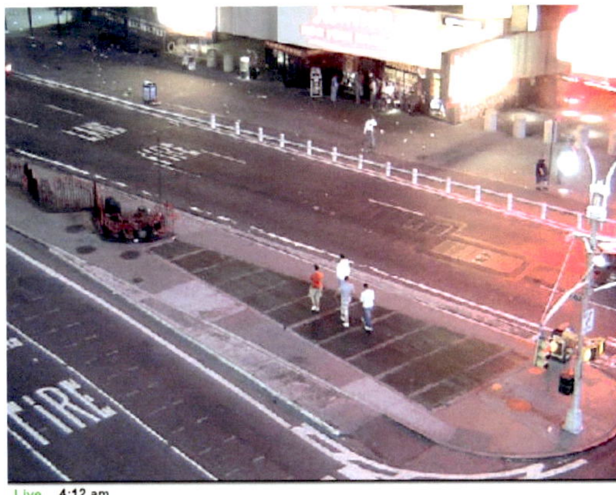

Live 4:12 am

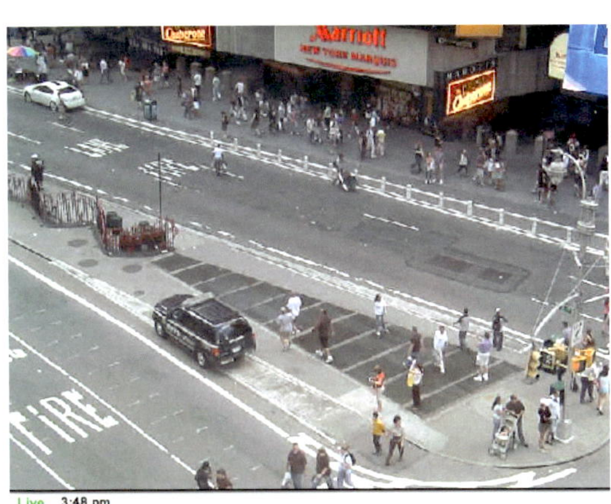

Live 3:48 pm

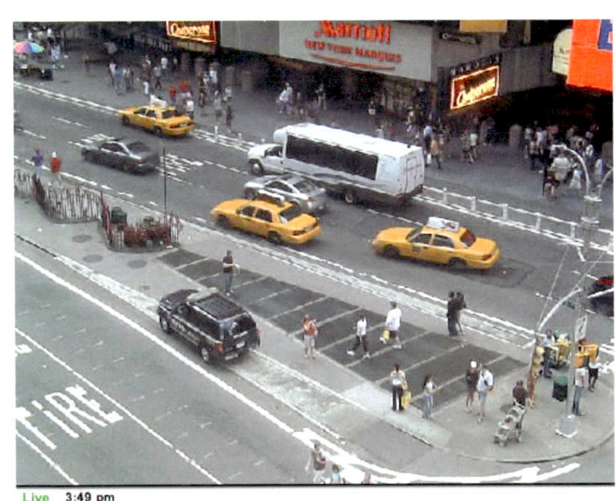

Live 3:49 pm

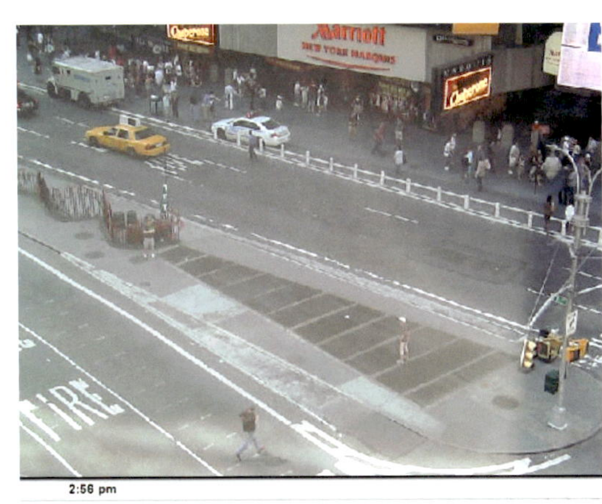

2:56 pm

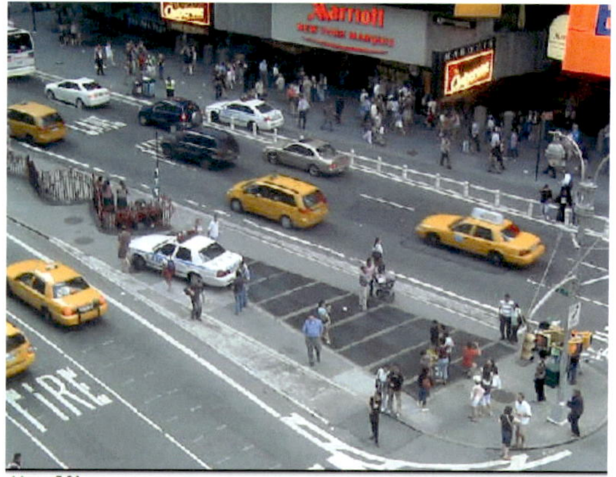
Marriott
NEW YORK MARQUIS

Live 5:01 pm

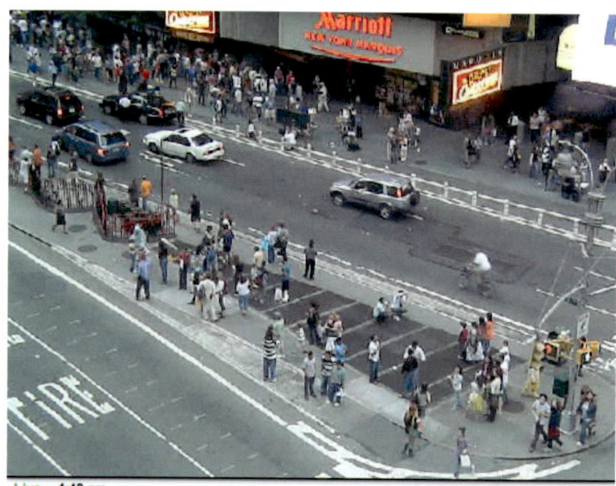
Marriott
NEW YORK MARQUIS
Live 4:42 pm

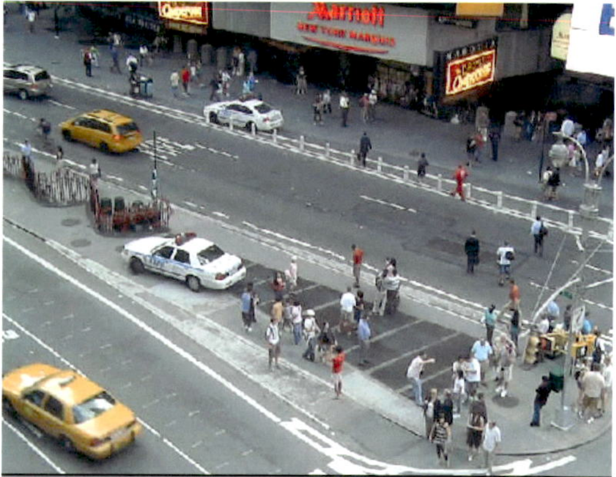
Marriott
NEW YORK MARQUIS
Live 5:03 pm

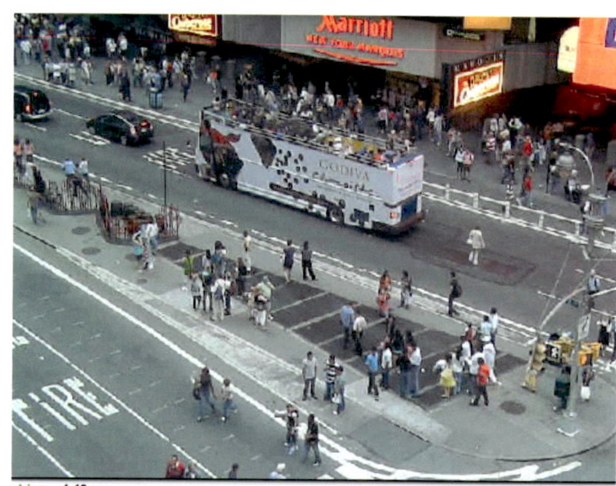
Marriott
NEW YORK MARQUIS
GODIVA
Live 4:43 pm

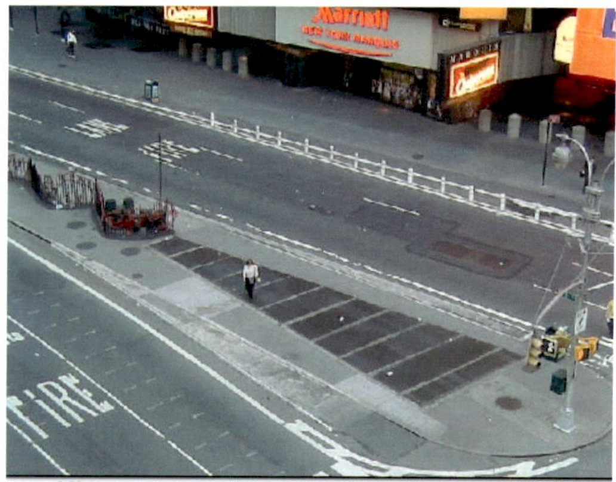
Marriott
NEW YORK MARQUIS
FIRE
Live 6:58 am

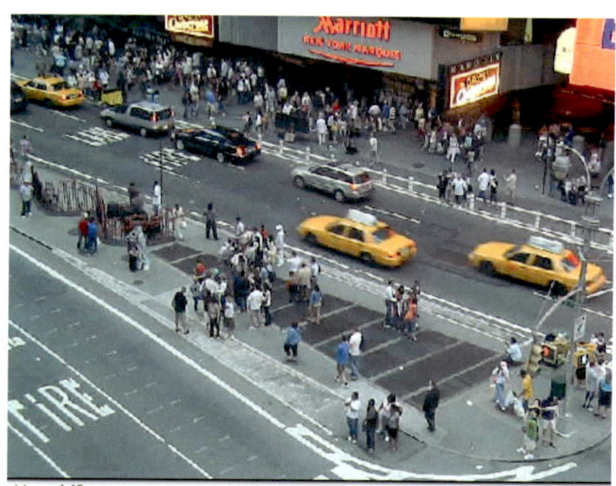
Marriott
NEW YORK MARQUIS
FIRE
Live 4:45 pm

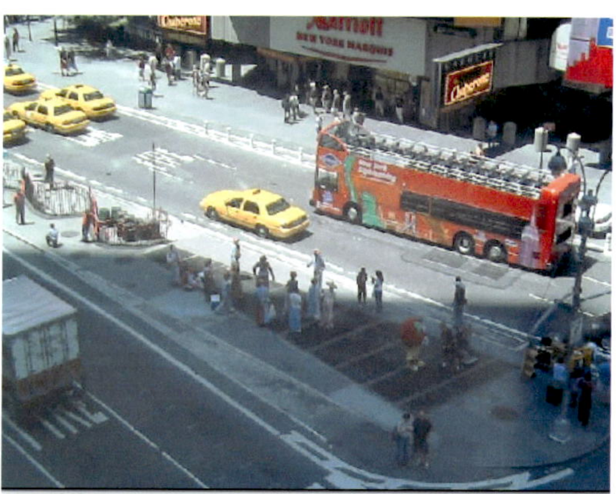
Marriott
NEW YORK MARQUIS
Live 12:32 pm

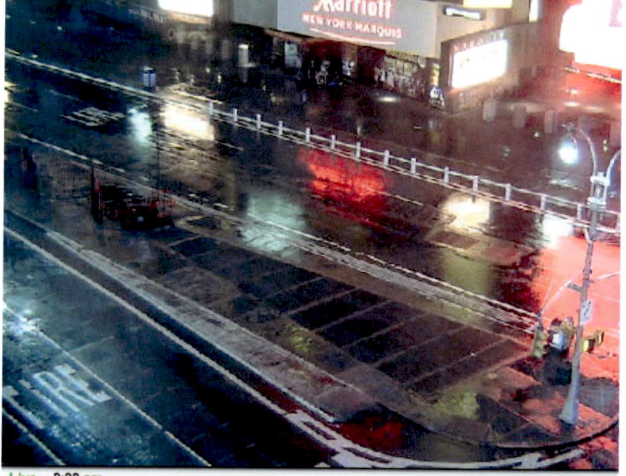
Marriott
NEW YORK MARQUIS
Live 2:22 am

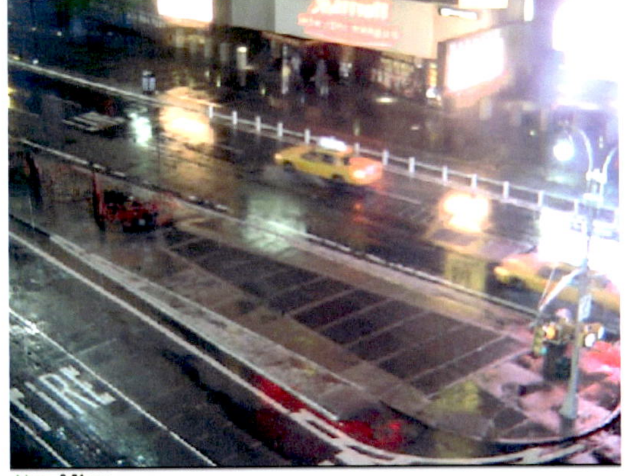

Live 2:51 am

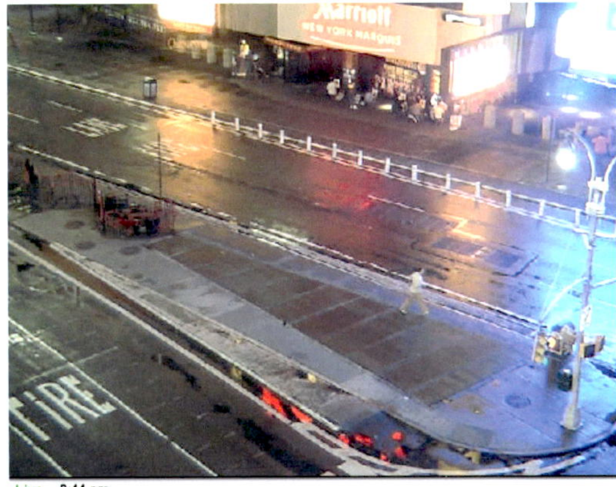

Live 2:44 am

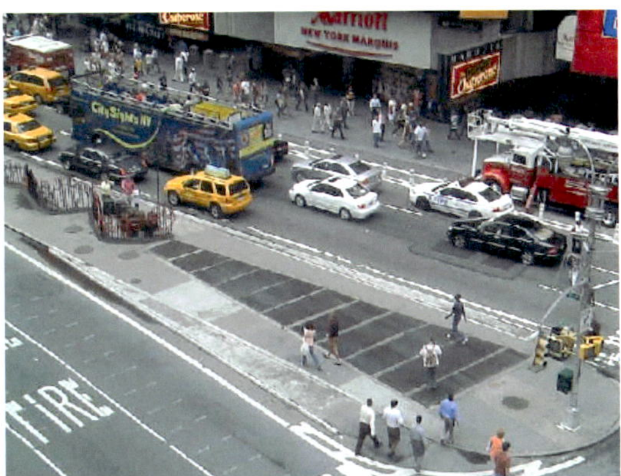

Live 12:37 pm

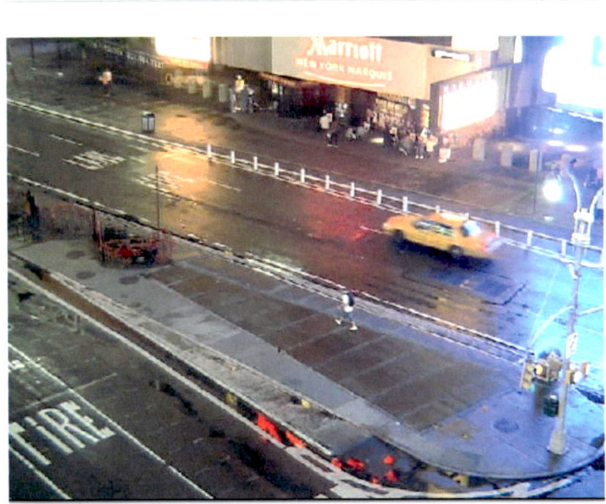

Live 2:45 am

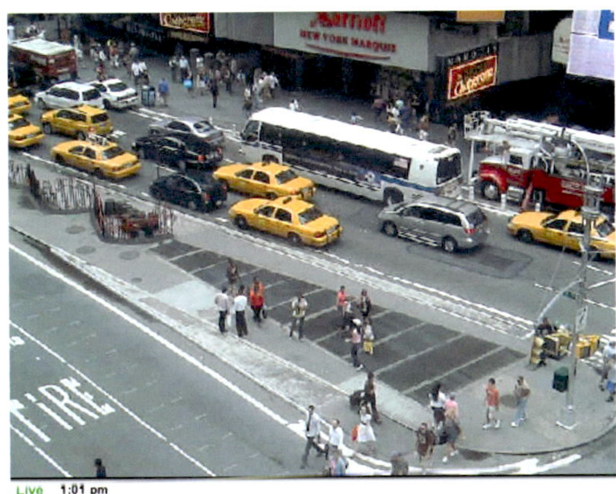

Live 1:01 pm

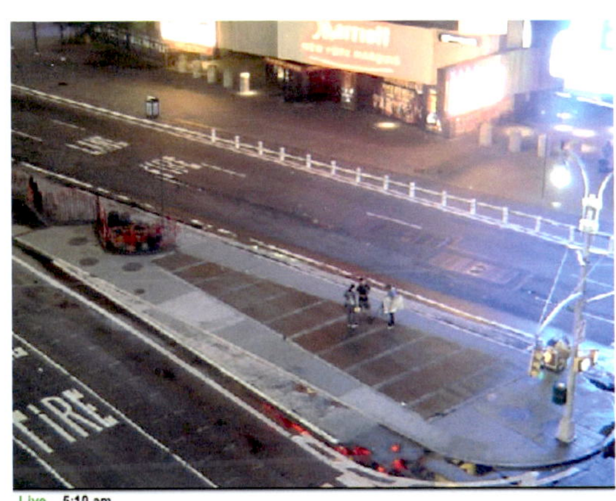

Live 5:10 am

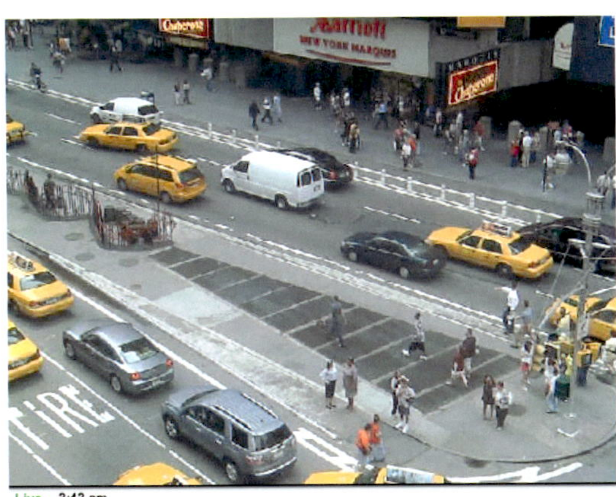

Live 2:42 pm

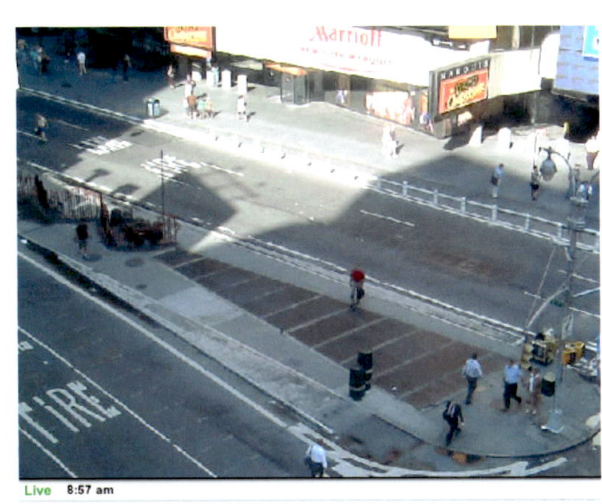

Live 8:57 am

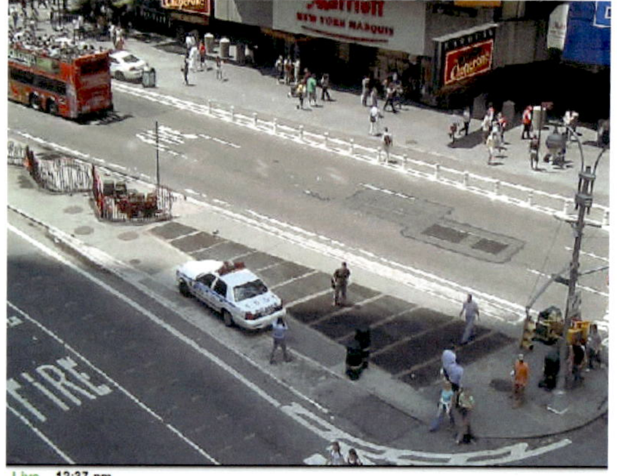
Live 12:37 pm

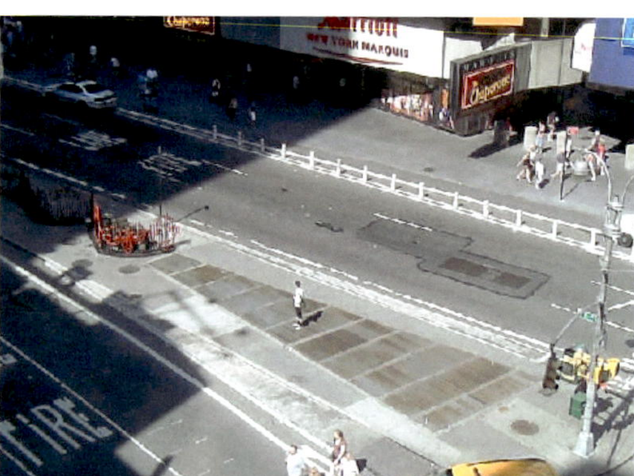
Live 9:58 am

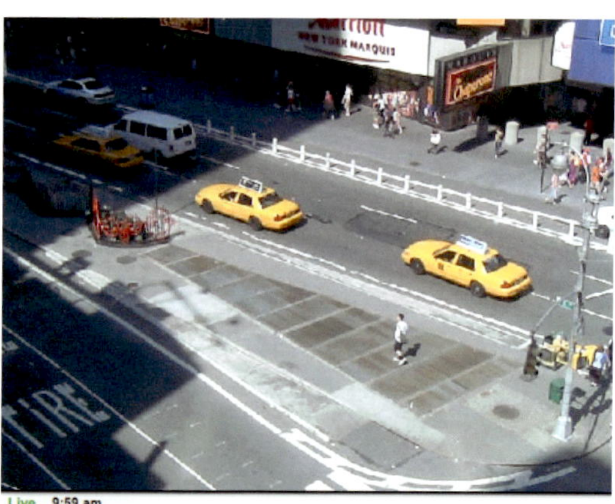
Live 9:59 am

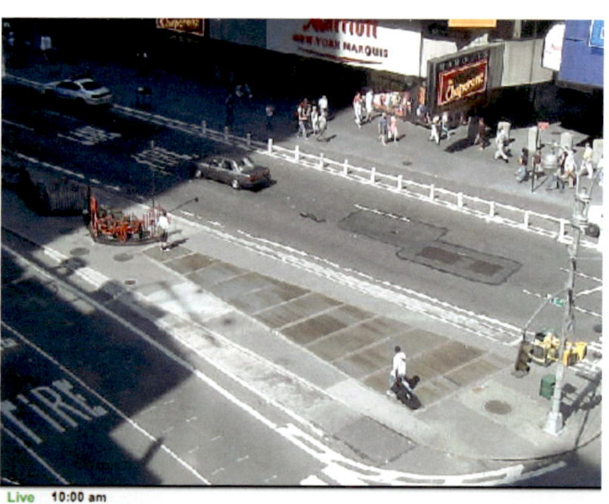
Live 10:00 am

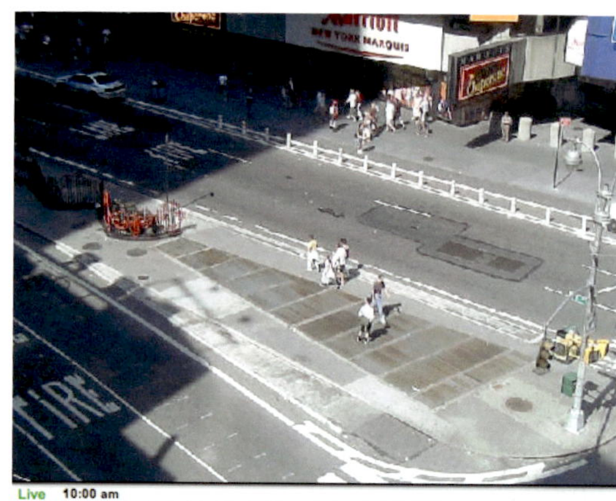
Live 10:00 am

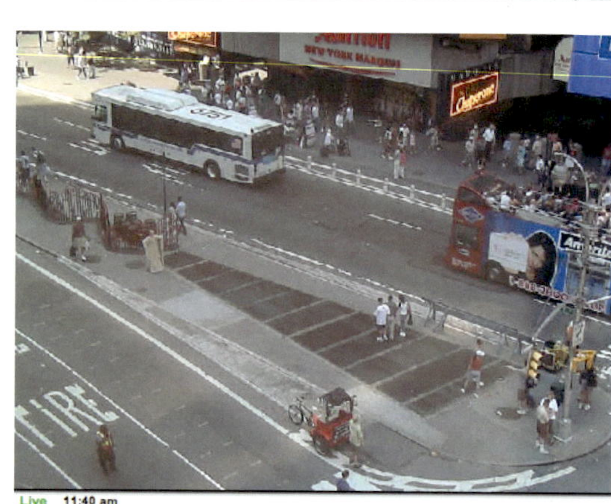
Live 11:40 am

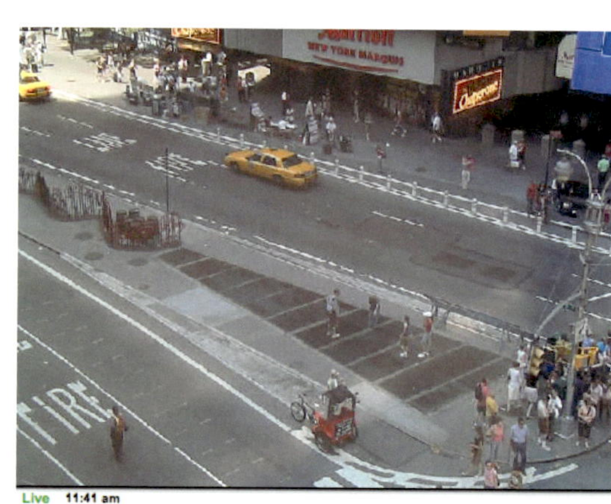
Live 11:41 am

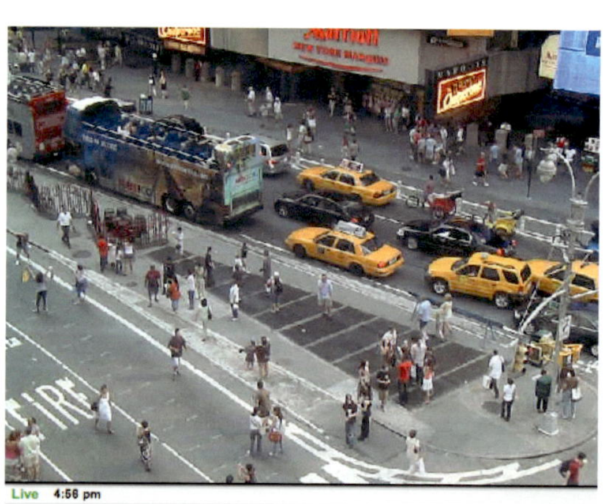
Live 4:56 pm

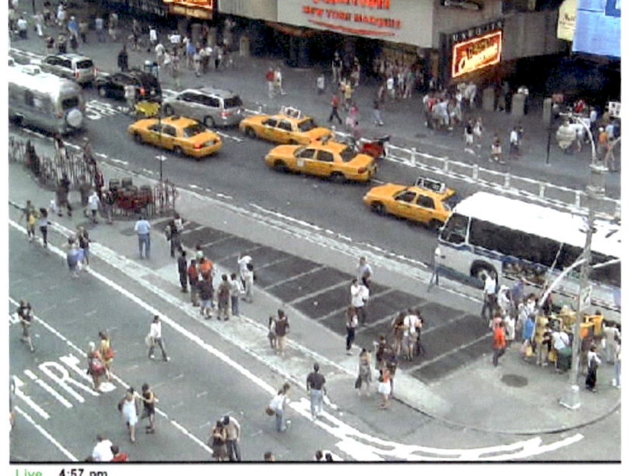

Live 4:57 pm

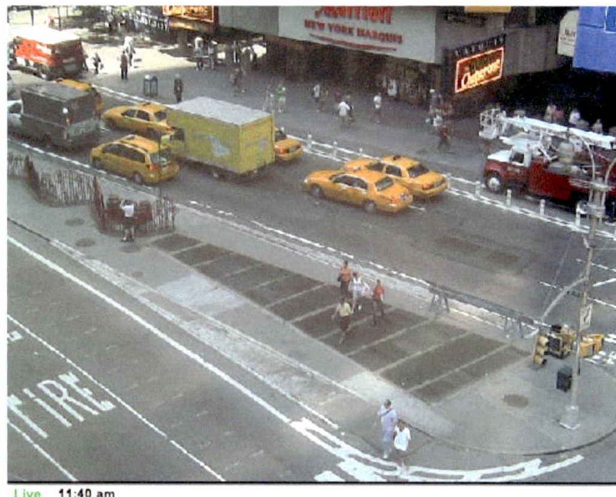

Live 11:40 am

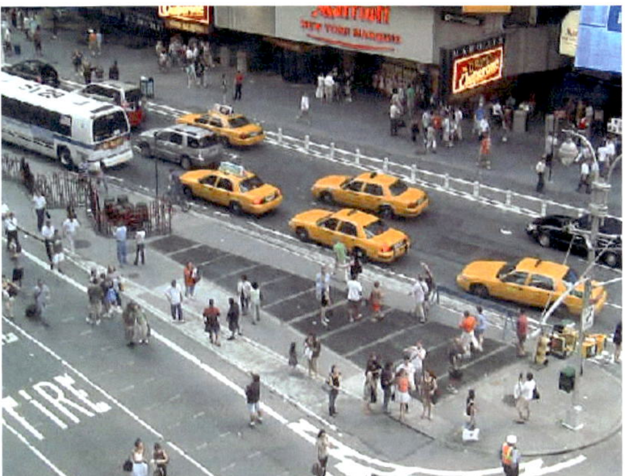

Live 4:58 pm

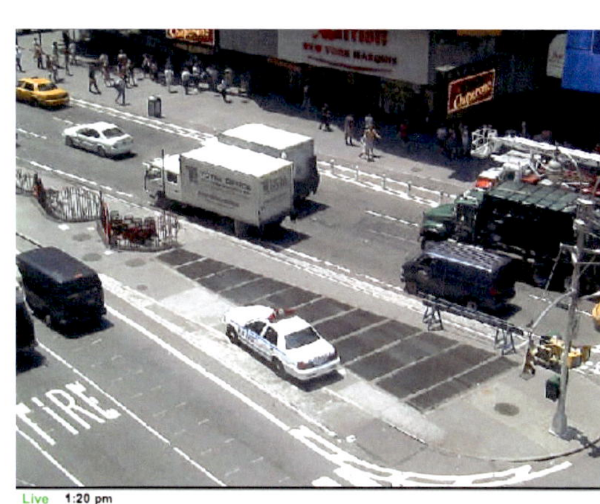

Live 1:20 pm

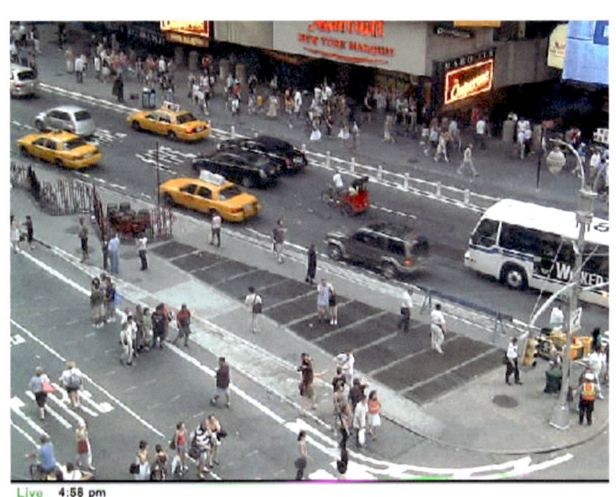

Live 4:58 pm

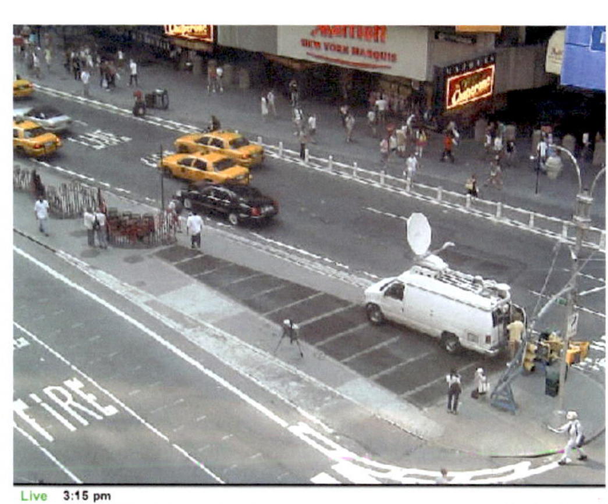

Live 3:15 pm

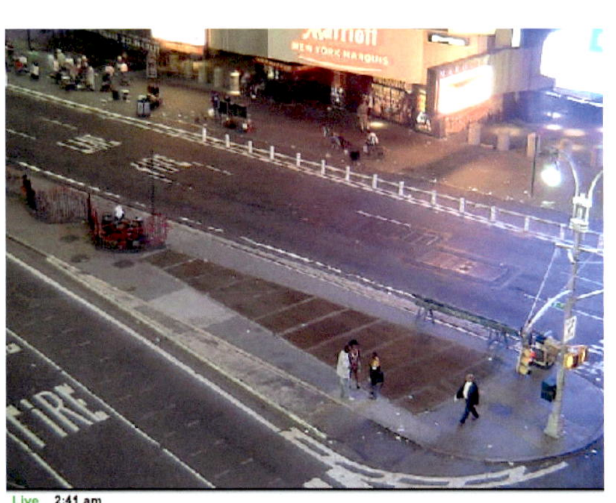

Live 2:41 am

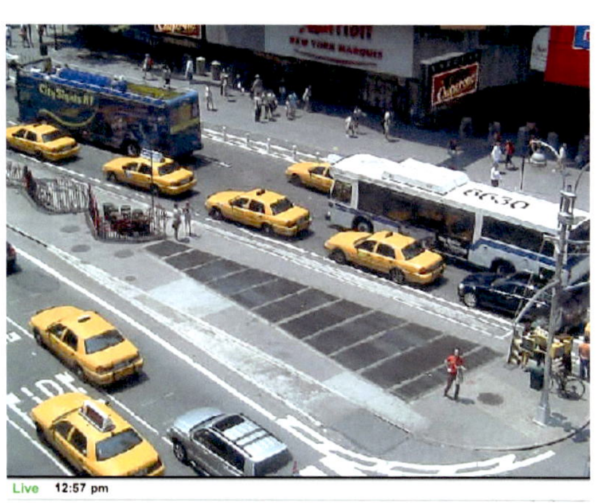

Live 12:57 pm

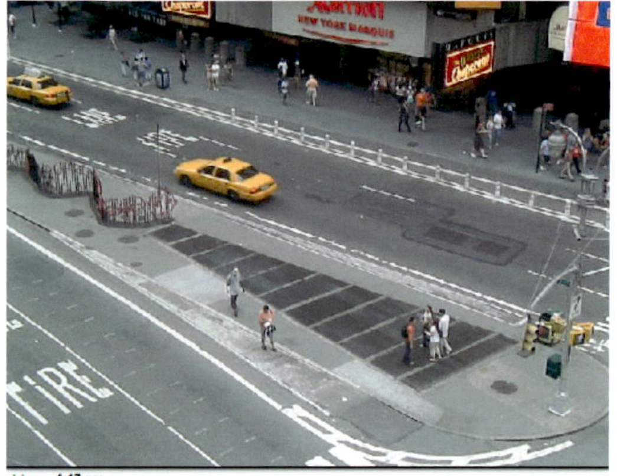

Live 4:47 pm

Live 2:09 pm

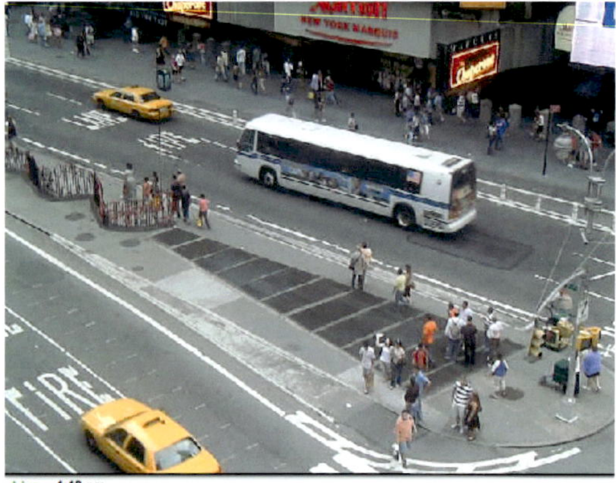

Live 4:48 pm

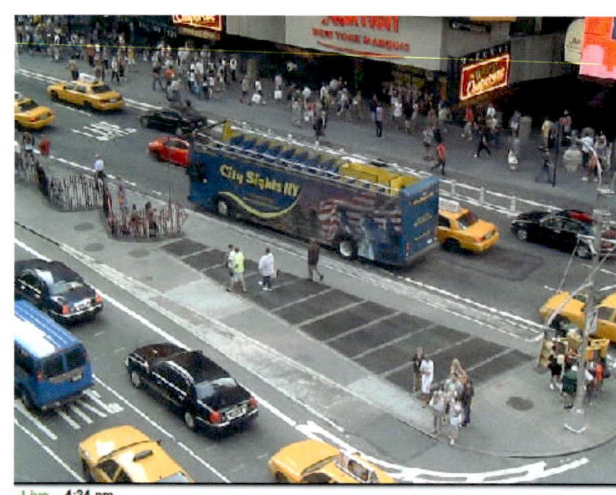

Live 4:24 pm

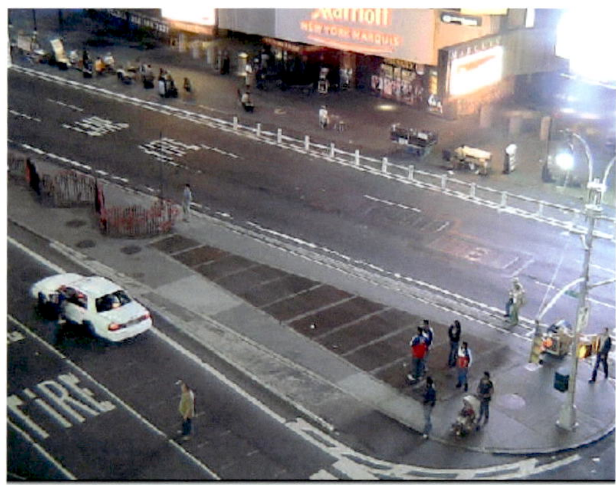

Live 2:16 am

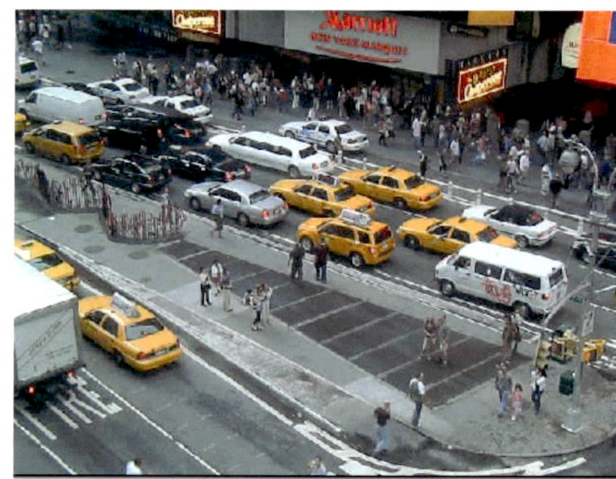

Live 12:58 pm

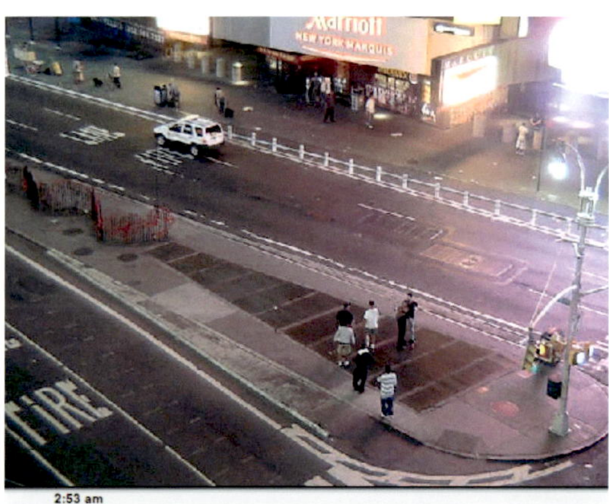

2:53 am

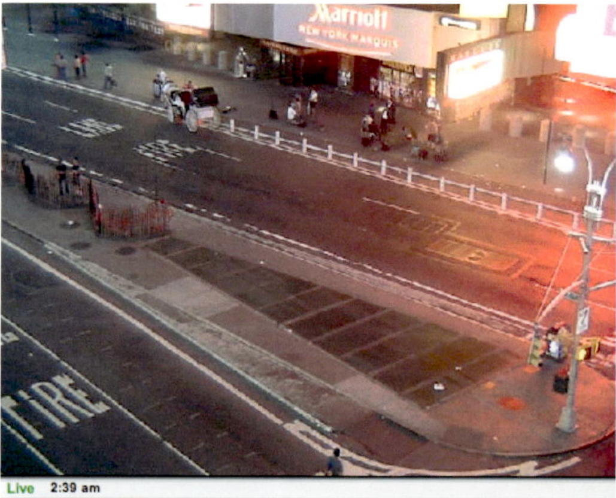

Live 2:39 am

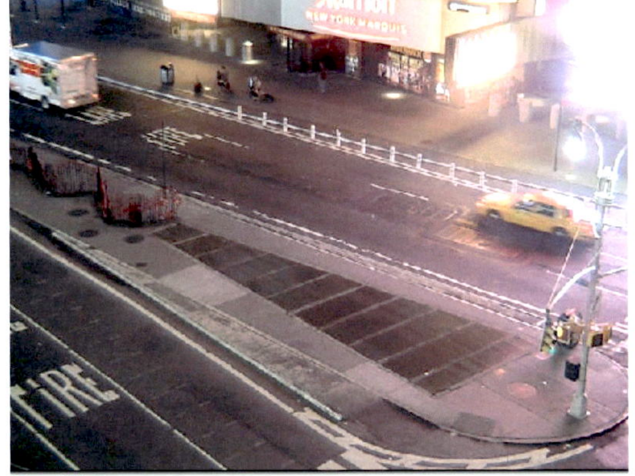
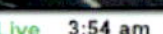
Live 3:54 am

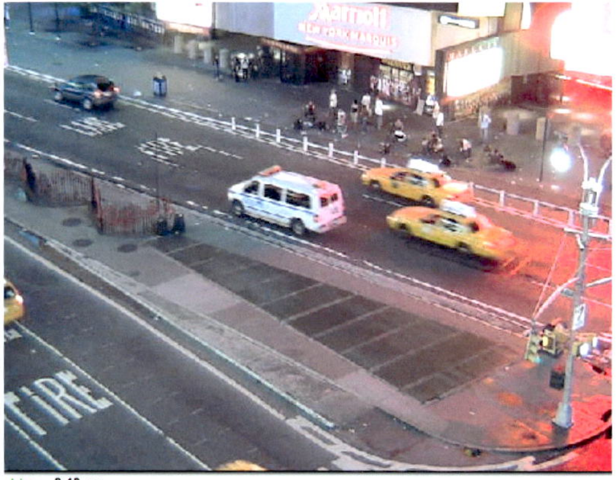
Live 2:40 am

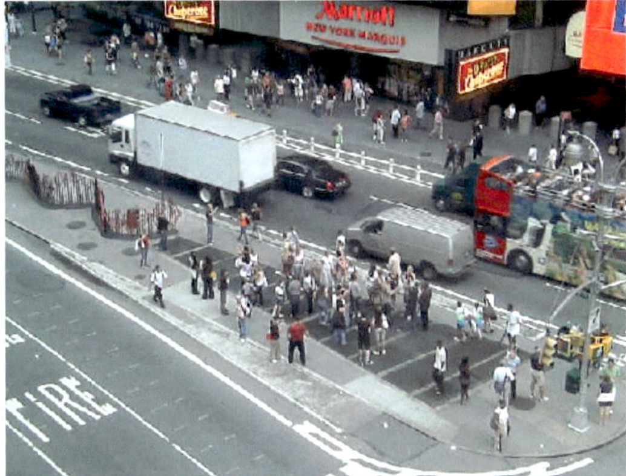
Live 3:40 pm

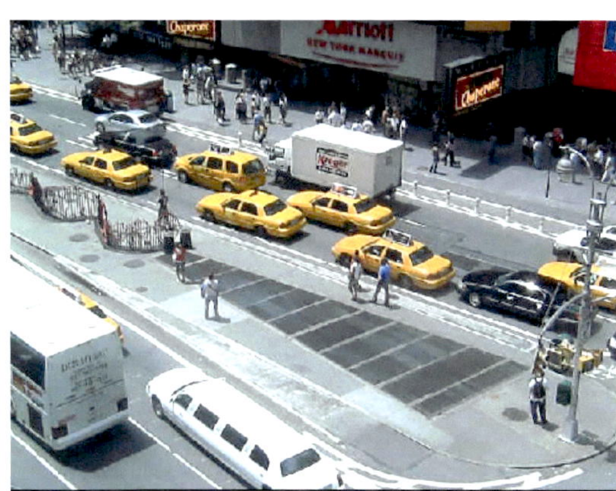
Live 1:08 pm

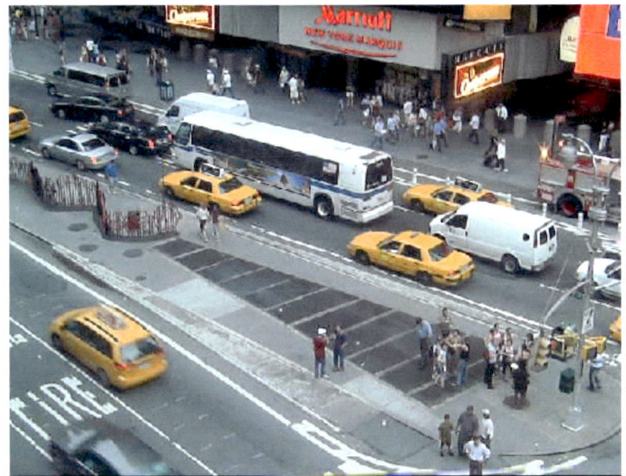
Live 3:46 pm

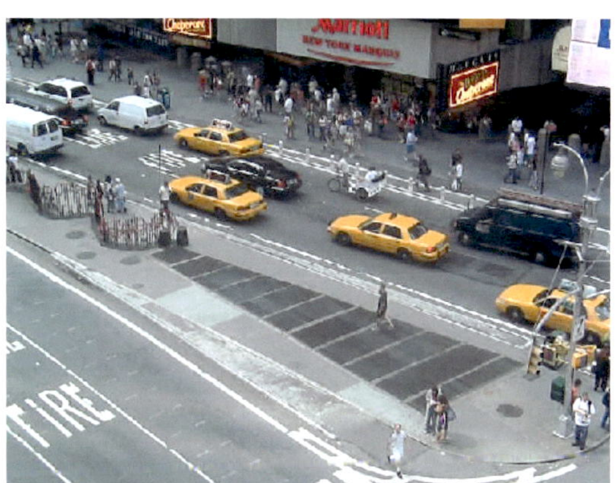
Live 3:23 pm

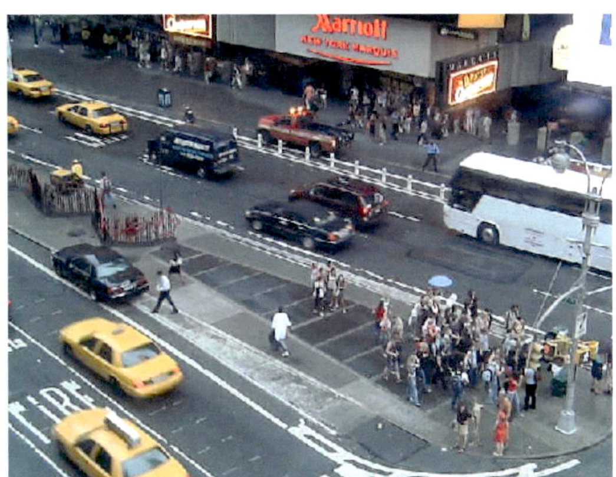
Live 3:50 pm

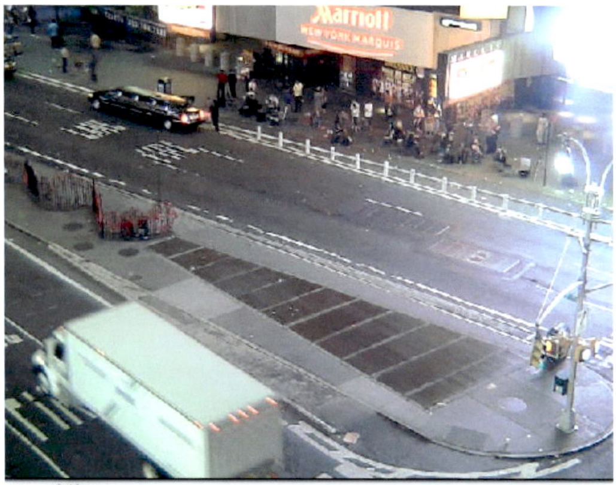
Live 2:10 am

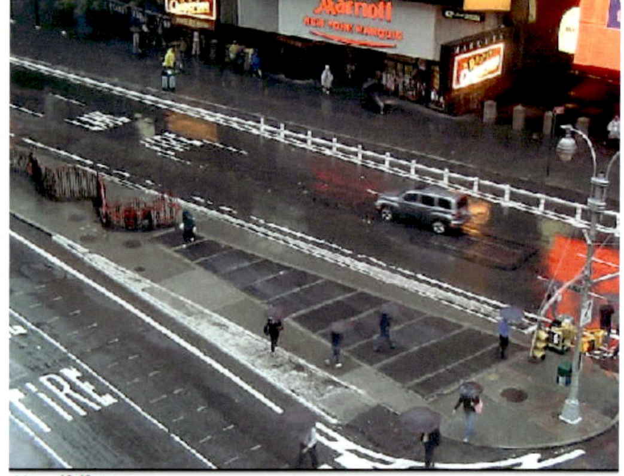

Live 10:49 am

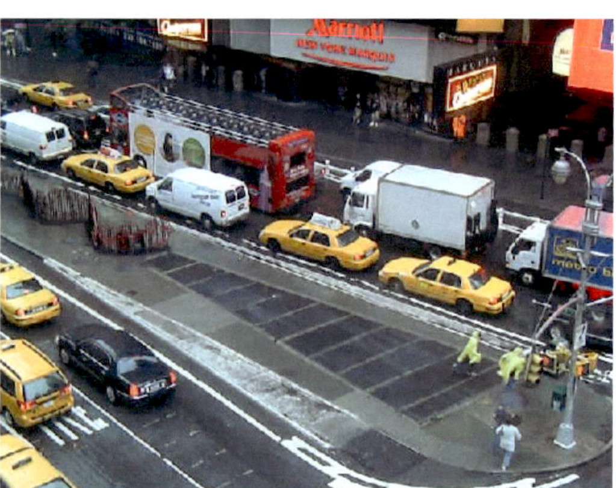

Live 1:21 pm

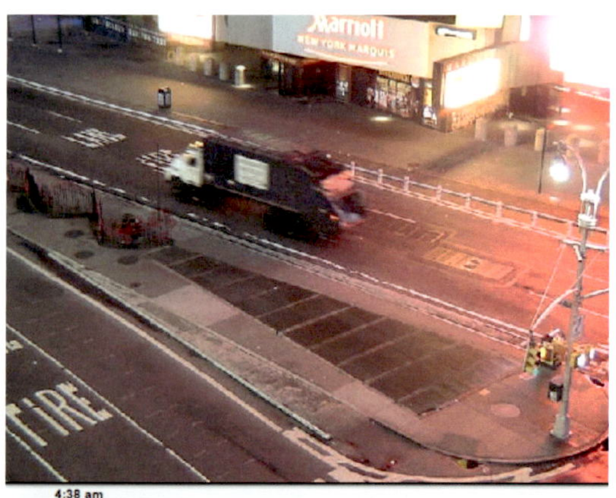

4:38 am

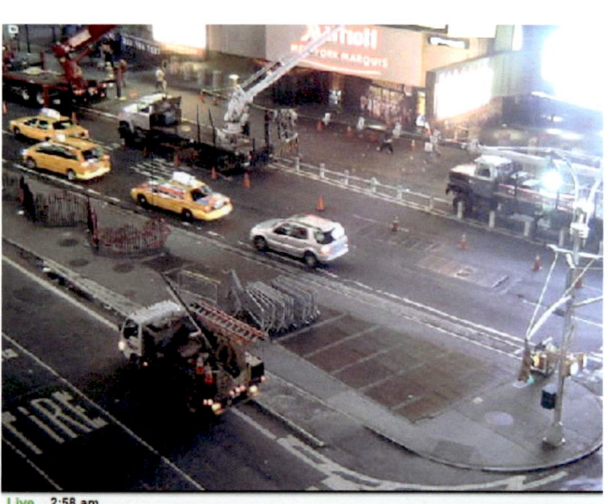

Live 2:58 am

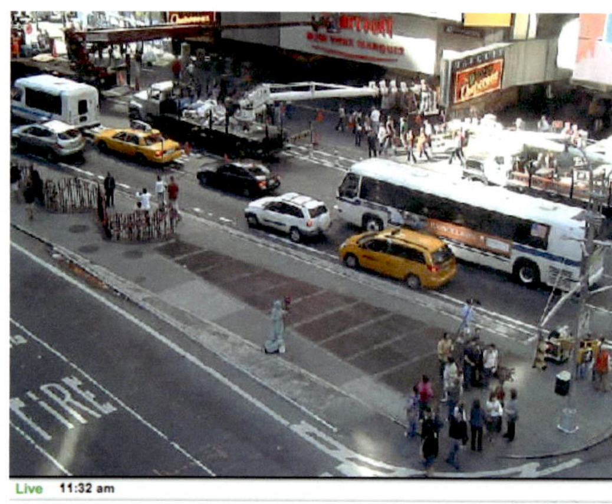

Live 11:32 am

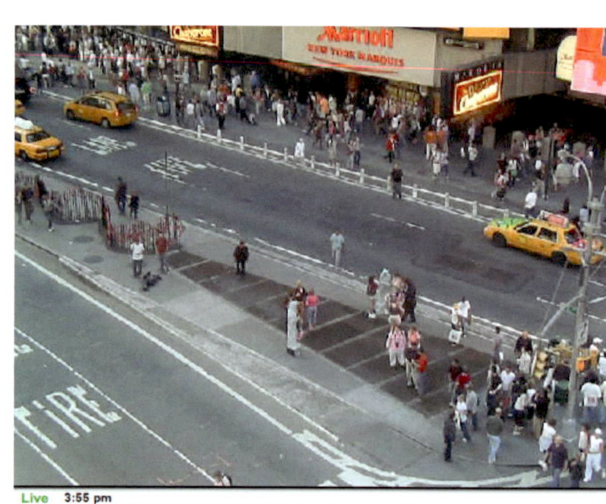

Live 3:55 pm

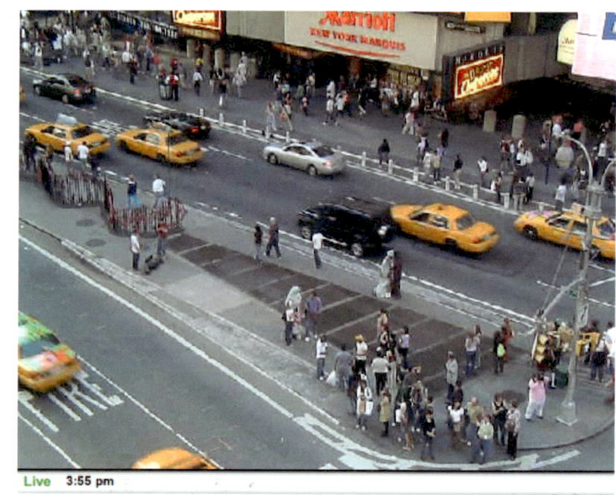

Live 3:55 pm

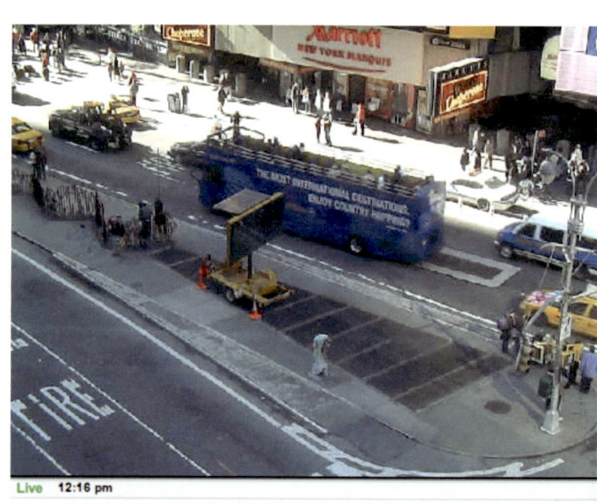

Live 12:16 pm

TIMES SQUARE

Max Neuhaus

TIME PIECE BEACON

Dia Art Foundation, New York
Distributed by Yale University Press,
New Haven and London
2009

The project to reinstate Max Neuhaus's *Times Square* in May 2002 was directed by Christine Burgin and sponsored by the Times Square BID in collaboration with Metropolitan Transportation Authority Arts for Transit. It was made possible through the generous help and financial support of the following residents of Times Square: Bertelsmann, Inc.; Condé Nast; Forest City Ratner Companies; New York Marriott Marquis; The New York Times Company, Inc.; and The Rudin Family. In 1977, the first installation of the work was realized with the cooperation of MTA New York City Transit and Sidney J. Frigand, and funding was provided by the National Endowment for the Arts and other donors.

Max Neuhaus's *Time Piece Beacon* was commissioned specifically for Dia Art Foundation's museum in Beacon, New York, where it was installed in 2005 and inaugurated on May 6, 2006. The work was made possible by Louise and Leonard Riggio.

Book design by Filiep Tacq, Madrid
Editors, Lynne Cooke and Karen Kelly, with Barbara Schröder
Editorial and Research Assistant, Jeanne Dreskin
Copyediting and proofreading by Sam Frank and Richard Gallin

535 West 22nd Street, New York, NY 10011
www.diaart.org

ISBN 978-0-300-15167-1 (Yale University Press)

Library of Congress Cataloging-in-Publication Data

Neuhaus, Max.
Max Neuhaus : Times Square, Time Piece Beacon / [editors, Lynne Cooke and Karen Kelly, with Barbara Schröder].
p. cm.
Includes bibliographical references.
ISBN 978-0-300-15167-1 (alk. paper)
1. Neuhaus, Max. Times Square. 2. Neuhaus, Max. Time Piece Beacon. 3. Neuhaus, Max—Criticism and interpretation. 4. Sound in art. I. Cooke, Lynne. II. Kelly, Karen J., 1964- III. Schröder, Barbara, 1969- IV. Title. V. Title: Times Square, Time Piece Beacon.
N6537.N47A75 2009
700.92—dc22
2009031902

Front cover: photos by Ken Goebel, based on a concept by Max Neuhaus
Endpapers (front): Max Neuhaus, Circumscription drawing for *Times Square* (1977–92; 2002–present), 1992. Colored pencil on paper; 2 parts, 29 ⅜ x 37 ¾ inches, 29 ⅜ x 31⅛ inches (74.5 x 96 cm, 74.5 x 79 cm). Collection Dia Art Foundation. Endpapers (back): Max Neuhaus, Circumscription drawing for *Time Piece Beacon* (2005–present), 2005. Colored pencil on paper; 2 parts, 34 ¼ x 47 ¼ inches, 34 ¼ x 12 ½ inches (87 x 120 cm, 87 x 32 cm). Collection Dia Art Foundation. Photos by Bill Jacobson.
Pages 1–17: Selection by Max Neuhaus of surveillance-camera stills of Times Square, 2008
Pages 141–172: Dia:Beacon, 2009, photos by Ken Goebel, based on a concept by Max Neuhaus

Distributed by Yale University Press, New Haven and London

Yale University Press
302 Temple Street
P.O. Box 209040
New Haven, CT 06520-9040
www.yalebooks.com

Printed and bound in Spain by Artes Graficas Palermo S.L.

Photo credits:
Pages 22, 25, 32, 44, 49, 53, 55, 58, 61, 66, 74, 82, 92, 94, 103, 118, 123 courtesy Estate of Max Neuhaus; pages 28, 31, 104, 112 photo by Peter Moore, courtesy Barbara Moore, © Estate of Peter Moore/VAGA, New York, NY; page 62 courtesy Princeton University Library; page 70 photo by Cathy Carver; page 48 courtesy Museum für Moderne Kunst, Frankfurt am Main, © Carl Andre/VAGA, New York, NY; page 50 courtesy Stephen Flavin, © 2009 Stephen Flavin / Artists Rights Society (ARS), New York; page 54 © 2009 Richard Serra / Artists Rights Society (ARS), New York; pages 95, 116 published by Henmar Press, C.F. Peters Corporation sole selling agent; all rights reserved; used by permission; page 96 © Pierre Henry, courtesy Pierre Henry and Electronic Music Foundation; page 97 © 2009 Artists Rights Society (ARS), New York / ADAGP, Paris / FLC, photo by Lucien Hervé; page 100 photo by Herve Gloaguen, courtesy John Cage Trust; page 99 © Estate of George Brecht, courtesy Liz Kotz; page 102 © Jung Hee Choi, photo by Jung Hee Choi; page 105 © 1976 Ruth Cummings, courtesy Estate of Max Neuhaus; page 122 © 2009 Robert Morris / Artists Rights Society (ARS), New York.

CONTENTS

Preface

Sadly last February, Max Neuhaus left us. He left us with his work and his far-from-conventional contribution to art and aesthetics. He left us with a new understanding and vision of what art can be. The minute Max emancipated himself from the traditional world of music, he also freed himself from disciplinary constrictions. Institutions animated by a progressive ambition and an experimental drive are only today attempting to redefine art across, beyond, and between disciplines. Max anticipated this conversation, but what he might not have anticipated was how long it would remain a virtual monologue; rare were ears that heard what he was loudly whispering. It would take years for institutions to meet him. Our institutional models are dusty, conventional to the point of being regressive. Our modes of representation are in crisis.

Neuhaus's works change the condition of sound, from its conception to its reception. His notion of art in a public space was not about decorum or about monumental celebration but about perception of oneself in the world. His notion of "public" was a truly democratic and necessary one; his *Times Square* (1977–92; 2002–present) might be the perfect embodiment of Jürgen Habermas's idea of the public sphere as an area of social life and discussion, in the sense of the Greek agora. Art for everyone, all the time, if one pays attention; the world might be flat and time might be square.

Neuhaus's art is not about sound, not about representation, not about time or space, but simultaneously about all of these. A different notion of time, nonlinear; a different notion of space, inhabited; a different notion of representation, beyond forms and objects. His art is about the continuum of sensory perception. His ethos suggests that art is uninterruptible, and only our perception is discontinuous. Neuhaus's art provides a philosophical incentive for us to be alert to the surrounding world.

This publication is a testimony to Max Neuhaus's work and to the way it has affected the lives of many passersby on Times Square, in Beacon, and in the many other places where his work is and has been installed.

I want to thank the authors, Lynne Cooke, Christoph Cox, Branden W. Joseph, Liz Kotz, Alex Potts, Ulrich Loock, and Peter Pakesch, for their contributions and for their dedication to the ideas of sound. Dia's publication department, Lynne Cooke, Karen Kelly, Barbara Schröder, and Jeanne Dreskin, has through this publication deepened the scholarship around Dia's permanent collection, allowing Max's voice and work to remain. We also appreciate Bettina Funcke's invaluable contributions to the planning of the book. Filiep Tacq took on the daunting task of translating the ideas Max sketched in the summer of 2008 into the form of this book. We are sincerely grateful for Filiep's sensitivity and insight, and feel sure that Max would have been thrilled with the subtlety of his design. This publication has also benefited from the contributions of many others, in particular Silvia Neuhaus, who generously opened Max's archive at a difficult time. Barbara Moore not only shared her memories but also led us to many previously unseen photographs by her late husband, Peter Moore, of Max's early work.

In 1977, the first installation of Max Neuhaus's *Times Square* was realized with the cooperation of MTA New York City Transit and Sidney J. Frigand, and funding was provided by the National Endowment for the Arts and other donors. By 1992 the piece was no longer active, and were it not for the vision and energy of Christine Burgin *Times Square* would not exist today. In 2002, Christine directed the effort to reinstate the artwork at its original site. She galvanized essential support from Tim Tomkins, President, Times Square Alliance, and Sandra Bloodworth, Director, Metropolitan Transportation Authority Arts for Transit, to reinstate the project. Vel Riberto, on behalf of Arts for Transit, worked diligently to coordinate logistics and access to the site. The 2002 reinstallation and this publication were made possible through the generous assistance and financial support of the following residents of Times Square: Bertelsmann, Inc.; Condé Nast; Forest City Ratner Companies; New York Marriott Marquis; The New York Times Company, Inc.; and The Rudin Family. The Times Square Alliance and MTA Arts for Transit continue to be invaluable partners in the maintenance of the artwork, which, thanks to Christine and Max, has since entered Dia's collection. Through the generosity of Louise and Leonard Riggio, the institution was able to commission *Time Piece Beacon* (2005–present) as a long-term installation at Dia:Beacon, Riggio Galleries, Dia's museum in Beacon, New York.

Sadly last February, Max Neuhaus left us. But his voice is ever present and will resonate with us and for us as an aesthetic immersion, independent from the yoke of physical and temporal manifestations. Ultimately this publication is dedicated to him: to his memory and to the acute actuality of his legacy.

Philippe Vergne, Director

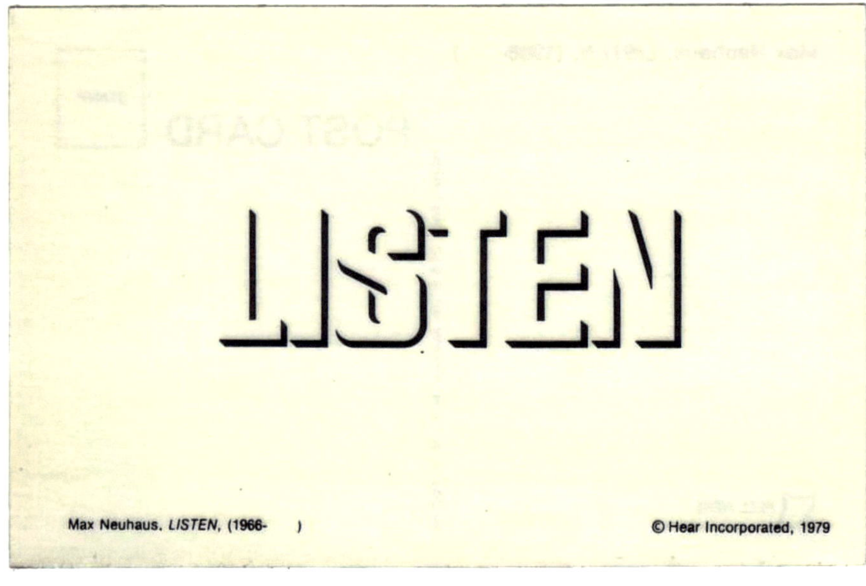

Max Neuhaus, *Listen*, postcard decal, 1979

Introduction

I see these works not as definers of a single frame of mind for all individuals, but as catalysts for shifts in frame of mind.
—Max Neuhaus

By his own account, Max Neuhaus decided at the age of fourteen to become the greatest drummer in the world, a decision duly recorded in most art books and catalogues devoted to his work. Also dutifully noted is the fact that within a decade he was on the national stage performing solo recitals of works by such great American experimental composers as John Cage and Morton Feldman, as well as touring internationally with Pierre Boulez, Karlheinz Stockhausen, and other luminaries. A prodigious percussionist, Neuhaus was unrivaled in his field when, in the mid-sixties, he decided to abandon music in favor of a career in the visual arts.[1]

A decade later, in 1977, he installed a public sculpture at one of New York City's most visible sites. This followed four years of negotiations with the New York City transit authority (during which the limits of his obstinate perseverance were fully tested) to allow him to install sound equipment in the ventilation chamber beneath a subway grate on a pedestrian island near Forty-sixth Street and Broadway and so create there a sound installation he would title *Times Square*. With this pioneering site-specific piece, Neuhaus more or less singlehandedly became the founding father of what is now known as sound art. Today—more than three decades later—*Times Square* (1977–92; 2002–present) remains the poster child for a rapidly expanding and well-established art form.

Mythologizing and simplistic, laced with heroic overtones of the kind endemic to great artists' biographies, this narrative has become standardized. The rampant ambition that vaulted the fourteen-year-old adolescent, living in a provincial American suburb in the mid-fifties, to the pinnacle of his chosen field continued to fuel his subsequent career. To land center stage in the early seventies in the contemporary art world—or, at least, its North American epicenter—took, however, not only this high quotient of ambition married to virtuosity and rigorous discipline but also an exigent intelligence.[2] Avidly curious, his sharp mind refined and filtered the cutting-edge discourses then framing Manhattan's downtown art scene, so that surprisingly few deviations or dead ends interrupted the trajectory of his artistic practice during its first decade. Reflecting its sophisticated, purposive evolution, this clearly focused body of work, which culminated in *Times Square*, deftly parses the concerns embedded in Happenings, Fluxus and environmental artworks, Minimalist and process-based aesthetics, as well as other emerging modes of dance and performance. Yet even as his artistic vision was shaped and honed by the protean scene into which he evidently plunged with gusto, he nonetheless greatly benefited from his former experience in the world of experimental music.

Times Square not only staked new ground for subsequent generations of sound artists, it formed the basis for much of Neuhaus's later practice, in which he prioritized sonic topographies over musical temporalities. Now quite extensive, the literature devoted to Neuhaus's work recounts his artistic formation prior to *Times Square*, one of the few extant pieces from his early career, by reference to dual legacies. First, there was the colossal and unavoidable presence of John Cage. For Neuhaus, the impact of Cage's compositions, which incorporated what Christoph Cox nicely terms "worldly sound," was complemented by the avant-garde composer's seminal theories, in which the determinants of chronological time were expanded to encompass duration, and listening was activated as it was freed from the filter of authorial voice.[3] Second, and equally influential for Neuhaus's nascent aesthetic, was his engagement with phenomenologically based art practices, exemplified by the works of Richard Serra, in particular, and with their theoretical substructure, as articulated in the writings of, inter alia, Robert Morris and Michael Fried.

The contributors to *Max Neuhaus: Times Square, Time Piece Beacon*, basing their arguments on a range of disciplinary perspectives, question the narrowness of these now well-rehearsed readings. Cox sets aside the emphasis provided by most commentators, including the artist himself, on spatiality over temporality and instead probes more deeply how notions of time, and of duration above all, informed Neuhaus's practice following his entrée into the visual arts. Liz Kotz's approach is twofold. On the one hand, she surveys the rarely explored terrain of spatialized music in post–World War II Europe and North America; on the other, she investigates the impact of the role of site as deployed across a broad range of postmodern art practices on Neuhaus's evolving aesthetic. Branden W. Joseph, who notes how little attention has been directed toward what he calls "the social dimension of sound within the 'public environment,'" contributes a pioneering study of the way that, for Neuhaus, the notion of "place" assumed a political dimension.[4] Among the most revealing aspects of Alex Potts's elucidation of Neuhaus's nascent aesthetic is his consideration of the role played by a nexus of three key notions: antielitism, pragmatism, accessibility. "Locational Listening," my own essay, examines Neuhaus's choice of a particular kind of urban location for works he made in New York City and its environs in the late sixties and seventies, specifically in relation to the preferences of his immediate peers, fellow artists living and working in downtown Manhattan who were similarly preoccupied with the public sphere.

Conceived in close collaboration with the artist, *Max Neuhaus: Times Square, Time Piece Beacon* is informed by the wide-ranging exchanges that Karen Kelly and I had with Max over many years. In a memorable meeting early in the process, he gently made it known that never before when making a publication had he felt the need for editors. Sometime later, he changed course, joined forces with us, and became our far-from-silent partner. Max's input was considerable. For example, during the intense discussions that surrounded the choice of authors, he dexterously vetted the range of topics that the book would address. Because he drew strict distinctions between his use of sound in his installations and contemporary musical composition and improvisation, this monograph contains no interdisciplinary examination of concurrent developments in vanguard music and no exploration of more recent developments in sound art. Other arenas, too, including his pioneering technological experimentation, warrant further study. The decision to include photographic images relating to the two key works under review—*Times Square* and

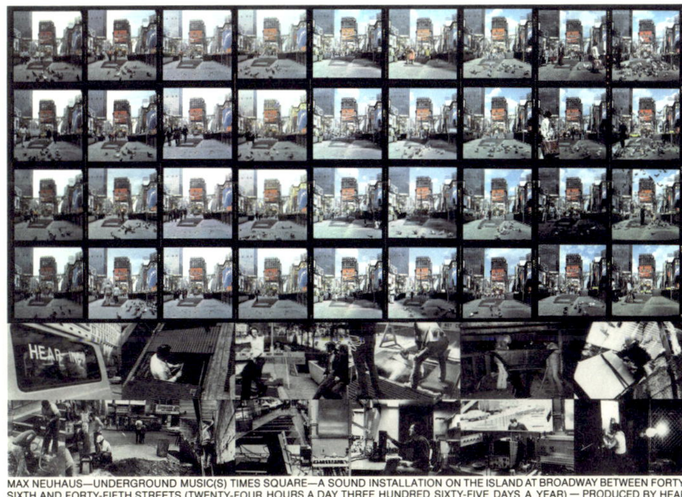

Max Neuhaus, poster for *Times Square*, 1977

Time Piece Beacon (2005–present)—was his. In general, Max rejected the use of photographs of the physical sites where his sound works were located. He favored what he termed Circumscription drawings, with the caveat that they are far from adequate. Beginning in the early nineties, diptychs composed of schematic diagrams and handwritten texts became the principal visual references for his works. The source for the images of *Times Square* is a webcam trained on the midtown site, which Max consulted daily to check on the work's well-being. Covering a twenty-four-hour period, our layout of images is informed by a design he used for a poster for *Times Square* in 1977. He chose to represent *Time Piece Beacon* by means of a series of shots of Dia:Beacon's roofline, from which the sound emanates, and sketched the vantage points in digital snapshots as guides for the professional photographer assigned the task. The fading-in of photographs to conjure metaphorically an audio counterpart is based on an idea he explored in "Time Pieces," a visual essay published in an exhibition catalogue in 1983.[5] By the time of his death in February 2009, *Max Neuhaus: Times Square, Time Piece Beacon*'s structure was fully in place. Unfortunately, Max did not live to read the essays, which would doubtless have occasioned further debate. Yet, as is proper, responsibility for this book remains ours. Originally devised to open the field he charted so ambitiously to wider scholarship, it assumed a supplementary function: to record as accurately as possible information that may otherwise soon be lost. Our research has benefited enormously from the assistance of many, above all Silvia Neuhaus, who generously and unstintingly opened her archives and records to us.

Lynne Cooke

Notes

1 Notwithstanding certain accounts to the contrary, this was not a Pauline conversion. Max Neuhaus continued to perform through 1968, when he released a record of solo performances with Columbia Masterworks. In an excellent review of *Water Whistle XV, XVI,* and *XVII* (all 1974) and related works, which he acknowledges are difficult to classify as "concert or sculpture or event," Al Brunelle describes Neuhaus as "a composer of electronic music and a percussionist of note." (Brunelle, "Deep Float: Neuhaus' Water Whistle," *Art in America* 62, no. 5 [September–October 1974], p. 91.) Neuhaus's broadcast works continue to this day to be discussed in relation to music. (See, for example, *Max Neuhaus: Evocare l'udible* [Milan: Charta, 1995], p. 37.) In a December 6, 1974, Op-Ed piece for the *New York Times*, he was identified simply as "a composer," and he originally called *Times Square* (1977–92; 2002–present) *Underground Music(s) I.*

2 For most vanguard artists in New York in the seventies, the measure of success was not selling all the works in a gallery show but rather realizing ambitious projects by means of public and private patronage. Measured by this (admittedly local) yardstick, Neuhaus's achievement is clear: three leading galleries of the day (Leo Castelli, Sonnabend, and John Weber) each sponsored unmarketable Water Whistle works, and the Museum of Modern Art presented an untitled work in its sculpture garden in 1978; his most notable public project in those years, *Times Square*, was created with the assistance of the New York Metropolitan Transportation Authority.

3 Christoph Cox, "Installing Duration: Time in the Sound Works of Max Neuhaus," in this book, p. 116.

4 Branden W. Joseph, "An Implication of an Implication," in this book, p. 60.

5 Max Neuhaus, "Time Pieces," in *Max Neuhaus: Sound Installation* (Basel: Kunsthalle Basel, 1983), pp. 25–33.

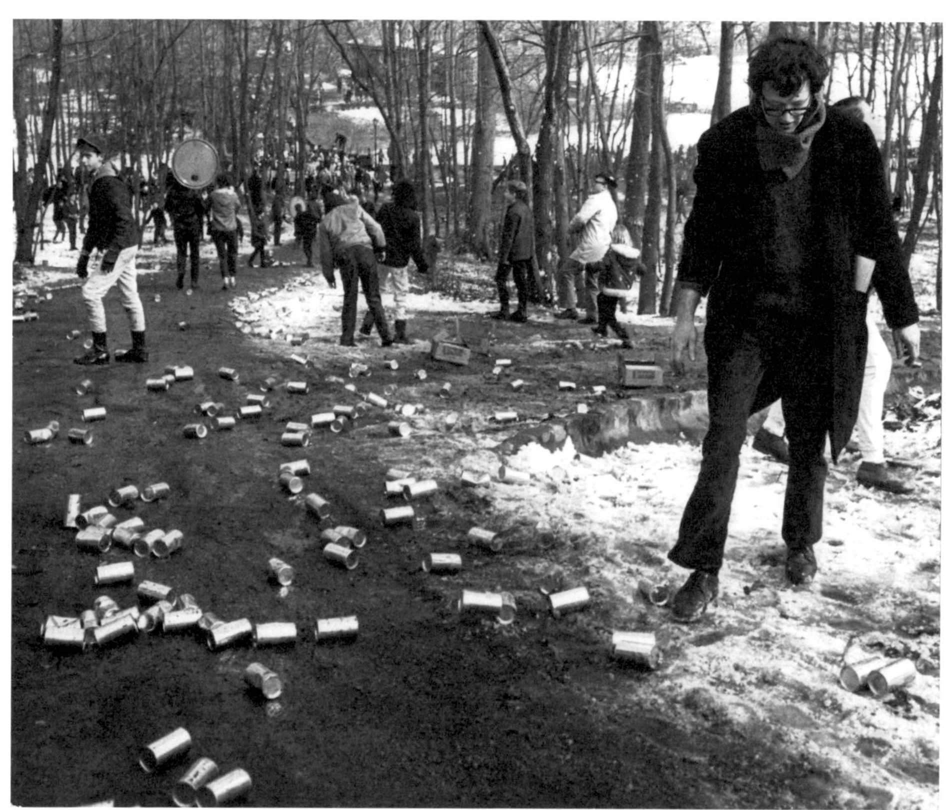

Max Neuhaus, *American Can*, Clove Lakes Park, Staten Island, New York, February 19, 1967, photo by Peter Moore

Locational Listening

Lynne Cooke

> *The sound is not the work; the sound is the material that I make the place out of. . . . The social context, the physical context, the architectural context, the acoustical context are my building blocks.*
> —Max Neuhaus

I.

In his own estimation, the first independent work Max Neuhaus made as a visual artist was also the first in what was to become a series of some fifteen works grouped under the collective title *Listen*. Inaugurated in February 1966, they continued intermittently for more than a decade. The earliest were promenades, their itineraries and schedules determined by the artist, who led the tours, offering no commentary.[1] Announced as concert programs, they were broadcast by word of mouth: participants were met by the artist at designated meeting points at prearranged times. After he had stamped the word *LISTEN* on their hands, Neuhaus took them on a walk that followed a carefully designated route, during which they encountered a series of soundscapes that included the heavy rumble generated by a Con Edison power plant, the vibrant street noise of a congested Puerto Rican neighborhood, and the roar of a freeway. Concluding the program was a solo performance at Neuhaus's studio comprising percussion pieces by John Cage, Morton Feldman, the artist himself, and others. Later *Listen* excursions, often to otherwise inaccessible industrial locations, took on the label "lecture demonstrations": like their predecessors, they were designed "to refocus people's aural perspective."[2] Each trip's aural composite was carefully scripted by the artist, though participants heard only whatever they individually concentrated on. Chance inevitably played a role in Neuhaus's art—given that horns blare, sirens scream, tires squeal, and children shriek, along with other uncontrollable and unpredictable explosions—but, compared with its part in the works of Cage in particular, its impact was strictly contained. Not only were the structures of his *Listen* "scores" predetermined, so were the basic acoustic materials. With that initial sortie, he galvanized his audience to leave the precincts of the auditorium and to enter the urban outdoors and thus to engage dynamically rather than passively as they did in a conventional concert situation; he limned a kind of manifesto. By "equating percussion music to urban environmental sounds and allying machine noise with the soundscape of an ethnic-minority neighborhood," Neuhaus announced the manmade urban realm was to be his preferred matrix, and its physical, architectural, and social contexts his building blocks, as Branden W. Joseph notes.[3] Of course, each pedestrian's experience would be subtly different: each would necessarily be subjective—but perhaps not more so than in any musical performance, where concentration, attention, focus, reflection, emotion, and memory shape and filter what is heard and how it is received, and possibly even less so, given that the title the artist chose for these polemical works was not simply a sign, a mark of attendance at a social situation like a hand stamp at a disco or club. Neuhaus's stencil is, instead, an injunction, one that is made all the more insistent by his use of a typeface of bold, blocky capital letters: "LISTEN."[4] The engaged, alert mode of hearing—"deep listening"—required to navigate his urban field trips transformed them into something more consequential than casual. A "more finely tuned and focused attentiveness . . . comes into play," Alex Potts argues, "once one apprehends something out of the ordinary and experiences the heightened level of awareness associated with aesthetic experience."[5]

Given that the artist himself led these field trips, he presumably set the pace, allocating a length of time to each particular soundscape. Moreover, since he issued neither maps nor sets of instructions for individuals to follow on their own, his lecture demonstrations could no more be imagined in advance than could they be independent of their creator. They consequently bear little in common with either contemporary Fluxus events or Happenings, to which they are sometimes compared. Neuhaus did not privilege the insignificant and humble, as did, say, Dick Higgins or Allan Kaprow; he did not desire to fuse art with life's mundanities, rely on the aleatory, or embrace an unbounded temporality that accommodated the whims of his participants.[6] And, even though he hoped to expand his audience beyond the elitist circles he associated with the customary concert-hall crowd, and though he, too, chose to work in free, readily accessible public spaces with what he would later term "uncodified" sounds, he essentially believed that the creation of great art was a stringent disciplinary practice.[7]

Since little documentation remains from those early field trips beyond cursory verbal accounts and sundry photographs, it is problematic to draw detailed conclusions about the aural life of their environments. Several photographs taken on these early field trips by Peter Moore, although probably not commissioned by the artist, are nonetheless revealing.[8] In one hitherto unpublished shot, a hand bearing Neuhaus's tell-tale stencil is framed against an industrial backdrop dominated by a smokestack

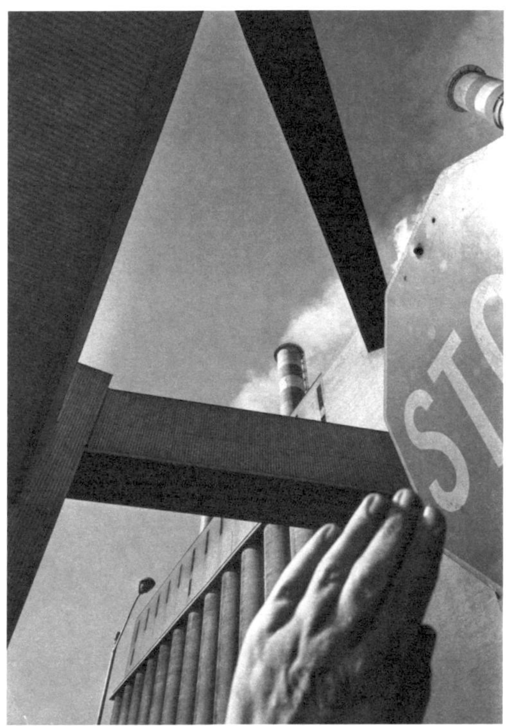

Photo by Peter Moore taken during Max Neuhaus's *Listen* sound walk, beginning on the corner of Avenue D and East 14th Street, New York, March 27, 1966

and juxtaposed with a street sign that commands the observer, or, better, the would-be listener, to "stop." The combination of asymmetrical composition, vertiginous viewpoint, and high-contrast black-and-white tonal range, together with the textual play, is in direct homage to Constructivist photography produced in the twenties and thirties in the Soviet Union by Alexander Rodchenko and his peers. Moore's knowing reference to a moment when industrialization was championed by artists and others as crucial to the process of modernization, and thereby key to implementing a modernist ideology, seems ironic in the context of New York City in the late sixties. For at that very moment, as witnessed in Danny Lyon's seminal series of images published in 1969, *The Destruction of Lower Manhattan*, the city was experiencing a phase of deindustrialization, which would result in the unprecedented decline and demolition of its waterfront, manufacturing districts, and even some residential neighborhoods (including those where Neuhaus and his peers lived and worked and where most of his Manhattan-based field trips would take place).

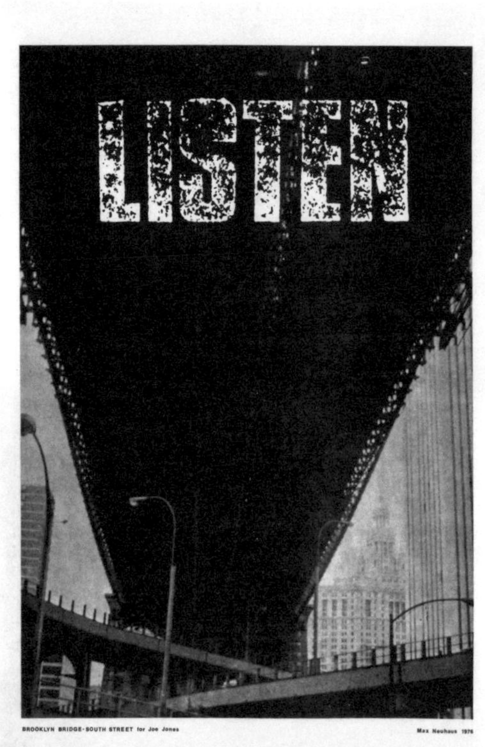

Max Neuhaus, *Listen* poster showing the Brooklyn Bridge taken from South Street, 1976

The *Listen* walks had been performative and participatory; more conceptual variants of the series then followed. One was an Op-Ed piece for the *New York Times*, published on December 6, 1974, which chastised the city's bureaucrats for unduly treating all urban sound as an irritant: "the basic point being that by arbitrarily condemning most man-made sounds as noise, they were making noise where it never existed before," Neuhaus wrote.[9] In addition, he made his own publications, notably posters and even a postcard in the form of a sticker, "a decal with the word outlined in open letters, to be placed in locations selected by its recipients."[10] With these last works in the *Listen* series, he finally relinquished agency to his audience, encouraging them, in turn, to engage others in an aural appreciation of the urban environment. Like Moore's photos, the images that Neuhaus used for his posters acknowledge the grandeur and drama of the city's industrial infrastructure. Among the most memorable is one, from 1976, that features the Brooklyn Bridge (which, when traffic flowed over its grated surfaces, emitted a deep tone that the artist relished): shot from below, the monumental steel structure pictured on the poster turns into an emphatic dark wedge that boldly bisects the composition; at its base, two freeways cross; over it float gritty letters spelling out *LISTEN*.[11]

During this first decade of his career (from about 1966 to 1977), Neuhaus preferred sites that encompassed both relatively neglected and highly trafficked outdoor urban locations; most had a markedly industrial timbre. Gradually, he eliminated all effects of the performative, which he saw as the province of music, and began to engage with his audience more collaboratively, as glimpsed in another of Moore's shots, this one taken during an event known as *American Can,* staged during the winter of 1966–67 in Staten Island's Clove Lakes Park and other locations around the city. Participants were invited to bounce or slide the cans that carpeted the ground, though whether they were given additional directions and temporal guidelines is no longer known.[12] A commonplace activity, usually associated with melancholic, aimless wandering and purposeless play, seems to have been detourned here by Neuhaus into a constructive collective action. Tellingly, the crowd generated the sound component of the work; it did not preexist as in his *Listen* series. It was no longer found sound.[13]

Shortly after, in *Fan Music* (1967), which he described as his first Place work, Neuhaus transferred performative agency to the site itself by harnessing solar power to generate sonic change. The artwork became responsive to atmospheric conditions, to humidity and temperature. Sited on the rooftops of four adjacent buildings on the Bowery, the piece comprised photovoltaic cells placed behind rotating fan blades, which, in turn, activated loudspeakers that broadcast sounds whose tone and volume were affected by a range of weather-related factors. Visitors could come and go at will over the four-day period of the work's installation; they could also experience it from multiple positions, from each of which the piece would sound different. Although *Fan Music* was installed only briefly, it signals a crucial shift away from "event" and toward "place," in that it utilized a fixed site (albeit temporary) and engaged immaterial features of that site. Moreover, for the first time in his practice, by amplifying and supplementing the existing soundscape, Neuhaus generated a new one.[14]

Leaving the skies in the early seventies, Neuhaus next immersed himself in aquatic realms. Creating a series titled *Water Whistle*, he allowed his audiences to access the works' acoustics while swimming or floating. After presenting fourteen of these works in pools across North America, he focused in late spring 1974 on New York City, where—with sponsorship from the three leading galleries of the day, Leo Castelli, Sonnabend, and John Weber—he launched new versions in a trio of outdoor facilities heated to a comfortable ninety-three degrees. By means of hoses of various lengths and diameters capped with whistlelike contraptions, Neuhaus created a sonic topography at once steady and full of subtle variations. "Being immersed in the musical experience was not a metaphor here but a fact," Al Brunelle wrote in a thoughtful analysis of these engaging public works.[15] Although initially struck by only the shrill sounds, swimmers soon honed their ability to discriminate among the more finely calibrated tones. Moreover, the comfortable warmth of the water induced a sensation that the acoustic element was being experienced not only through the ears but through the skin, to the point where, Brunelle writes, it finally appeared as though "the music didn't have much to do any more with either ears or skin and seemed to be dreamy, dark shifting vapors of mood."[16] Eluding easy classification, these concert events once again freed participants to orchestrate their own experience, finding and fine-tuning the range of available sounds as they moved through the water, exploring the sculptural topography.

At about this time, Neuhaus finally circumvented the event-based character of many of his previous works by returning to more anonymous, transitional urban spaces. *Walkthrough* (1973–77), the first of two related installations, occupied an overtly transitional space, the arcade of the Jay Street–Borough Hall subway station in Brooklyn. There he introduced a series of pings and clicks, some more hollow than others, which seemed to move around the space. Unsigned and unmarked, this piece lasted some four years, until a subway official, irritated by its invasion of what he considered his terrain, dismantled it. That same year, 1977, Neuhaus turned his attention to a remarkable acoustic chamber in a subway ventilation shaft in midtown Manhattan. Installing equipment at this public and yet undefined, "leftover," and easily accessible Manhattan site again required the approval of the Metropolitan Transportation Authority. Located on the north end of a triangular pedestrian island between Forty-fifth and Forty-sixth streets at the intersection of Broadway and Seventh Avenue, it was part of an area long celebrated as the "Crossroads of the World" but run-down and seedy by the early seventies. Well known for its illicit traffic, it was home to porn cinemas, drug dealing, prostitution, cruising, petty crime, and vagrants. Neuhaus's plan to install a public sculpture—albeit an invisible one—in what remained a glamorous and legendary, though tarnished, location required considerable bravura.

The artistic ethos that inflected his bold gesture of (re)claiming this landmark for the wider public was one he now shared with a number of his peers. Neuhaus could no longer feel himself isolated, if he ever had.[17] In 1970, Richard Serra had persuaded the local police to allow him to install a sculpture in a cul-de-sac in the South Bronx. This neglected, crime-ridden area proved to be a place that most of the artist's friends and peers considered too dangerous to visit, so few actually saw the sculpture. It is unlikely that the local inhabitants paid any attention either to this unmarked and anonymous industrial artifact, whether or not they considered it an artwork. (Anonymity would be the key term that, several years later, Neuhaus hoped would frame his similarly unmarked sound piece in midtown Manhattan.[18]) That same year, 1970, independent curator and artist Willoughby Sharp initiated a series of projects with twenty-seven artists, including Vito Acconci, Dan Graham, and Serra, on Pier 18, one of many deserted and decaying piers then lining the Hudson.[19] And, though he had previously only found suitable places in the outer boroughs and cities elsewhere in the country, Gordon Matta-Clark also decided on the abandoned West Side piers as the most appropriate location for a major work in Manhattan. In a clandestine, unauthorized guerrilla action, he created one of his most ambitious works, *Day's End*, on Pier 52 in the summer of 1975.[20] So inaccessible and dangerous was its site that when his friends and other art-world avatars wished to see it, he was obliged to allow only guided tours.[21] Not long after, the police denied all access. Douglas Crimp writes in a groundbreaking evocation of the deindustrializing city as the prime site for artists and others to engage: "the subject and site of Matta-Clark's art was the city itself, the city experienced simultaneously as neglected and usable, as dilapidated and beautiful, as loss and possibility."[22] In contrast to the dramatic, even heroic, portrayal of the Brooklyn Bridge in his 1976 poster, Neuhaus discerned in Times Square an ambience more aligned with that of sites favored by Matta-Clark and Serra. The grimy and neglected physical context of the work was conjured in the poster he designed to mark its inauguration by a series of repeating images, like a filmstrip, that limns the transient, ever-changing nature of the locale. (Another sequence of images shows the installation of the equipment, a focus on physical labor that is exceptional in the artist's oeuvre.)

While Neuhaus, Matta-Clark, and Serra (with his *St. John's Rotary Arc* [1980]) would all make their most ambitious and remarkable public works for New York City in what might then have been described as "leftover" public space,[23] none of these artists were opposed in principle to institutional venues or to public patronage. All responded opportunistically—that is, pragmatically rather than ideologically—to commissions and invitations of diverse kinds.[24] For all three, the spatial and physical character of a site in effect constituted its aesthetic potential, but also crucial was its accessibility (hypothetically, at least) by a wide range of people. In pursuit of an antielitist stance, no markers indicating the entity as an artwork were deemed necessary: it was up to each individual to experience it in any terms he or she chose. The radical politic informing Neuhaus's realization of *Times Square* in 1977 was not just a product of that antiestablishment era but also his recurrent concern. When, in 2002, *Times Square* was restored and relaunched under the auspices of Dia Art Foundation, Neuhaus was still adamant that there be no signage.[25] With no plaque recording the name of the piece, the artist, the sponsors, or the owners on the site, there is nothing to signify the presence of an artwork.

If a low public profile was essential to the identity and ethos of this work, the question of its maintenance was of the highest order; strict vigilance was required from the institution to which it had been entrusted. Dia's technician and the artist himself would inspect the site daily via a webcam.[26] While Neuhaus embraced the myriad activities and temporary interventions that now make this one of the most highly trafficked vehicular and pedestrian areas in the city, he could not abide the ongoing presence of street musicians, in particular the self-styled Naked Cowboy, who regularly used the triangular grating as a makeshift stage. Frequent email and telephone bulletins would arrive from southern Italy (where Neuhaus had been living since the 1990s), advising Dia of ingenious ways in which it might discourage, if not forcibly evict, the busker from his daily perch. At first, this barrage of missives was mistakenly received as humorous, petulant grandstanding rather than as deadly serious demands; however, their persistence and increasingly aggravated tone—rare lapses in the artist's usual courtly demeanor—revealed them as products of principle. More was at issue than the gimmickry in the ersatz popular entertainer's pose designed to attract tourists. His long-term presence on the site was anathema to Neuhaus because in giving a focus to the pedestrian island it transformed that nondescript, mundane place of transit, where passersby, if attentive to their aural environment, could encounter an unexpectedly resonant presence. By destabilizing the aural and visual ecology of the site, the constant presence of the Naked Cowboy became, for the artist, not only an affront but a violation.

As the economic climate in the United States worsened in the later seventies and public arts funding in large part dried up, Neuhaus and his peers began to receive more commissions from European institutions for works in public venues. Partly as a result of finding himself working more frequently there, Neuhaus relocated to Europe in the mid-eighties. Neither he, Serra (after his controversial *Tilted Arc* was installed in Federal Plaza in 1981), nor Matta-Clark (who died in 1978) would again make large-scale outdoor works in New York City.[27] During the eighties and nineties, Neuhaus, who occasionally created works for commercial galleries and for international group shows like Documenta, sought whenever possible to ensure that his pieces would become permanent, as had occurred in 1992 with *Three to One*, a piece he installed in the AOK health-insurance building in Kassel. Among his key commissions from this period were a number of what he termed Place works that were sited in more or less transitional spaces—that is, sites that were not, in themselves, destinations, but were thoroughfares to places elsewhere: a small park adjacent to the Musée Rath, Geneva

(*Promenade du Pin* [2002–present]); a footbridge in Bern (*Suspended Sound Line* [1999–present]); and the historic atrium that marked the entrance to the Castello di Rivoli, Turin (*Untitled* [1996–present]). Writing of these Place works in 1997, Neuhaus stated: "Unlike music where the sound is the artwork, here sound is used as a subtle tool to shape a new perception of space."[28] Two words are critical here: "subtle" and "perception." The works were subtle because they were made of and from their site—that is, with the constituents of their site as their bricks and mortar. Hence the sounds were not easily recognized as aberrant, unlike, say, the clicks at Jay Street. And they offered an unprecedented way of perceiving the site. That is, because their invisibility and muted acoustics rendered them elusive, the audience was required to be proactive rather than simply reactive, as was the audience for the early *Listen* pieces, when it was the percussive barrage of sound that characterized each work as much as the aural environment. By the mid-seventies it was less the work of Cage than that of Morton Feldman that seems to have offered Neuhaus fresh guidance. Writing about Feldman's piano works of the early sixties, the British composer Cornelius Cardew had argued that "Feldman sees the sounds as reverberating endlessly, never getting lost, changing their resonances as they die away, or rather do not die away, but recede from our ears, and soft because softness is compelling, because an insidious invasion of our senses is more effective than a frontal attack, because our ears must strain to catch the music." In Cardew's opinion, audiences "must become more sensitive before they [can] perceive the world of sound in which Feldman's music takes place."[29] Something similar may be said of the soundscapes that followed *Times Square*. Whether in Geneva, Bern, or outside Turin, Neuhaus's Place pieces are most often found in natural or rural settings, with none of the textural qualities of dense, bustling midtown Manhattan. Even so, what they share with Times Square is more significant than how they differ, for the same methodology is employed in each context. The soundscape is constructed from the location's acoustic and other features; it is then introduced on site in such a way that a bystander must pay close attention, first, to apprehend it and, then, to explore its sonic topography—the means to a new apprehension of the context.

II.

In recent years, Neuhaus divided his time mostly between Place and Moment works. In the latter group, to which *Time Piece Beacon* (2005–present) belongs, periodic, almost imperceptible, sonic tones gradually build up over several minutes, then abruptly cease at a designated moment—the hour, in the case of Dia's piece. This sudden absence produces what at first seems to be a silence, a silence that to many people proves more audible than was the sound's presence. For, in what is perceived as silence is the ambient sound particular to that site in that particular instant. The last Moment work Neuhaus created, in 2007, was commissioned by the small German town of Stommeln-Pulheim. The arrest of the low, almost inaudible, hum, again created from and in relation to its sonic environment—a site fronting a former synagogue—marks the halachic hours of the Jewish ritual day.[30] Recalling another absence—that of the town's former Jewish population—this work, in addressing historical memory, takes on an overtly memorializing dimension rare in Neuhaus's oeuvre. Previously, issues relating to a site's history concerned him less than its sociopolitics.[31]

As issues of identity and history come to the fore in the Moment pieces, so do notions of community. Whatever sense of collectivity is generated by a Place work like *Times Square* is a function of serendipity, of coexistence and contiguity; it automatically involves those who recognize and engage with the work. Yet, as Branden Joseph argues, referencing Giorgio Agamben's *The Coming Community*, this fugitive community implies and entails nothing beyond itself at that moment: it is built on "adjacency rather than identification with whatever exclusionary ideal."[32] In contrast to the Place pieces, the Moment works operate on two distinct registers. The uninitiated, the casual passersby, attend to the silence, which they experience more in their bodies than in their minds. However, for those who become familiar with a Moment piece, and who therefore experience it as a part of their daily soundscape, the sound, too, plays a role. Sometimes consciously, often almost unconsciously, its iteration is registered as each hour approaches.

The regular and frequent whistles from passing trains, counterpoints to *Time Piece Beacon*'s precisely scheduled interventions, are similarly impossible to ignore: they, too, are integral to the site's sonic texture. Yet, though also periodic, they do not share the invincible regularity—the reliability—of this Moment piece and so lack its deterministic authority. Moreover, their sound is commonplace and generic, whereas that of *Time Piece Beacon* is singular. At once unique and instantly identifiable, Neuhaus's piece functions as a timekeeper whose auditory code imparts identity to the terrain within its sonic reach, effecting a kind of social bond, however rudimentary its basis.

While *Time Piece Beacon* has a distinctive acoustic signature, its low, ringing harmonic tone has been likened, by the artist himself as well as others, to the sound of bells: it evokes not merely the function but the character and rhetoric of campanology in rural places in times past.[33] As Alain Corbin reveals in his fascinating study *Village Bells: Sound and Meaning in the 19th-Century French Countryside*, the ringing of bells traditionally served multiple roles—in addition to providing an index of collective sensibilities, it fulfilled various communicative agendas: public and private, secular and religious, exceptional and mundane, singular and regulatory, festive and tragic.[34] The unique sound of a hand-cast bell in a clarion ensured that the compass of its reach would identify the community when no other form of communication could range so far so fast and none could prove so resourceful and distinctive. Audible to virtually everyone within its sonic field, it demarcated space acoustically and imparted identity by drawing boundaries to shared territory.[35]

The people who frequent Dia:Beacon could be said to constitute a small, temporary, and quite specialized community, in contrast to, say, the considerably larger, stable, and more diverse citizenry of Graz, Austria, whose town square is the site of another work in the Moment series. By reactivating older notions of community, both works provide an occasion for thinking about the identity, desirability, and viability of community: to its current relevance as well as its historical legacy. In one of his few statements about historical change, Neuhaus argued that by about AD 1100, "the church bell had become united with the mechanical clock. The bell no longer just announced special events but provided a communal time base for the general coordination of activities." He noted that today "most of these minute by minute functions have been taken over by radio and television." By his reckoning, this change entailed a loss measurable in terms of the particularity and individuality of place and, hence, of community: "The intrinsic nature of these media generalizes and depersonalizes functions," he concluded.[36] His succinct overview contains a clear expression of the sociopolitical dimension at the core of this final series of works and implies a potentially stronger notion of community than that which, pace Joseph, pertains to the Place pieces. For, in addition to confirming the value Neuhaus attributed to any significant work of art in the public sphere, this statement highlights a key function he now required of locational—and even, perhaps, localized—listening.

Notes

1 Note, by contrast, the earliest of Max Neuhaus's installation pieces, the drive-by sound work titled *Drive-in Music* (1967), heard by tuning a car radio to a specified frequency while driving along a mile of the Lincoln Parkway near the Albright-Knox Art Gallery in Buffalo. The freeway was a popular trope at this time, following Tony Smith's account of his transformative experience on the New Jersey Turnpike, a narrative that featured prominently in Michael Fried's seminal essay, "Art and Objecthood," *Artforum* 5, no. 10 (June 1967), pp. 12–23; reprinted in Michael Fried, *Art and Objecthood: Essays and Reviews* (Chicago: University of Chicago Press, 1998), pp. 148–72. See, for another example, Robert Smithson's *New York, New Jersey* (1967) illustrated in *Robert Smithson* (Berkeley: University of California Press, 2004), p. 130.

2 Neuhaus, "Listen," in *Max Neuhaus: Elusive Sources and "Like" Spaces* (Turin: Giorgio Persano, 1990), p. 21; also at http://www.maxneuhaus.info/soundworks/vectors/walks/LISTEN. A comparison should also be made with Smithson's contemporaneous field trips to New Jersey's Pine Barrens and other sites that he felt were underappreciated. "The Crystal Land," Smithson's first important article, published in *Harper's Bazaar* in May 1966, followed an outing to a quarry with Nancy Holt and Donald and Julie Judd. The field trip provided the basis for the multilayered text, which filtered, through a highly subjective lens, speculative references garnered from geology, natural history, and other subjects. Subsequent trips led to further works, notably his 1967 essay "The Monuments of Passaic," *Artforum* 6, no. 4 (December 1967), pp. 48–51.

3 Branden W. Joseph, "An Implication of an Implication," in this book, p. 63.

4 By linking noise pollution to urban sounds, public officials "in effect robbed us of the ability to listen to our environment," Neuhaus argued in a *New York Times* Op-Ed piece, which he considered a work in the *Listen* series. (Neuhaus, "BANG, BOOooom, ThumP, EEEK, tinkle," *New York Times*, December 6, 1974, p. 39.) Neither then nor later did he wish to elicit a meditative response from his audience. While he categorically rejected that notion on account of the "baggage" it contained, he also separated himself from the idea of providing a spiritual retreat of the kind that characterized the sound and light environments of La Monte Young and Marian Zazeela, their Dream Houses in particular. At the same time, Neuhaus eschewed a provocative polemical stance like that of Bruce Nauman, who abrasively and sometimes sadistically taunted his audience: "Pay attention motherfuckers" (see his lithograph *Pay Attention* from 1973, illustrated in *Bruce Nauman* [Minneapolis: Walker Art Center, in association with the Hirshhorn Museum and Sculpture Garden, Washington, D.C., 1993], p. 68).

5 Alex Potts, "Moment and Place: Art in the Arena of the Everyday," in this book, p. 50.

6 The ideas behind Neuhaus's *Listen* works are thus diametrically opposed to those of a piece La Monte Young describes in his "Lecture 1960," which consisted only of the word *listen* but "was entirely indeterminacy and left the composer out of it." (See Young, "Lecture 1960," in *Happenings and Other Acts*, ed. Mariellen R. Sandford [New York: Routledge, 1995], p. 75.) Because Neuhaus's body of work might be described as directorial, it might be related to the contemporaneous sound pieces of Nauman, who, though never present in public as a performer, set up situations in which he could not only determine but could also closely monitor those who engaged with his work, whether it be in a narrow corridor that required careful negotiation to pass within its constricted frame or an audio installation with sound that emerged from walls stripped of any architectural features.

7 See Neuhaus, discussion with members of the International Academy of Philosophy of Art, Bern (1998), http://max-neuhaus.info/bibliography/IAPA.htm; also published as

"Vortrag Neuhaus," in *End of Art—Endings in Art,* ed. Gerhard Seel (Basel: Schwabe Verlag, 2006).

8 Neuhaus tended to avoid documentary photography, since it recorded neither the sound nor the phenomenological and kinaesthetic means by which the work was experienced. This stance reflects the attitudes of contemporaries like Robert Irwin, who refused to have his installations documented, but it diverges from that of such Conceptual artists as Robert Barry, who was famously pictured releasing inert gases in documentary photographs alongside texts, which then were sold as the material component of the artworks (for example, *Inert Gas: Neon* [1969]).

9 Neuhaus, "Listen," p. 21.

10 Ibid., p. 22.

11 The black-and-white grainy aesthetic, the subject matter, and even the typography in the poster might be seen as reminiscent of Richard Serra's documentation of his work. Also like Serra, Neuhaus seems to have been opposed to forms of mediation, preferring instead a phenomenologically based experience. Note that there are no references in Neuhaus's posters to uptown areas, such as cross streets lined with brownstones or bucolic parts of Central Park, suggesting that these held no attraction as sites for Neuhaus's sonic field trips. This differentiates them from Richard Long's walks, known through text pieces and still photographs, which gained considerable attention in New York in the late sixties. In his romantic approach to nature, Long avoided any reference to either the contemporary world or its industrial manifestations. Undertaken by the artist alone in remote, often wild and inaccessible landscapes, Long's works could only be experienced vicariously, like those of On Kawara in his series *I Met* (1968–79) and Stanley Brouwn in *This Way Brouwn* (1960–64). All three of these artists used textual, diagrammatic, and/or visual forms of representation.

12 "The ground upon which the product is distributed should be hard enough to insure that a sound is made when the product is bounced or slid along it." (Quoted from text on a flyer that Neuhaus produced in September 1966 for *American Can.*)

13 A comparison with two Fluxus works is telling: *Violin with String* (1961), in which Nam June Paik dragged a violin on a string through the street until it disintegrated, and a piece by Robin Page in which he solicited the help of his audience in kicking his guitar, past both the Museum of Modern Art and the Whitney Museum of American Art, during the May 1963 Yam Festival in New York.

14 In taking to the roofs of downtown Manhattan, Neuhaus was soon followed by others. For example, in 1970, the roof of a building on Broadway had provided the point of departure for Trisha Brown's *Man Walking down the Side of a Building*; three years later, she choreographed *Roof Piece*, a work that incorporated a number of downtown rooftops. The audiences of both pieces congregated informally, choosing whatever seemed to them the most convenient vantage point.

15 Al Brunelle, "Deep Float: Neuhaus' 'Water Whistle,'" *Art in America* 62, no. 5 (September–October 1974), p. 91.

16 Ibid.

17 Many artists at the time were increasingly finding and even preferring sites outside major institutions, which they attacked on the grounds that they were exclusive, elitist, and conservative. For more on the political solidarity at this time among New York artists, many of whom were members of the Art Workers' Coalition, see Alistair Rider, "Arts of Isolation, Arts of Coalition," in *On Location: Siting Robert Smithson and his Contemporaries* (London: Blackdog, 2008), pp. 132–49.

18 Serra is the artist whom Neuhaus most consistently discussed in relation to his own practice. In addition to the phenomenologically based character of both their practices, they defined the public character of their works in similar terms. Serra was not able to realize large-scale works downtown for several years, but he eventually installed three major pieces: *St. John's Rotary Arc*, at the Holland Tunnel exit,

in 1980; *T.W.U.*, on West Broadway between Franklin and Leonard streets, in 1981; and *Tilted Arc*, in Federal Plaza, also in 1981. Serra described the first of these in terms that echo those Neuhaus could have used vis-à-vis *Times Square* (1977–92; 2002–present): arguing that it responded to the topography of the site, Serra described how the work gave "sculptural definition" to the site. And, like Neuhaus, he sought to avoid ideological cooptation by choosing what he termed "leftover sites which cannot be the object of misinterpretation": "The Rotary is totally defined by its multiple traffic regulatory functions, which in themselves create a useless central area," he wrote. "This central area, unstructured and empty, is open to pedestrian and vehicular viewing." (Serra, "*Tilted Arc* Destroyed," p. 203, and "St. John's Rotary Arc," pp. 119–123, in *Richard Serra: Writings, Interviews* [Chicago: University of Chicago Press, 1994].)

19 Harry Shunk and Janos Kender documented these projects in photographs that were shown the following year at the Museum of Modern Art. See Harry Shunk, *Projects: Pier 18* (Nice: Musée d'art moderne et contemporain, 1992).

20 In an interview given after completing *Day's End* (1975), Gordon Matta-Clark described spending his days "hunting for emptiness, for a quiet abandoned spot on which to concentrate my piercing attention." In reality, the abandoned piers were far from empty in the seventies, being a well-known and much frequented site for cruising by gay men. (Matta-Clark, *Gordon Matta-Clark: Works and Collected Writings*, ed. Gloria Moure [Barcelona: Ediciones Polìgrafa, 2006], p. 141.)

21 Neuhaus's *Times Square* was often similarly but erroneously described—obliquely by the artist, more directly by other writers such as David Toop—as a kind of guerrilla intervention. See Toop, *Haunted Weather: Music, Silence and Memory* (London: Serpent's Tail, 2004), p. 116. During the following year—1978—Neuhaus launched a study involving urban planners and city politicians, his Sirens project.

22 Douglas Crimp, "Action around the Edges," unpublished manuscript.

23 Note that in his seminal 1967 text, "Art and Objecthood," Fried had already characterized the places that would be integral to such work as "empty" or "abandoned." (Fried, "Art and Objecthood," in *Art and Objecthood*, p. 159.)

24 The result for Neuhaus was that he would install his work in a range of sites, from ad hoc situations to alternative spaces, galleries, and mainstream museums, such as the Museum of Modern Art, where an untitled work originally referred to as *Underground Music(s) II* was installed in a ventilation shaft in the institution's garden in 1978. The work was related to *Times Square*, which was originally called *Underground Music(s) I*.

25 The sole change Neuhaus made when the work was reinstalled in 2002 was that the volume of the piece increased, since he felt that the overall sound levels at the site were considerably louder than when the work was first installed.

26 In addition to requiring that the piece receive daily oversight, Neuhaus instituted a program of long-term preservation and maintenance. Fail-safe measures ensured that were there any technical malfunctions both parties—Dia and the artist—would be instantly alerted. Biannual on-site visits would further ensure against technical breakdowns, and a sophisticated software program was written to guarantee long-term accuracy.

27 Indeed, there have been very few such ambitious open-air works—Dan Graham's Rooftop Urban Park Project at Dia Art Foundation (1991), at Dia's exhibition facility on West Twenty-second Street, and Rachel Whiteread's *Water Tower* (1998) in SoHo. More recent projects, such as Olafur Eliasson's *The New York City Waterfalls* (2008), Doug Aitken's *Sleepwalkers* (2007), and Christo and Jeanne-Claude's *The Gates* in Central Park (1975/2005), were all not only temporary but high-profile marketing and media extravaganzas, the opposite of the anonymous, low-profile works created by the earlier generation.

28 Neuhaus, in *Max Neuhaus: La Collezione,*

The Collection (Milan: Charta, in association with Castello di Rivoli, Museo d'Arte Contemporanea, 1997), p. 24.

[29] Cornelius Cardew, quoted in Toop, p. 91.

[30] One of the few synagogues in the area of Cologne that survived World War II intact, this venue has been hosting contemporary art projects for almost twenty years. Neuhaus's *Time Piece Stommeln* (2007–present) is the only one to date to have become a permanent piece. (Serra's sculpture *The Drowned and the Saved*, first shown there in 1992, was later installed permanently in a related site, the Gothic sacristy of the former St. Kolumba church, which was partially destroyed by World War II bombing and now is part of the museum of the Roman Catholic Archdiocese of Cologne.)

[31] As Christoph Cox argues in "Installing Duration: Time in the Sound Works of Max Neuhaus," published in this volume, duration involves not only a concentration on the present moment but also a recognition of how the past coexists with the present, hence of how memory informs being in the moment. In his Circumscription drawing for the untitled sound work for the Castello di Rivoli, Neuhaus, exceptionally, alludes to this issue. See Neuhaus, in *Max Neuhaus: La Collezione, The Collection*, p. 34.

[32] Joseph, p. 76.

[33] This reference applies to the tonal color of many of Neuhaus's later works, most evidently *A Bell for Saint Cäcilien* (1989–91), which he installed in a disused Catholic chapel in Cologne.

[34] See Alain Corbin, *Village Bells: Sound and Meaning in the 19th-Century French Countryside* (New York: Columbia University Press, 1998).

[35] According to Neuhaus's biography published in *Max Neuhaus: La Collezione, The Collection*: "In a series of large scale works for whole communities, he utilizes the cessation of sound to create a periodic sense of silence throughout the community both marking time and creating reflective moments" (p. 37).

[36] Neuhaus, "Time Piece Series," in *Max Neuhaus: Two Sound Works 1989* (Bern: Kunsthalle Bern and Kölnischer Kunstverein, 1989), pp. 9–10.

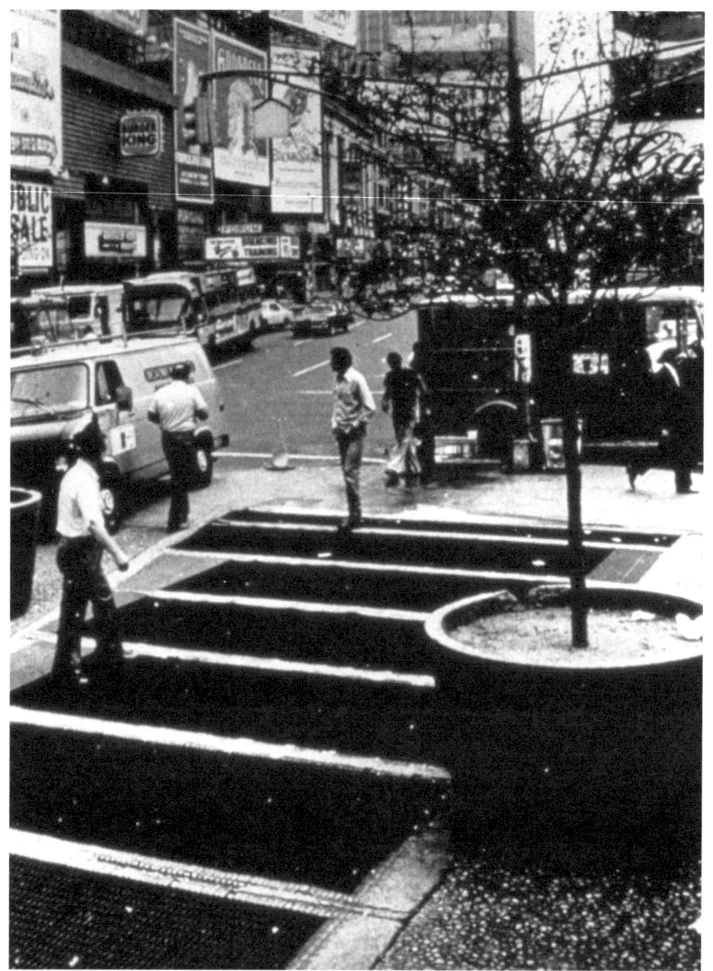

Max Neuhaus in Times Square, 1977

Moment and Place: Art in the Arena of the Everyday

Alex Potts

Max Neuhaus is a rather special case. In the 1960s and early 1970s, he established his practice—first as a performing musician and then as an artist—at a time when the idea of breaking down boundaries between art forms was being widely promoted. However, he stands out in this moment of avant-garde experimentation as one of the few figures whose work truly straddled the separate arenas of music or sound performance and art based on what Neuhaus called a "plastic sense."[1] His earlier professional involvement with sound production was brought to bear on a practice that conventionally stayed within the visual, spatial, and tactile parameters specific to three-dimensional art. Like many phenomenologically oriented visual artists, he saw his work as constituted through the audience's immediate perceptual engagement with it. As it operated at several different levels of sensory awareness, however, a problem also facing a number of other artists at the time became particularly acute in his case: his work could not be reproduced, even inadequately, in photographic images.[2]

Neuhaus's attempt to "shape, transform, create specific place, with sound only," echoes important tendencies in Minimalist and Postminimalist sculpture, site-specific art, and Land Art of the late 1960s and early 1970s—work conceived as an intervention in space rather than as a sculpted, modeled, or found object. It is important to stress these affinities because the formal and phenomenological aspects of Neuhaus's work set it apart from the Antiform and Conceptualist currents that were also prevalent at the time. Two tendencies operate in his work. Its more formal-seeming aspect relates to the Minimalist and Postminimalist preoccupation with the way a work shapes its immediate environment and with the kinesthetic rather than purely visual effects this produces.[3] There is also a more politically charged side to his work, rooted in the libertarian avant-garde of the earlier 1960s, the moment of Fluxus and Happenings and of free interchange between visual art and performance. He shared with figures such as John Cage and Allan Kaprow a strong commitment to renegotiating the boundaries between art and life.

Neuhaus systematically pursued a project that situated itself within the arena of the everyday at the same time that it activated a heightened sensory awareness. In political terms, this meant he needed to find a way to radically democratize an audience's mode of engagement with his work, without selling out to consumerist demands for entertainment. Neuhaus was fascinated by the idea of staging an aesthetic experience that was so embedded in an everyday experience of a place that one could choose to attend to the work or simply let it pass by. If it enhanced one's attentiveness, this effect was not to be felt as imposed but as generated from a willing engagement with the specific environment of the work. Along with this commitment to democratizing the artwork's address came Neuhaus's particular interest in conceiving projects for heavily trafficked public areas. Without a doubt, he authored some of the most significant projects of this kind, managing to operate largely without the ideological baggage that art fashioned for a high-profile urban site tends to carry.[4]

Space and Time

Space and *place* are key terms in Neuhaus's writing about the principles of his art, and he was explicit that these were preoccupations he shared primarily with sculptors and other artists working in three dimensions. He explained this bond in a 1982 interview, when he was still using the term *sound installation* for his work:

> In terms of classification, I'd move the [sound] installations into the purview of the visual arts even though they have no visual component, because the visual arts, in the plastic sense, have dealt with space. Sculptors define and transform spaces. I create, transform, and change spaces by adding sound.[5]

Succinctly: "I use sound to change the way we perceive a space."[6] This idea that an artwork should change one's apprehension of the space it occupies echoes the concerns of Minimalist artists such as Donald Judd, Robert Morris, and Carl Andre, who attempted to activate a temporal dynamic that played out in a viewer's circulation around or through their work.[7] A significant difference, however, in Neuhaus's case, is the medium; the sound in his work engages issues of temporality at a different level. At the same time, he was driven by a desire to distinguish his practice clearly from musical performance and its distinctive time-based character. He argued that the continuity of sound in his work differentiated it from the temporal articulation of a piece of music, in that there was no definable beginning or end and no cumulative progression, even when the sound varied in time. There was, too, no identifiable moment of performance. For him, the spatial location of sound was paramount, so that, in contrast to musical performance, sound did not entirely constitute the work. Rather, it functioned as a means of realizing ends that ultimately manifested themselves in spatial terms.[8] Even so, he did not dispute that a temporal dynamic entered into an audience's spatial experience of his sound work. Tracing a trajectory through the environment that a work defined, he or she would inevitably find that the tenor of the sound, and, hence, the distinctive apprehension of space created by the sound, changed over time.

Neuhaus was fascinated by this temporal dynamic because it was not preprogrammed but instead set by the listener-viewer's relatively freewheeling and self-determined journey through a work's spatial arena. Unlike a performance event, it provided an experience that the viewer could initiate and sever more or less at will, and was anchored in a sense of something unchanging and persistent and clearly located in space. Neuhaus summarized this in a program note he wrote in 1974: "Traditionally composers have located the elements of a composition in time. One idea which I am interested in is locating them, instead, in space, and letting the listener place them in his own time."[9]

In his later projects, Neuhaus sometimes experimented with punctuating the audience's spatial experience with sound events. Sound would emerge slowly from the ambience, growing from barely perceptible tones, and would then suddenly cut off, at which point the listener would perceive the presence of sound through its cessation, an effect comparable to that of an afterimage. Neuhaus came to distinguish between these "Moment" works and what he came to call "Place" works, where the sound, even if changing, was continuous, with no clear temporal articulation. His explanation of this distinction indicates that he did not separate out spatial from temporal works; rather, he was differentiating modalities of work that combined spatial and temporal effects. With the Moment pieces, the sound event permeates the entire area of the work at the same time it stimulates a heightened awareness of the particular place one happens to be occupying while listening to it. With the Place works, the sound varies slightly if one moves around but does not if one stands in one place. In mapping out the work's spatial parameters, however, one becomes acutely aware of the temporal nature of the particular trajectory one is tracing. Just as Moment pieces focus attention on an individually experienced sense of space, so Place pieces make one aware of being caught up in an individually experienced sense of time. As Neuhaus put it,

> The thing that makes moment pieces different from place pieces is that the moment pieces are all in places, but only occur for a moment in all those places; while the place pieces are only in one place, but are continuums which are always there.

The moment pieces don't construct places, but they cause this realization of place to happen when they disappear; in the same way that the place pieces do not construct time, but they allow your own realization of time to happen within their static nature. Each one generates in the perceiver the opposite of what it is: the moment pieces generate an instant of being in one's own place; place pieces generate a period of being in one's own time. They are two opposites; each one is what the other is not.[10]

Neuhaus's description of place in his work is reminiscent of Andre's famous designation of his work as place.[11] While Neuhaus used sound, Andre deployed low-profile, minimal sculptural interventions to create a sense of place within a relatively neutral spatial environment. One might also compare the way one approaches Andre's floor pieces, particularly those made from thin copper or steel "tiles," to the way one comes upon Neuhaus's sound pieces. Flat on the floor and, hence, out of any immediate sight lines, Andre's floor works are at first inconspicuous, almost invisible. Yet in time they become strongly present, charging the space they occupy. Similarly, Neuhaus designed his sound pieces with minimal means, low-level sounds that almost blend into the ambient noise. On first entering the arena in which the sound can be heard, one may not be at all aware of anything other than the noises normally associated with the place. But once one notices the sound, it can become engrossing to the point that one believes one still hears it even after having moved outside its range.

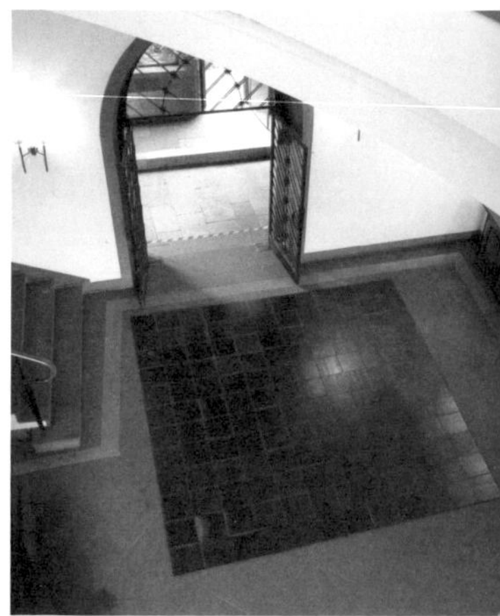

Carl Andre, *144 Steel Square*, 1969. Collection Museum für Moderne Kunst, Frankfurt am Main, as installed in the Karmeliterkloster, Frankfurt a. M., in 1991

There are also clear differences in the aims of the two artists—for one thing, in works by Andre, the source of one's reconfigured sense of space is visible and tangible. By contrast, the sources of Neuhaus's sound are hidden. The way the sound spreads through the environment and changes direction by bouncing off surfaces, and the way it mingles with, interferes with, and is disrupted by sounds coming from other sources, make it impossible to pinpoint its source. The ear cannot locate the source of a sound with anything like the accuracy that the eye can situate an object it sees. With Neuhaus, the aesthetic experience is not based in or focused on an object. The perceptible materiality of the work is constituted entirely by sound effects and the inflection they give to the place where one happens to be standing. Minimalist art, such as Andre's tiles, Judd's "specific objects," Morris's ultracool geometric shapes, or Richard Serra's massive sheets of Cor-Ten steel, may partially dismantle the conventional habit of locating the essence of a work of art in an object of some kind because

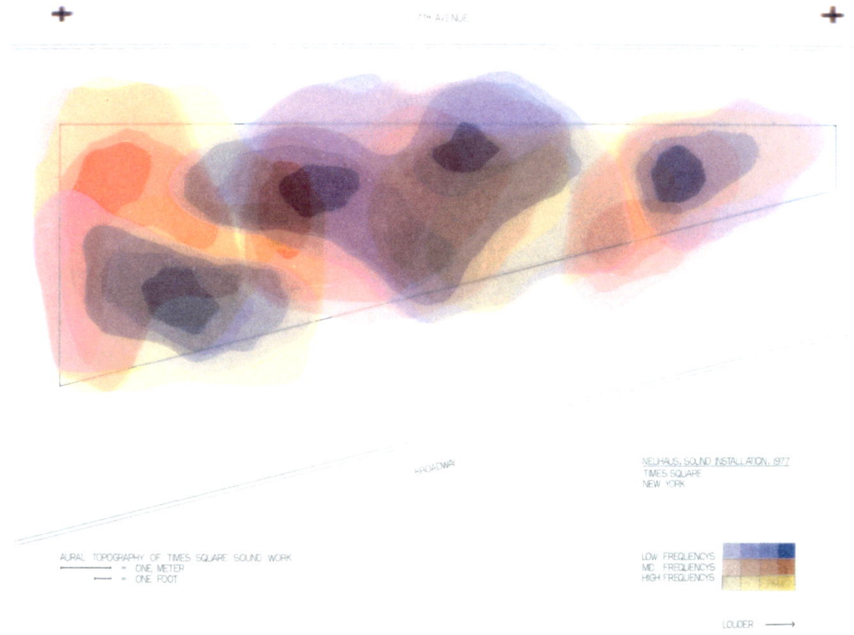

Rendering of the aural topography of *Times Square,* 1977

the intensity and interest of the perceptual experience being offered are incommensurate with the bare simplicity of the visual form. An object, though, still plays a significant role in one's experience of the work.

There is one further important distinction to be made between Neuhaus's Place pieces and most Minimalist art, and that is the all-enveloping nature of the former. A work of his sets up an aural-spatial environment that surrounds one upon entering its ambit. The sound infuses a fairly extensive space around its source. The spatial effect of most Minimalist art, by contrast, is more circumscribed, usually only being fully felt in a delimited area in the immediate vicinity of the object or structure defining it, at least before the fashion for large-scale integrated installations took over in the 1980s. The closest contemporaneous parallels are to be found in Dan Flavin's installations with fluorescent lights. His installation in New York's Kornblee Gallery in 1967, for example, was designed to reshape one's visual sense of a whole room through strategically placed fluorescent-light fixtures. Their green light permeated the whole space, rather like a sound, diffusing over the surfaces—to the point that, after a period of time, the eye's accommodation to the green coloration made it seem as if the interior of the room were neutral in color and anything outside took on a complementary rose tint. The light almost dissolved the enclosing walls and ceiling, while its varying intensity and cast shadows created a ghost spatial structuring that Judd once aptly described as an "interior exoskeleton."[12] Nevertheless, Flavin's fluorescent tubes are definable objects that could still be seen to constitute the core of the work.

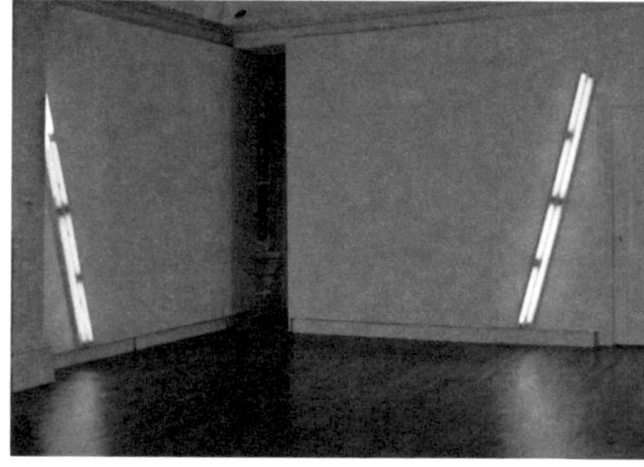

Dan Flavin, installation view, Kornblee Gallery, New York, January 7–February 2, 1967

Art and Life

On numerous occasions, Neuhaus suggested that he envisioned his work as impinging on everyday experience. Such comments are as attuned to the political dynamic of the interactions he set up as they are to the phenomenological refinements of the experience he offered. This political dimension comes out of a democratic desire to break down, blur, or thoroughly reconfigure the boundary between art and the everyday. This imperative played an important role in avant-garde initiatives of the 1960s, particularly in the earlier part of the decade. Unlike Kaprow, however, who was one of the more radical proponents of an art that would integrate with everyday life, Neuhaus did not have in mind work that would be taken as non-art. Though his sound pieces can easily be ignored or neglected by someone who passes through them and does not attend to their subtle modifications of the aural environment (even works made for museum settings can be disregarded), once a work does enter one's consciousness, it only achieves its effect, in Neuhaus's view, if it is listened to closely and given the focused attention one would accord a work of art. He thus conceived his work as both merging into the everyday aural ambience of a place and clearly differentiating itself from background noise. Appropriately, then, he consistently deployed "artificial" electronic sounds that he generated himself rather than recordings of noises from the lived environment.

In sum, his work involves its audience in an experience that moves between the low-level attentiveness that operates as one casually navigates an environment and the more finely tuned and focused attentiveness that comes into play once one apprehends something out of the ordinary and experiences the heightened level of awareness associated with aesthetic experience. What prompts someone passing through one of his sound works to take note of it is an awareness of the artificiality or implausibility of a sound effect that at first seems part of a relatively uniform continuum of ambient noise but then stands out from this background because of its slight incongruity.[13] This holds, too, for the Moment pieces, where a sound that blends with the aural texture of an environment suddenly draws attention to itself by coming to an end. Neuhaus was seeking an alternative to the deliberately staged performance, wanting to get away from "the onus of entertainment."[14] He was also suspicious of the contemplative or meditative refinements associated with work realized in the concert hall or gallery. The attentiveness he had in mind was of a different kind: "Some people call my work meditative because of this need to focus. I don't like the baggage the word carries."[15]

It is in his more public work, like *Times Square* (1977–92; 2002–present), located in a heavily used urban environment, that the democratizing of aesthetic experience he was seeking becomes particularly evident. He was not critiquing the aesthetic as inherently elitist but instead seeking to reconfigure it so that it would be rooted in one's more open and freely experienced interactions with things. Such an understanding sets his work within an American tradition of democratic pragmatism, but it also has affinities with the matter-of-fact, empirical outlook of early speculation, during the Enlightenment period, about aesthetic experience. In a passage from an interview titled "The Institutional Beast," he explains:

> I am always surprised when people ask me why I am interested in working in such places [on the street or in mass-transit systems]—as if these places were somehow unworthy of serious aesthetic endeavors. The idea being, I suppose, that unless we carefully prepare and maintain special places like museums and concert halls, and educate audiences in how to perceive works of art within them, the aesthetic experience cannot occur.
>
> I feel the opposite, i.e. that the aesthetic experience is natural to the human being, a phenomenon of living, and further that it is highly unique to each individual.[16]

This critique of the conventional isolation of aesthetic experience within specialized art spaces was not something that Neuhaus took at absolute face value; he has made many works for art-world contexts, if usually marginal, nondisplay spaces, such as exteriors and entrances, stairwells, and other avenues of circulation. Furthermore, the politics informing his comments on the quasi-elitist isolation of art in specially designated spaces can only be understood properly if seen in relation to his equally negative statements about ersatz antiaesthetic and antielitist gestures toward egalitarianism spewed by commercialized culture and globalism. Public art, as typically conceived, he thought of as "urban decor" that had become part of the "cultural muck of the mainstream." Attacking the contemporary political debasement of democracy, he protested:

> This poor word, recently mauled as a euphemism for capitalism by the free booters to justify global economic exploitation . . . in the process applied to the arts as a justification for mediocrity (a more broad based line of products). And leading then, through further semantic confusion, to "non-elitist" art—not a bad idea if applied to the audience of art (why should the appreciation of art be limited to those with insider knowledge?)—but becomes a disaster when applied to the art itself. . . . The accomplishment of a work of art is not a common occurrence; it is rare because it is difficult. When it happens it is always extraordinary.[17]

A nagging question intrudes here. Let's take Neuhaus's best-known piece, the humming sound emerging from beneath the grating of a subway ventilator shaft on a traffic island in New York's Times Square, as an example: are casual passersby actually unexpectedly arrested by the sound, and do they find it in any way unusual or special? Or does its public effectiveness largely derive from the impact it has on art-world people who know something is there and consciously seek out an aesthetic experience in this visually and aurally dense environment? They are given the opportunity to apprehend the work in such a way that it does not seem "deliberately made" and so can "claim the work as a place of their own discovering."[18] That was certainly how I experienced it when I first came across it. I spent a good deal of time wandering one evening around the wrong end of Times Square, near the army recruiting center, at times imagining I was hearing the work. I only happened to come across it just as I had given up hope of ever finding it. So it was a kind of discovery. I did not feel compelled to take note of it or see it as something special; the sound I heard could simply have been ambient noise coming from machinery below the grate, yet it had a subtly pleasurable, enveloping quality that couldn't be assimilated to the hum of a machine.

The democratic aspiration embodied in the conception of this work, however, has little to do with the actual impact it makes on the majority of people circulating through Times Square. It has much more to do with its informal mode of address. Its subtleties are such that someone from outside the art world might conceivably pick up on them and become intrigued by them. This apparent openness to the perceptual awareness of the casual passerby is more a utopian aspiration than something that could be substantiated by a survey of audience responses.[19]

Particularly intriguing is the nature of the "public" experience the work offers. There one is, loitering over a subway grate (and possibly, for some passersby, loitering to no good intent), exposed to a hyperactive urban environment and somewhat distracted by the visual stimulation, especially that emitted from electronic signage. Yet one is also caught up in a world of one's own, engrossed in listening to a just-perceptible sound

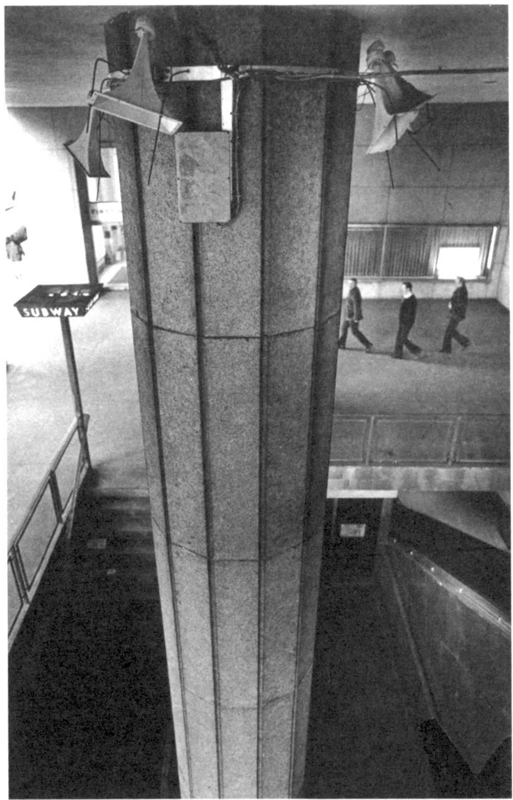

Site of Max Neuhaus's *Walkthrough* (1973–77), Jay Street–Borough Hall subway station, Brooklyn, New York

whose tonalities are a little indeterminate and unstable, shifting as one moves around yet insistently there once one has tuned into them. This is a peculiarly telling instance of a common experience in a public environment—momentarily feeling isolated by one's own response to something that catches one's attention. A work of art sited in the public sphere is public in character usually only in a very limited sense, in that it is designed to attract attention and occupy a public space. Actual responses to it, however, inasmuch as they occur, are hardly public in character. If perchance a work makes an impression on a passerby, it does so by way of that person's private, individual responses to it, even as these are played out in a public arena. Neuhaus's *Times Square* highlights this alternation between public siting and private awareness, which might be seen as the very condition of art situated in the urban spaces of a mass society that is also profoundly individualistic.

For all its weighty substance and extent, Serra's *Tilted Arc* (1981), which was removed from New York's Federal Plaza after a controversial public protest, has certain affinities with Neuhaus's *Times Square*. In many ways, it would have been similarly apprehended by passersby, at least by those who were not consumed by blind indignation at the obstacle looming before them. Serra's work was conceived not only as a thing or object but as an intervention that would alter one's perception of the space in which it was sited. The work was not simply a curved piece of steel in a city square; it was also the sense of place its presence created for those encountering and walking around it, a localized reshaping of the urban environment that operated at an intangible visual and spatial, as well as at a more literal tactile, level. Neuhaus's account of how one might ideally engage with a sound work situated in a public place offers a quite plausible way of imagining the experience to be had in a sympathetic encounter with *Tilted Arc*: "one can move through [the] topography [of a work] at one's own pace, stop where one wants to. One has the freedom to form an experience of the work for oneself but not impose it on anyone else."[20]

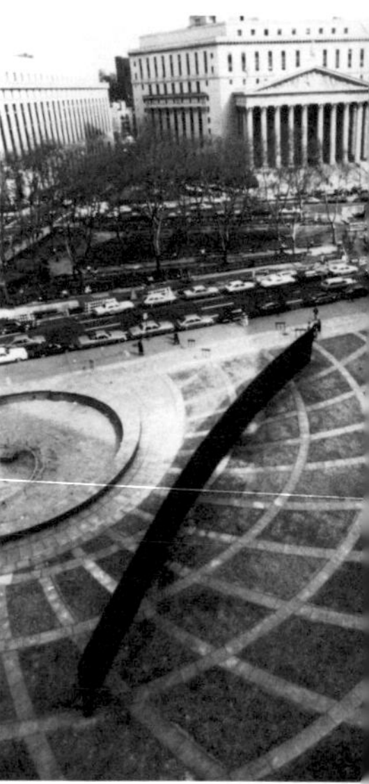

Richard Serra, *Tilted Arc*, 1981. Collection U.S. General Services Administration, Washington, D.C., destroyed by the United States government, 1989, photo by Anne Chauvet

However, the rhetorical mode of address that would have operated in a close encounter between *Tilted Arc* and a passerby clearly differentiates it from *Times Square*. Neuhaus explained how in working "in the public sphere, I am not interested in generating a confrontation. I feel like I am working in a space which is theirs [that is, belonging to the people who are using the space]. The public works are all deliberately pitched at a threshold of perception, a point where people can notice them or not notice them."[21]

In producing work that does not strive to transform the environment where it is placed, Neuhaus was effectively abandoning the revolutionary and radically progressive, collectivist aspirations that motivated many of the early modernists, aspirations that still reverberated in the post–World War II period of reconstruction and social-democratic reform. Neuhaus's works create minor interruptions or hiatuses in the sensory fabric of the everyday environment that may only be noticed by the occasional passerby. However, even assertive large-scale public sculpture nowadays is largely ignored as part of the background visual noise of a cityscape. A public sound work by Neuhaus at least offers the possibility for a compelling aesthetic experience, unadulterated by vacuous pretensions of moralizing public purpose or by the banalities of consumerist entertainment.

Neuhaus's work could be seen as an attempt, which has proved successful, to square the circle of creating contemporary public art. How is one to make public art for a society that is intensely individualistic and whose public spaces, while shared by and open to a multitude of people, atomize the perceptual and mental world of those passing through it? Compounding this problem is the issue of sustaining a commitment to making work that is genuinely democratic in its address, while operating in a context regulated by a hierarchical network of politics and finance. Neuhaus negotiated this situation by producing work that is both there and not there, almost imperceptible yet insistently present for the individual who happens to focus on it.

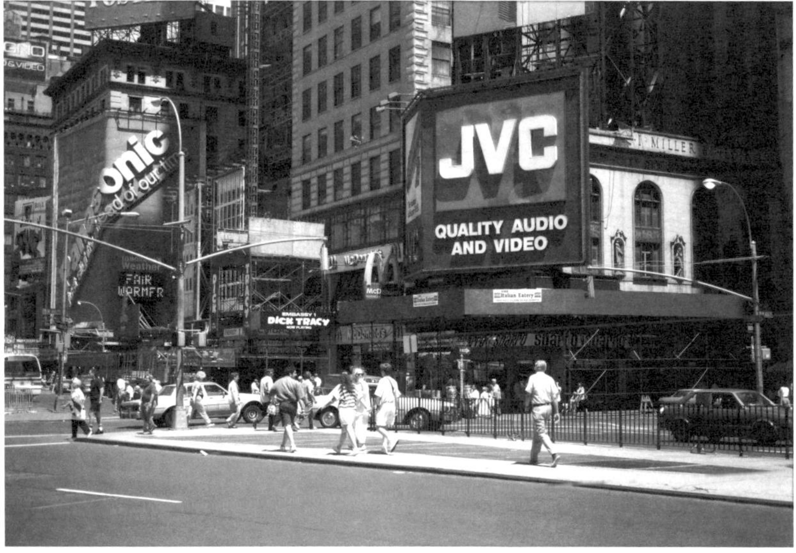

Times Square, c. 1990

Notes

1 Max Neuhaus, interview by William Duckworth (1982), in *Max Neuhaus: Sound Works*, vol. 1, *Inscription* (Ostfildern-Ruit, Germany: Cantz, 1994), p. 42. Also at http://www.max-neuhaus.info/bibliography/Duckworth.pdf. In addition to providing a collection of interviews and writings by Max Neuhaus, *Inscription* contains illuminating critical commentaries on Neuhaus's work, such as those by Calvin Tomkins and Jean-Christophe Ammann. Several of the commentators describe various sound installations in detail. Verbal description is thus the primary medium for recording these works, records that take the form of evocation or recollection rather than reproduction.

2 Neuhaus was more systematic in his refusal of photographic reproduction than almost any of his phenomenologically orientated contemporaries, devising a schema for presenting his work that actively blocks the works being considered in terms of a single image or sound recording and instead takes the form of an interplay between different levels of representation, schematic drawings on the one hand and verbal narration on the other. See Neuhaus, conversation with Ulrich Loock (1990), in *Max Neuhaus: Sound Works*, vol. 1, *Inscription*, p. 132; and Neuhaus, "Notes on the Drawings," in *Max Neuhaus: Sound Works*, vol. 2, *Drawings* (Ostfildern-Ruit, Germany: Cantz, 1994), pp. 9–11. On the often carefully contrived photographic imaging of Minimalist work, see my "The Minimalist Object and the Photographic Image," in *Sculpture and Photography: Envisioning the Third Dimension*, ed. Geraldine Johnson (Cambridge, U.K.: Cambridge University Press, 1998), pp. 181–98.

3 The new explorations into the kinesthetic experience of sculpture were formulated most explicitly by Robert Morris in his "Notes on Sculpture," *Artforum* 4, no. 6 (February 1966), p. 44; and "Notes on Sculpture, Part II," *Artforum* 5, no. 2 (October 1966), pp. 21–23.

4 For a particularly acute analysis of this problematic, see Miwon Kwon, *One Place after Another: Site-Specific Art and Locational Identity* (Cambridge, Mass.: MIT Press, 2002).

5 Neuhaus, interview by Duckworth, p. 42.

6 Neuhaus, "Lecture at the Seibu Museum Tokyo," in *Max Neuhaus: Sound Works*, vol. 1, *Inscription*, p. 60; also at http://www.max-neuhaus.info/bibliography/Tokyo.htm; from a question-and-answer session after a lecture he gave in 1982. See also Alex Potts, *The Sculptural Imagination: Figurative, Modernist, Minimalist* (New Haven, Conn.: Yale University Press, 2000), pp. 296–98, 371.

7 See, for example, Rosalind E. Krauss, *Passages in Modern Sculpture* (Cambridge, Mass.: MIT Press, 1981), pp. 266–67; and Alex Potts, *Sculptural Imagination*, pp. 236–42, 263, 312–13, 302–4.

8 Neuhaus spells this out in a conversation with Ulrich Loock, conducted in 1990 (see conversation with Loock, in *Max Neuhaus: Sound Works*, vol. 1, *Inscription*, p. 124).

9 Neuhaus, "Program Notes" (1974), in *Max Neuhaus: Sound Works*, vol. 1, *Inscription*, p. 34.

10 Neuhaus, "Notes on Place and Moment" (1992), in *Max Neuhaus: Sound Works*, vol. 1, *Inscription*, pp. 100–1; also at http://www.max-neuhaus.info/soundworks/vectors/moment/notes/.

11 See Carl Andre, interview by Phyllis Tuchman, *Artforum* 8, no. 10 (June 1970), p. 55.

12 Donald Judd, "Aspects of Flavin's Work" (1969), in *Complete Writings 1955–1975*, (Halifax: Press of the Nova Scotia College of Art and Design, in association with New York University Press, New York, 1975), p. 200.

13 Neuhaus, "Notes on Place and Moment," p. 98.

14 Neuhaus, "Modus Operandi" (1980), in *Max Neuhaus: Sound Works*, vol. 1, *Inscription*, p. 18; also at http://www. max-neuhaus.info/soundworks/vectors/passage/modusoperandi/.

15 Neuhaus, "Notes on Place and Moment," p. 98.

16 Neuhaus, "The Institutional Beast" (1994), in *Max Neuhaus: Sound Works*, vol. 1, *Inscription*, p. 82; also at http://www.max-neuhaus.info/

bibliography/InstitutionalBeast.htm. Some of Neuhaus's earliest works, such as the series of "sound walks" titled *Listen* (1966–76), when he was working in a more informal mode similar to that of Happenings and Fluxus artists, involved activities in which audiences were asked to listen. See Allan Kaprow, "Education of the Un-Artist, Part III," in *Essays on the Blurring of Art and Life* (Berkeley: University of California Press, 1993), pp. 138–39.

[17] Neuhaus, "The Institutional Beast," p. 83. Compare his comments from the conversation with Loock, in *Max Neuhaus: Sound Works*, vol. 1, *Inscription*, p. 134.

[18] Neuhaus, *Max Neuhaus: Sound Works*, vol. 3, *Place* (Ostfildern-Ruit, Germany: Cantz, 1994), p. 20.

[19] Neuhaus often argued that there was no real way of understanding audience response, given its volatile, unpredictable, and individual nature. (See, for example, "Lecture at the Seibu Museum Tokyo," p. 62, and "Lecture at the University of Miami," in *Max Neuhaus: Sound Works*, vol. 1, *Inscription*, p. 74; also at http://www.max-neuhaus.info/bibliography/miami.htm.)

[20] Neuhaus, "Lecture at the University of Miami," p. 75. The comments were made in 1984, the same year the controversy around *Tilted Arc* was raging.

[21] Neuhaus, "Lecture at the Seibu Museum Tokyo," p. 64. See also his comments specifically on *Times Square* ("Lecture at the University of Miami," p. 72).

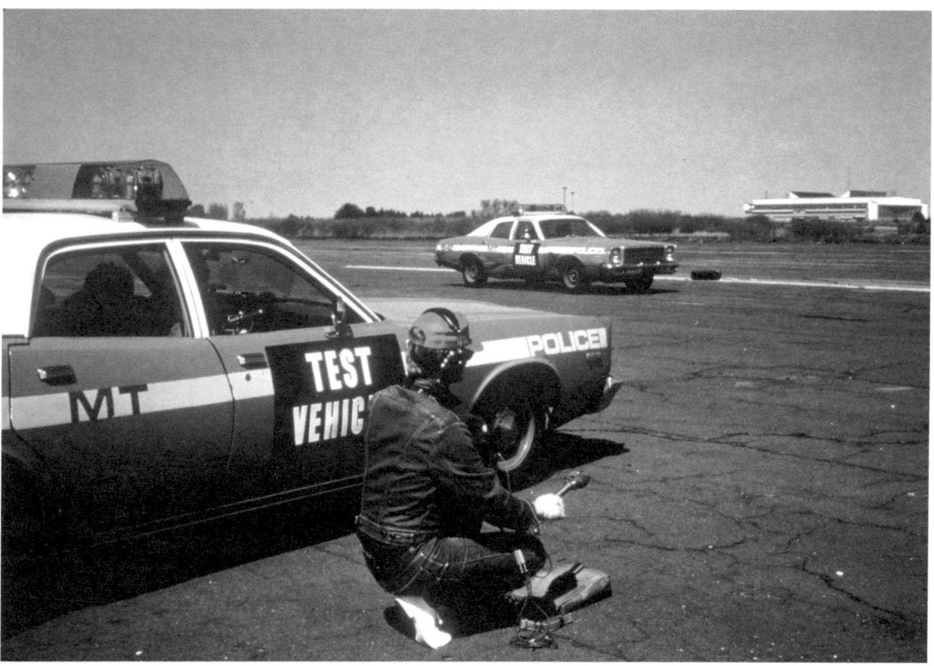

Max Neuhaus testing his Sirens project

An Implication of an Implication

Branden W. Joseph

Carter Ratcliff, one of the most frequent commentators on Max Neuhaus's art, once characterized its politics as "an implication of an implication."[1] Reading through the not-insignificant literature devoted to Neuhaus's sound works only reinforces such an impression. On account, perhaps, of the formal, even formalist nature of his molding of acoustic material—an impression additionally fostered by the elegant drawings by which his sound works are insufficiently (as the artist noted) represented—critics have been led to discuss his work predominantly, if not solely, in aesthetic and experiential terms.[2] Yet, as with others of Neuhaus's generation of Minimal and Postminimal sculptors, composers, and filmmakers, the impetus behind his art was, in fact, thoroughly political; indeed, politics, as we shall see, was the very precondition of his move from the realm of music into that of art. It is therefore worth while to investigate Neuhaus's practice, as it emerged in the 1960s and continued until his death in February 2009, from this angle. In order to bring out this aspect of his production, however, we will begin neither with an artwork nor with a musical performance but with a *New York Times* editorial Neuhaus published on December 6, 1974.

I. Listen

Submitted as "Noise Pollution Propaganda Makes Noise" and appearing under the unfortunately cartoonish title "BANG, BOOooom, ThumP, EEEK, tinkle," the editorial by Neuhaus, identified only as "a composer," responded to a pamphlet published by the Department of Air Resources of the New York City Environmental Protection Agency (EPA), "Noise Makes You Sick."[3] Noise pollution had been in the news frequently over the preceding months, owing to the repercussions of the federal Noise Control Act of 1972. New Jersey public-utilities officials opened 1974 with an inquiry into excessive noise produced by the Erie Lackawanna Railway's freight lines.[4] In March, the nation's first toll-road noise regulations were implemented on the New Jersey Turnpike, an action followed in October by the federal EPA's issuing noise-control standards for interstate-highway trucking.[5] In June, the U.S. Department of Housing and Urban Development misapplied noise regulations intended for airport traffic in order to refuse funding for government-subsidized housing in the predominantly African American New York neighborhoods of Harlem, Bedford-Stuyvesant, and Brownsville.[6] Earlier that month, the *New York Times* had weighed in with an editorial against excessive automobile horns during parade-route traffic jams, declaring that "noise pollution is a serious affront to city dwellers" and that there was no "excuse for allowing a flagrant and unnecessary assault on the population's ears and nerves."[7] Reports in October indicated that the city EPA was in turmoil under incoming mayor Abraham David "Abe" Beame, with "Civil Servant clerks . . . from the Air Resources Department's Bureau of Noise Abatement . . . doing nothing, because . . . the professionals they worked for are gone," a situation that did little to deter letter writers from likening noise to smoking and calling for suppression of "the plague of transistor radios" in public space.[8]

Neuhaus's Op-Ed ran distinctly counter to the tide of public opinion, declaring in its first line, "The popular concept of 'noise pollution' is a dangerously misleading one."[9] Neuhaus indicated that the Department of Air Resources's pamphlet discussed noise in purely physiological terms, bypassing the social dimension of sound within the "public environment." According to the city EPA, loud sounds, regardless of source or context, have detrimental effects on the ear, brain, glands, and internal organs. (In actuality, as Neuhaus noted, "the reaction doesn't normally go as far as the glands and internal organs.") "Through extreme exaggeration of the effects of sound on the human mind and body," he contended, "this propaganda has so frightened people that it has created 'noise' in many places where there was none before, and in effect robbed us of the ability to listen to our environment." In contrast to physiology, Neuhaus emphasized people's capacity to adapt to acoustic shocks, observing, "A human being conditions himself fairly quickly to what is 'loud or unexpected' in his particular environment," and, "certainly the modern urban dweller is not put in a state of fright (except of course when there is actual danger) very often by the sounds around him."

Neuhaus did not speak out indiscriminately against noise abatement. He noted that the environment contained truly "ear-damaging sounds" and granted an evident "need to be able to rest from sound just as we do from visual stimulation." Instead, what he contested was the establishment of rigid distinctions between proper and improper sounds, allowable and excluded noises. "Surely," he maintained, "several hundred years of musical history can be of value: At the very least, they can show us that our response to sound

BANG, BOOooom, ThumP, EEEK, tinkle

By Max Neuhaus

The popular concept of "noise pollution" is a dangerously misleading one. In reality, dangers to hearing do exist in prolonged, excessively loud sound levels. However, the residue of the idea that has ended up in the mind of the public because of misleading publicity is that sound in general is harmful to people.

A brief examination of a pamphlet, "Noise Makes You Sick," published by the Department of Air Resources of the city's Environmental Protection Agency, is typical of the literature and clearly illustrates the problem.

The first sentence, "Sound is instantly transmitted from your ears to your brain and then to your nerves, glands and organs," is of course literally true. Actually the reaction doesn't normally go as far as the glands and internal organs.

However, we are left with the impression that we have absolutely no defense against unwanted sound. This is untrue. The body has automatic reflex barriers, both physical and psychological, to deal with sounds it does not wish to react to.

The pamphlet goes on, "Any loud or unexpected sounds put your body on alert." This is true with a newborn child or in primitive societies, both of which need this reaction to survive, but certainly the modern urban dweller is not put into a state of fright (except of course when there is actual danger) very often by the sounds around him.

A human being conditions himself fairly quickly to what is "loud or unexpected" in his particular environment.

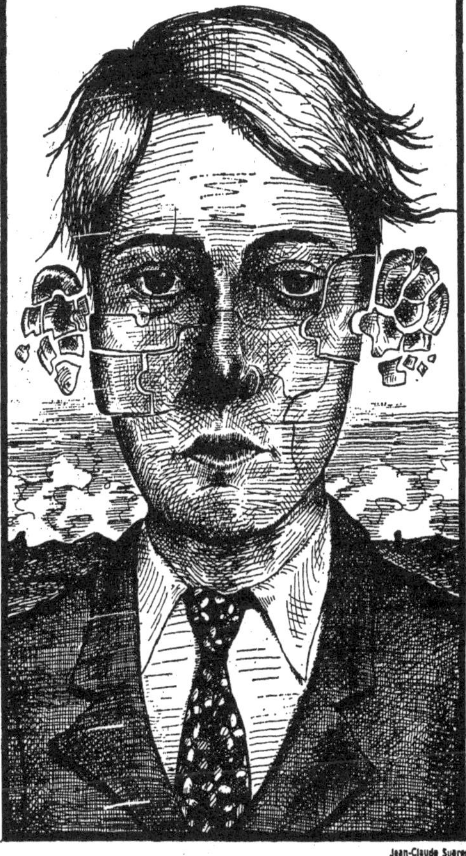

Jean-Claude Suares

Once having "established" the impression that we are constantly in a state of "fright" though, the brochure goes on to extrapolate in august pseudo-medical terms: "Adrenalin, an energy-producing hormone, is released into your blood stream. Your heart beats faster, your muscles tense, and your blood pressure rises. Sudden spasms occur in your stomach and intestines." This finally gives the impression that every honking horn brings us a little bit closer to death.

The law defines noise as "any unwanted sound." Surely several hundred years of musical history can be of value: At the very least, they can show us that our response to sound is subjective—that no sound is intrinsically bad. How we hear it depends a great deal on how we have been conditioned to **hear it.**

Through extreme exaggeration of the effects of sound on the human mind and body, this propaganda has so frightened people that it has created "noise" in many places where there was none before; and in effect robbed us of the ability to listen to our environment.

Admittedly it may be necessary to oversimplify an idea to bring enough public pressure to bear on the producers of ear-damaging sounds in our environment to stop this victimization of the public. This degree of misrepresentation is not only unnecessary, but irresponsible and ultimately negative.

This present concept of noise pollution condemns all sounds by leaving, in the public mind, the impression that sound itself is physiologically and psychologically harmful.

It is this exaggerated and oversimplified concept that is doing most of the damage, not sound—damage that can and should be rectified by curtailing misleading propaganda and showing people other ways to listen to their surroundings.

Obviously we need to be able to rest from sound just as we do from visual stimulation, we need aural as well as visual privacy, but silencing our public environment is the acoustic equivalent of painting it black. Certainly just as our eyes are for seeing, our ears are for hearing.

Max Neuhaus is a composer.

New York Times Op-Ed by Max Neuhaus, December 6, 1974

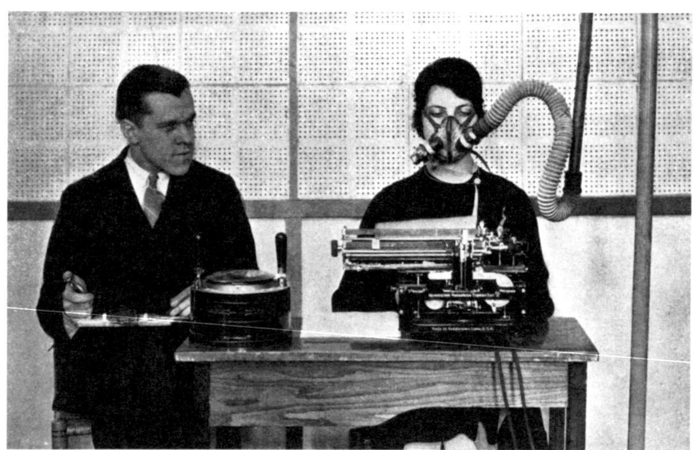

Donald Laird, "Experiments on the Physiological Cost of Noise," 1929. From the *Journal of the National Institute of Industrial Psychology*, no. 4 (January 1929), p. 253, fig. 1.

is subjective—that no sound is intrinsically bad. How we hear it depends a great deal on how we have been conditioned to hear it." Needless to say, the subtlety of Neuhaus's argument was lost on many readers. Nicholas Bergman of Citizens for a Quieter City responded angrily, denouncing Neuhaus's position and, citing the dangers of hearing loss, all but proposing a ban on amplified music in the name of public safety.[10]

Neuhaus was entering an area of long-standing contention. The Society for the Suppression of Unnecessary Noise was founded in New York City in 1906, and in 1929 New York's health commissioner appointed the nation's first noise-abatement commission in response to studies such as those by Donald Laird, which documented a connection between noise, inefficiency, and detrimental physiological response.[11] Despite economic and physiological justifications, however, civic noise regulations, as Emily Thompson has argued, were thoroughly political and disproportionately applied to lower-class and minority populations. In the 1930s, as Thompson has shown, distinct anxieties about recent demographic changes crystallized around the discursive treatment of jazz, which likened the urban mechanical noise of modernization to the music of the city's increasing African American population.[12] Legal constraints on so-called noise pollution were written and subjectively enforced so as to target populations and avocations that did not fit with the white "middle-class vision of a well-ordered city."[13]

As a virtuoso percussionist, Neuhaus had participated throughout the 1960s in an avant-garde music scene wherein issues of noise, sound, and social discrimination were explicitly debated.[14] In "Lecture on Nothing," of 1950, avant-garde composer John Cage had pointedly, if subtly, likened the issue of noise to that of social justice, declaring, "I liked noises just as much as I had liked single sounds. Noises, too, had been discriminated against; and being American, having been trained to be sentimental, I fought for noises. I liked being on the side of the underdog."[15] Earlier in his career, Cage had briefly aligned his percussion aesthetic with that of jazz, seeing in the latter both advanced rhythmic structures and a laudable political model of collective improvisation.[16] By the late 1940s, however, he had distanced himself from jazz, subtly disparaging it (and folk music) as "not cultivated species, growing best when left wild."[17] By 1964, the political implications of avant-garde music had been taken up by artist, composer, and radical philosopher Henry Flynt, who pressed Cage and others by arguing that a truly progressive avant-garde had to ally itself explicitly with oppressed populations, particularly African Americans, by approaching not only jazz but also indigenous forms of blues and rock and roll. Anything less could only be considered—as Flynt charged in public protests against Karlheinz Stockhausen—"Racism in Music."[18] Neuhaus could hardly have been unaware of Flynt's position; not only did the two travel in some of the same circles but Neuhaus performed in both concerts that Flynt and associates had picketed under the guise of Action against Cultural Imperialism.[19] By the end of 1974, when Neuhaus's Op-Ed appeared, both Stockhausen and Cage would be under attack from an increasingly politicized group of composers, most notably Cornelius Cardew, whose positions Neuhaus would likely also have known.[20]

In addition to resonating with the contentious history of noise abatement in New York and the political debates in the musical avant-garde, Neuhaus's Op-Ed also alluded to his own contemporary production. His call to rectify misleading antinoise propaganda by "showing people other ways to listen to their surroundings" indirectly referenced his *Listen* pieces (1966–76), in which he postered acoustically interesting sites such as the Brooklyn Bridge with signs reading "LISTEN" or stamped the word on individuals' hands and led them on "field trips thru found sound environments" to enhance their auditory appreciation.[21] Neuhaus's initial *Listen* event—which he considered his "first independent work as an artist"—took place in February 1966.[22] Beginning on East Fourteenth Street in Manhattan's East Village, Neuhaus led listeners through the "spectacularly massive rumbling" of the Con Edison power plant that rises on both sides of the street between Avenues C and D, continued along the automobile-filled East River Drive, passed "through the Puerto Rican street life of the lower east side," and ended at his studio for a percussion concert.[23] The itinerary formed an implicit manifesto, equating percussion music to urban environmental sounds and allying machine noise with the soundscape of an ethnic-minority neighborhood. Such interconnections made explicit what was tacit in Neuhaus's Op-Ed: the aesthetic refusal to distinguish between proper and improper sounds relates to a political refusal to discriminate between "proper" and "improper" inhabitants of the urban public sphere.

II. Times Square

By the end of 1974, when his Op-Ed appeared, Neuhaus had been planning the sound work that would become known as *Times Square* (1977–92; 2002–present) for more than a year. Located at the north end of a small triangular traffic island between Forty-fifth and Forty-sixth streets at the intersection of Broadway and Seventh Avenue in Manhattan, the piece, completed in 1977, consists of a range of closely related tones that well up from beneath a metal subway grating. In today's art world, filled with officially sanctioned, site-specific Postminimal sculpture, it is difficult to conceive of how odd Neuhaus's proposal initially seemed. Henry Romney called it "the zaniest" proposition ever received by the Rockefeller Foundation (which nonetheless awarded Neuhaus a grant of $4,525 toward its completion).[24]

As Neuhaus explained to fellow sound artist Christina Kubisch, his decision to leave concert performance behind to erect soundscapes within more freely accessible public spaces was "political," conditioned by "his realization that music had to communicate with a different public in different spaces."[25] Voicing an anti-institutional position at one with the times, Neuhaus told Amy Hiffner in 1974 that it was "ridiculous to be cooped up in a concert hall situation" when there were "tremendous opportunities for making music accessible to people."[26] As he reiterated his thinking more recently:

> My premise in leaving Carnegie Hall and going to Times Square was that I felt that I could deal, in a serious way, with a broad spectrum of people who were not necessarily culturally initiated, not by reducing or simplifying what I did but by using an uncodified language, not assuming any specific knowledge of the listener and taking the new context seriously, building upon what was really there, not for a context that was not, like a museum or concert hall.[27]

Unmarked, unsigned, apparently unauthored, *Times Square* aims to instantiate an explicitly antiauthoritarian form of public art, refusing to dictate the terms of aesthetic experience or even that the experience is, per se, aesthetic. Kubisch described the effect as advancing a "strong tendency towards Intimism . . . excluding any personal relationship with the author. Thus, after having been in the spotlight for a long time, the artist is running away from the field of action, leaving his work to stand on its own."[28] "Having no way of knowing that it has been deliberately made," asserted Neuhaus of *Times Square*, uninformed percipients "usually claim the work as a place of their own discovering."[29]

By the time he conceived of *Times Square*, Neuhaus had already created several works that would come to be called sound installations: *Fan Music* (1967), in which photovoltaic cells behind rotating fan blades activated loudspeakers across the rooftops of four buildings on the Bowery, the sounds' volume and tonal color dependent on the sun's brightness and angle; *Drive-in Music* (1967), in which radio transmitters placed along a roadway leading from the Albright-Knox Art Gallery in Buffalo, New York, constructed a topography of sound heard only on car stereos; *Southwest Stairwell* (1968), at Ryerson University in Toronto, where visitors in making their way up or down a four-story staircase could perceive a succession of graduating timbres; and *Walkthrough* (1973–77), where partially weather-controlled acoustic clicks and pings filled an entryway of Brooklyn's Jay Street–Borough Hall subway station. Neuhaus had also experimented with installation-like situations within the context of musical performances, as in *Three Hours of Sound Construction* (1968), an audiovisual presentation involving "14 speakers positioned strategically—diabolically, even—about the auditorium" of Carnegie Hall's Weill Recital Hall, and a 1966 rendition of Morton Feldman's *King of Denmark* (1964) performed, not onstage, but in the stairwell of the Arts Club of Chicago.[30] Thomas Willis of the *Chicago Tribune* reported of the latter, "The audience obediently sat on the steps, clustered along the railings, and stood near the exit door. The percussionist was playing the blocks and bells with his fingers from a score taped to the wall. What was audible made an interesting obbligato to the traffic noise coming thru the glass wall."[31]

Neuhaus's most sustained investigation of what he called a "sound-oriented piece in a situation other than the concert hall" would be the seventeen Water Whistle events, staged in swimming pools between 1971 and 1974 and continued by three Underwater Music "concerts" between 1976 and 1977.[32] In them, Neuhaus rigged up a series of underwater hoses capped with whistles of various pitches. Lasting up to fifteen hours, and leaving the swim-trunk-clad audience free to enter and leave at will, Neuhaus's underwater concerts were already, as he called them, "sound environment[s]."[33] According to the comments of those who experienced them, the pieces rewarded sustained auditory attention (a form of attentiveness that would appropriately be described, were it not for the unfortunate pun, by composer Pauline Oliveros's term "deep listening"). Al Brunelle wrote in *Art in America*, "The ear, focused effortlessly on the ongoing stimulus, reacted with increasing discrimination. After five or ten minutes, the increase in interior variation of the drone was startling, and it moved toward further differentiation of already tiny parts. Microscopic dramas flooded the sound and were themselves invaded or effaced."[34] The geometric enclosures of water defined by the contours of the pools—labeled on Neuhaus's related drawings "polyhedric

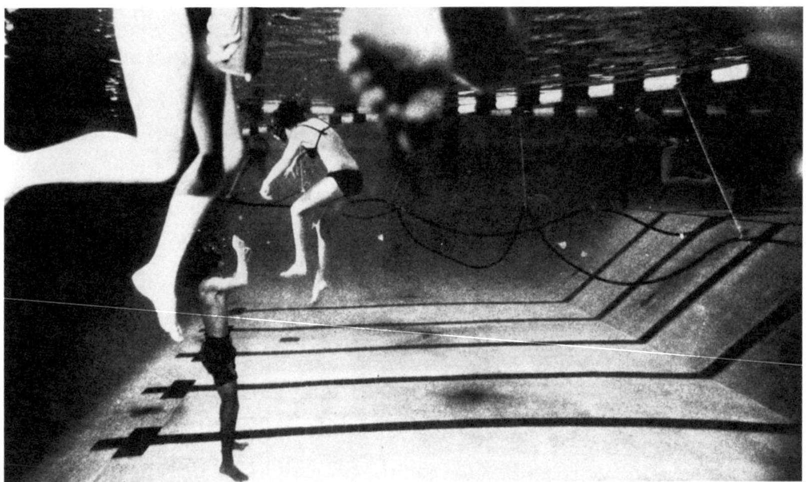

Photo by Tom Bennett of Max Neuhaus's *Water Whistle*, 1974

volumes"—along with the implicit recreational invitation to swim, emphasize the spatialization of the acoustic phenomena, which could only be heard underwater. Swimmers dived or floated through overlapping zones of acoustic variation caused by the whipping, water-filled hoses, variations that brought to mind not only spatial and environmental associations but also specifically sculptural and architectural ones:

> Texture is not just a metaphor with underwater sound; this sound had a tactile quality that slowly became quite apparent to Neuhaus' audience. The flux of his music was set against the stability of architecture, so that the entire volume of water in the pool seemed completely charged with sound. At first, the undifferentiated tactile sensation was felt uniformly by the body; when this progressed to differentiation, the sculptural responses set in; somehow the musical variations seemed volumetric or at least sculptural; different parts of the body seemed to touch different frequencies.[35]

Neuhaus's *Times Square* was originally presented under the title *Underground Music(s) I*, indicating the connection between it and the earlier Underwater Music series.[36] Like its aquatic predecessors, *Times Square* activates a virtual space, in this case above the traffic island, as though the air-filled "polyhedric volume" of a swimming pool has been upended. The result is a topography of sound waves through which listeners swim, albeit on dry land. Within an environment such as *Times Square*, it is not solely the electronically produced sound that is the focus of perception, nor even the interaction of the sound with the site's acoustic (and visual) context, but the very act of perceiving itself, as differences in frequency and timbre slowly and subtly reveal themselves, less by their own transformation than by the force of concentration and as a result of perambulations across the acoustically activated zone. The listener is surrounded by acoustic material, and the locus of the experience is his or her own corporeality. As Hal Foster wrote of Neuhaus's *Five Russians (A Tuned Room)* (1979), "In effect, one's body became the index to one's perception as, say, a weathervane is an index to the wind's direction; and yet because one was 'inside' the signification process, it was impossible to orient oneself in the space by the pitches." "One felt," he concluded, "at once very fine and very inadequate as a register."[37]

Implicitly linking Neuhaus to the concerns of a number of Minimalist musicians and sculptors, Brunelle observed, "What is especially admirable is that the underlying foundation for [Neuhaus's] work is not esthetic convention or philosophical theory but basic human perceptual structure."[38] In a way that parallels Robert Morris's appraisal of viewers' interactions with his sculpture, Neuhaus understood the phenomenological perceptual engagement induced by his sound installations to be integral to their political character.[39] In addition to shedding the elitist confines of the musical establishment for a public space accessible to all, regardless of musical skill or knowledge, *Times Square* allows the listener, rather than the composer or artist, to instigate and control the ultimate acoustic experience, to the point even—and this was important to Neuhaus—of ignoring or bypassing it altogether.[40] Neuhaus distanced himself from popular notions of interactivity (particularly attractive, he said, to "culture bureaucrats"), which instrumentalize subjects in the name of participation.[41] "The ideas that I am involved with," he explained,

> are contrary to that—giving each person the possibility to make a work for himself, but for himself only. For instance, by making a work that has a topography, one can move through that topography at one's own pace, stop where one wants to. One has the freedom to form an experience of the work for oneself but not impose it on anyone else.[42]

Far from incidental, Neuhaus's concern to free the listener from authorial imposition underlay what was for him the fundamental distinction between music and sound art: placing sounds in the realm of space rather than that of time. "Traditionally composers have located the elements of a composition in time. One idea which I am interested in is locating them, instead, in space, and *letting the listener place them in his own time*."[43]

To a certain degree, Neuhaus's sound installations resemble La Monte Young and Marian Zazeela's Dream Houses, proposed as early as 1962 and first realized at the Pasadena Art Museum in 1968. In a Dream House, standing waves produced by amplified chords of varying complexity transform an architectural enclosure into an acoustic environment tinted by Zazeela's intricate, psychedelic lighting effects.[44]

Young and Zazeela aim to control the sensory atmosphere of sound, light, and (via incense) smell to produce an otherworldly setting, one with its own impression of space and time. Carefully adhering to the mathematical ratios of just intonation, which represent for Young something akin to the harmony of the spheres, a Dream House is to induce specific and repeatable affective states and transport visitors into transcendental realms. "There is evidence that each time a particular frequency is repeated it is transmitted through the same parts of our auditory system," Young has explained. "When these frequencies are continuous, as in my music, we can conceive even more easily how, if part of our circuitry is performing the same operation continuously, this could be considered to be or to simulate a psychological state. My own feeling has always been that if people just aren't carried away to heaven I'm failing. They should be moved to strong spiritual feeling."[45]

Commentators have often approached Neuhaus's installations, including *Times Square*, from a similar perspective, as meditative and even transcendental. Shortly after its inauguration, Richard Lorber of *Artforum* described *Times Square* in terms suggesting spiritual union:

> In the cacophonous ambience of Times Square, mecca of the honky-tonk world, *Times Square* functions as something of an oracle, an autochthonous voice which makes sacred the profane environment. Passers-by in earshot of the unexpected, groaning drone often looked distractedly about, up into the air, or into the traffic, seeking some mechanical, if not ethereal, source. . . . Those few who were diverted from their passage seemed to engage in a most private dialogue with the sound, as though in an insulated environment, introspectively detached from assaulting sensations in the most exhibitionistic of public spaces.[46]

Despite such a reception, Neuhaus's work always related more firmly to a Cagean aesthetic of acoustic immanence, accepting and exploring indeterminate responses and a "transparency" between his installations and the sites they inhabit (recall his stairway percussion concert at the Arts Club of Chicago that incorporated the outside traffic noise).[47] Rather than deducing his sonorities from transcendent harmonic ideals, Neuhaus derived them inductively from the sounds inherent to the sites themselves. In the case of *Times Square*, electronically processed traffic sounds form part of the piece's ringing tones, which further resemble the sounds that might issue from the kinds of machinery expected to exist beneath such metal grates. Neuhaus's acoustic material was, as he said, "almost plausible within its context."[48]

Although the sounds Neuhaus added to the environment could be so unobtrusive as to be missed, they were not, for all that, identical to those issuing from the site before his intervention. As he explained, "The sounds I build grow out of that situation, but they aren't of that situation."[49] Jean-Christophe Ammann well characterized this aspect of experiencing Neuhaus's installations:

> We first perceive noises and sounds and we are quick to identify them with what we already know. Only later do we discover a displacement—sometimes more, sometimes less apparent—between our perception and that with which we have identified it. This displacement is like a gap, a sonority-space-image that becomes fixed in our minds as a memory.[50]

It is such a doubly split attentiveness—between the actual acoustic environment and the addition of artificial tones, on the side of the sound work, and between perceptual immediacy and mnemonic comparison, on the side of the listener—that defines (at minimum) any encounter with Neuhaus's art.

Entering a Neuhaus installation, then, one is within neither a meditative, transcendent sphere nor a pure state of perceptual immediacy, the two poles between which so much writing on the artist unsteadily vacillates.[51] At the same time, however, while one is undeniably within a mundane environment, one's perception is nonetheless slightly displaced. Rather than outside this world, in a state of transcendence, one finds oneself both within and beside it, in a space neither sacred nor profane. Such a state, in all its complexities and from which religious associations cannot entirely be eliminated, may be likened to what Italian philosopher Giorgio Agamben has described by the prefix *para-*:

> neither a simple existence nor a transcendence; it is a paraexistence or a paratranscendence that dwells beside the thing (in all the sense of the prefix "para-"), so close that it *almost* merges with it, giving it a halo. It is not the identity of the thing and yet it is nothing other than the thing (it is *none-other*).[52]

Neuhaus's so-called Place installations may be described in much the same manner: almost but not quite merging with the sites from which they are nonetheless inextricable and which they provide with an acoustic "halo."

III. Max-Feed

Neuhaus's first art object was the *Max-Feed* (1966), a small electronic device produced by MassArt, a company that pioneered the artist's multiple.[53] MassArt, which also issued Allan Kaprow's LP *How to Make a Happening* (1966), as well as an inflatable chair, shared many of Neuhaus's goals: antielitism, accessibility to a wider audience, and a presence outside recognized cultural institutions. In the words of cofounder Phil Orenstein, "You have no idea how exciting it is to get a product out of your studio and into, say, a supermarket."[54] Despite its populist ambitions, however, the *Max-Feed* did not integrate itself seamlessly into the commercial realm; it inhabited it only to *detourn* it. Neuhaus's contraption operated via much the same means as his *Fontana Mix—Feed* performances (1965–68), in which he "played" the feedback caused by placing contact microphones on percussion instruments just in front of loudspeakers. Nominally realizing Cage's score for *Fontana Mix* (1958), Neuhaus manipulated the volume levels of the waves of amplified feedback, which varied at each performance because of the spatial configuration of the concert hall (or, in one instance, Central Park).[55] The high volume and spatial conditioning of the piece were duly noted by Theodore Strongin, who wrote that it "was not the kind of electronic music that emanates distantly from the speakers. It felt as though one's own head were part of the feedback circuit."[56]

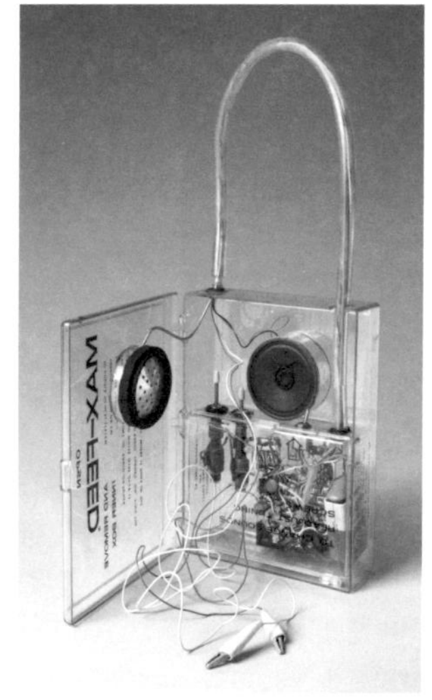

Max Neuhaus, *Max-Feed*, 1966

With the *Max-Feed*, Neuhaus aimed to incorporate a similar effect into a convenient, take-home package. Set beside a hi-fi stereo, Neuhaus's box would distort its sound into a wail of amplified feedback. No longer a passive forum for commercial radio, the *Max-Feed* purchaser's living room was transformed into an indeterminate and phenomenologically activated installation. (Not limited to radio, the *Max-Feed* could also "infiltrate a TV set with a clap of thunder.")[57] The *Max-Feed* was, in effect, a portable avant-gardizer that went well beyond the indeterminate manipulations of treble, bass, and volume dials proposed by Cage and Lejaren Hiller's *HPSCHD* LP (1971) and formed a domestic counterpart to Neuhaus's interventions into radio broadcasting such as *Public Supply I*, which also debuted in 1966.[58]

Although nearly forgotten within the literature, *Max-Feed* proves symptomatic of Neuhaus's project as a whole. Set within an increasingly commercially mediated public realm, in which, via both advertising and entertainment, listeners are interpellated into preformed acoustic imaginaries, Neuhaus's small electronic device provides a contrasting perceptual experience: indeterminate and individual, contingent on the time and space of the listener's particular phenomenological engagement. Approached from this perspective, Neuhaus's selection of Times Square as the site for his first permanent sound installation also reveals itself as symptomatic: often referred to as the

"Crossroads of the World," Times Square is one of the most commercialized of public spaces, an arena of incessant advertising, entertainment, and solicitation, of kinds licit and, at the time of the work's construction, illicit.

Neuhaus's principal rhetorical adversary, however, was neither advertising nor commercial radio, but their more insistently instrumentalized acoustic conflation, Muzak.[59] In this, Neuhaus once again proved close to Cage, who repeatedly proclaimed his distaste for Muzak's piped-in background music.[60] Indeed, the earliest version of Cage's infamous silent composition *4'33"* (1952) explicitly sought to provide a momentary reprieve from the corporation's soundscape. Cage described the work in terms of his desire "to compose a piece of uninterrupted silence and sell it to Muzak Co. It will be 3 or 4 1/2 minutes long—those being the standard lengths of 'canned' music—and its title will be *Silent Prayer*. . . . The ending will approach imperceptibility."[61]

Muzak is nothing other than the instrumentalization of sound for the aims of increased production and profitability. The corporation makes its goals explicit under the banner of the term "Audio Architecture":

> Audio Architecture is emotion by design. Our innovation and our inspiration, it is the integration of music, voice and sound to create experiences that link customers with companies. Its power lies in its subtlety. It bypasses the resistance of the mind and targets the receptiveness of the heart. When people are made to feel good in, say, a store, they feel good about that store. They like it. Remember it. Go back to it. Audio Architecture builds a bridge to loyalty. And loyalty is what keeps brands alive.[62]

By its own admission, Muzak manipulatively targets listeners' sense of place (which it defines as a commercial space, the store), affect (as a noncognitive response, an almost subliminal inducement of mood), and memory (converted into feel-good brand loyalty).

Neuhaus explicitly objected to Muzak's acoustic management, its "claims that these melodies raise production in factories and calm people" and its support of such claims with "dubious scientific studies," the extension and counterpart, no doubt, of Laird's efficiency analyses of the 1920s.[63] It is against the backdrop of an increasingly regulated and commercialized public sphere (exemplified by, but by no means limited to, Muzak) that Neuhaus's sound installations—which are almost point-by-point inversions or refutations of Audio Architecture—achieve their full import and potentially critical vocation.

Neuhaus was concerned with noncognitive, affective responses to auditory stimuli, akin to the effects of Muzak. He termed the nonreferential, uncodified acoustic material with which he worked "sound character" and saw it as a powerful, though nearly subliminal, communicator of information and impressions.[64] Unlike Muzak, however,

Neuhaus's installations are indeterminate of the listener's response. As he wrote about his Place works in general:

> I see these works not as definers of a single frame of mind for all individuals, but as catalysts for shifts in frame of mind. I am not concerned with a specific individual's frame of mind. . . . I am concerned with the catalyst, the initiator; their individual pathways are very private, their own.[65]

Intricately and inextricably drawn from the environmental noises, incidental sounds, and unique acoustic resonances of a place, Neuhaus's installations are site-specific in a way that explicitly opposes the infinitely replicable acoustic environments that Muzak fashions for the commercial realm. Ultimately determined by the visitors (by how attentive they are to the sound, how they happen to move through the environment, how long they stay), the impact of Neuhaus's installations differs for each person, catalyzing in them individual responses—responses that are substantively theirs and not the result of any interpellation or identification with a commercial enterprise or brand.

Through manipulating acoustic affect, Muzak aims to link consumers' memories to particular commercial spaces, producing an automatic and indelible bond between them. Neuhaus, by contrast, engaged memory not only to draw listeners' attention to the site, thereby connecting the two, but also simultaneously to induce a slight distinction. As Ratcliff has perspicaciously noted, however close the acoustic connection between the site and the installation, Neuhaus's "need" was always "to establish a difference—not a telling similarity—between the sounds of the piece and the sounds of its place."[66] Memory, as described by Ammann above, is invoked via the comparison of Neuhaus's acoustic additions, once discerned, with the listener's previous (mis)perception of the sounds as belonging to the environment. Memory is also involved, as Brandon LaBelle explains, in providing depth to the type of phenomenological engagement Neuhaus's installations necessitate:

> The activation of perception through sound may draw attention to space, its material presence, and any perceptual phenomena, and it does so by activating our memory of spatial experience, of the event-space happening there, for sound installation is distinct by offering up information that is simultaneous and yet durational, present and passing: I glimpse the given installation as a set of information that is there all at once and yet that only comes to the fore through my movements, through my listening to, my attending to its evolution, as embedded within and conversant with space.[67]

In more recent works, such as *A Bell for St. Cäcilien* (1989–91), in which a sound reminiscent of a carillon issues from the vicinity of a disused church in Cologne, and *Time*

Piece Stommeln (2007–present), situated at the site of one of the few German synagogues to avoid Nazi destruction, Neuhaus further linked his work to issues of historical memory and memorialization. If, as Guy Debord maintained, the "pseudo-cyclical time" of spectacle (which would almost certainly have to include Muzak) is marked by a false immediacy, which bears the spectator along without access to either history or a conceptualization of their situation, Neuhaus's installations allow memory to operate differently, effecting a more complex perceptual experience, involving splits and shifts that contribute not only to a certain depth (phenomenological and, potentially, historical) but also to a cognitive difference, the type of heightened perception necessary for any form of critical reception.[68]

IV. Moment

Although all Neuhaus's installations operate similarly according to acoustic shifts, bifurcations, divisions, and doublings, the subtleties of their invocations of perception and memory are often overlooked in accounts that build up (or, rather, reduce) the experience to one of pure presence: an almost mystical resolution of the listener with the site (whether immanent or transcendent) and with themselves via the agency of the sound. As though in response to such readings, Neuhaus's so-called Moment works, such as *Time Piece Graz* (2003–present) and *Time Piece Beacon* (2005–present), revolve not around presence but rather around absence.[69] Like the *Max-Feed*, Neuhaus's Moment works initially took the form of an unusual consumer product (never put into production): a silent alarm clock he designed in 1979. As Neuhaus described it, the device measured "two by sixteen by one inches with a time display and control buttons on the left side of the larger surface and a round screen covering a small speaker on the far right."[70] Before the time set to awake its listener, the alarm would begin to emit a continuous tone, carefully pitched at the upper limit of the sleeper's range of hearing, a frequency that, Neuhaus explained, "has a very special character. It is there but at the same time almost not there—more of a presence than a sound."[71] Starting at an almost imperceptibly low level, the tone would gradually increase in volume until, at the appointed time, it would suddenly shut off, the abrupt cessation of acoustic stimulus being what would induce wakefulness. Neuhaus's seemingly paradoxical device brings to mind Walter Benjamin's description of "an alarm clock that in each minute rings for sixty seconds."[72] Invoked at the end of his essay on Surrealism, Benjamin's image illustrated the revolutionary face of the new human subject, in whom media technologies thoroughly interpenetrated and enervated the body. Muzak's affective management, which began five years after the publication

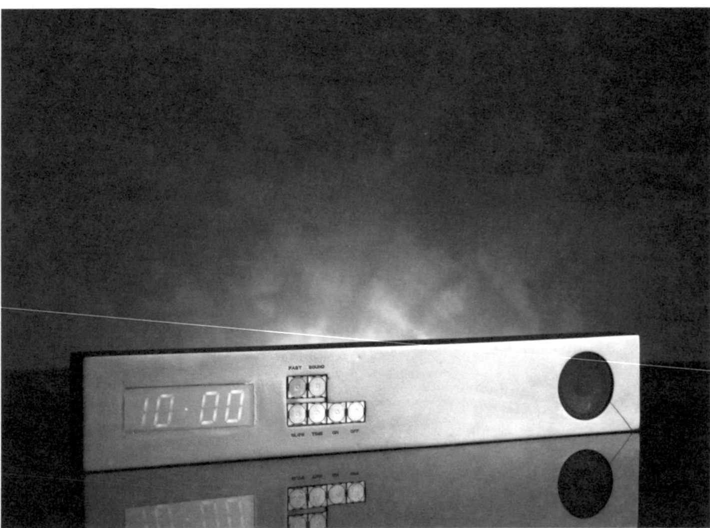

Max Neuhaus's 1979 design for a silent alarm clock

of Benjamin's essay, is only one, and not the most nefarious, technological attempt to regulate the body on a micropolitical register. Neuhaus's alarm clock, however, reverses the effect of such enervation: the acoustic stimulus is noticed, jolting the sleeper awake, only when it abruptly ceases.

Neuhaus's Moment works instigate the same process on a much larger scale, addressing a collective audience within a public realm. Beginning at a nearly inaudible volume, which increases progressively but so slowly as to avoid conscious notice, a tone is suddenly removed, leaving what the artist described as an "aural afterimage . . . superimposed on the sounds of the environment—a spontaneous aural memory or reconstruction perhaps, subtle and transparent, engendered by the sound's disappearance."[73] Felt by the body more than perceived by the mind, the sound, which disappears even though one did not realize it was there (much as, one imagines, how Cage's *Silent Prayer* might have impacted a restaurant or shopping mall), is doubly imperceptible: "inaudibility follows inaudibility, for the absence of sound comes after sounds produced but unheard."[74]

In describing the Moment works, Neuhaus invariably emphasized the relationship between the works' acoustic reach and the geographic expanse of a community:

> By the late 700s in western civilization, the church bell had become a dominant force in European communities. It not only announced church services, deaths, births, fire,

revolt and festivals but it was such a strong unifying force that in many cases the limits of the community were defined by its range. Four hundred years later the church bell had become united with the mechanical clock. The bell no longer just announced special events but provided a communal time base for the general coordination of activities. In present day society most of these minute by minute functions have been taken over by radio and television. The intrinsic nature of these media generalize and depersonalize these functions.[75]

Faced with the replacement of the church bell by the mass media, Neuhaus's Moment works are, to some extent, compensatory. His aim was to restore "a common moment within a community, periodically throughout the day," outside the mediation of commercial spectacle.[76] The impetus was not, however, reactionary. For unlike the Christian church bell (or the voice of the muezzin calling the Muslim faithful to prayer from the minaret of a mosque), a Moment work does not seek to instill identification with any particular structure or ideal: civic, national, religious, or otherwise. Members of the community addressed or instated by Neuhaus's work are united solely by the sound's presence or—more correctly and specifically—by the periodic, collective experience of its disappearance. If there is any community formation, it is on the basis of this shared sense of absence alone. In *Time Piece Stommeln*, Neuhaus related the absence of the acoustic tone to mourning and loss, as the sound's disappearance recalls the eradication of the Jewish community that once congregated at the Stommeln synagogue. Yet, the notion of communion that Neuhaus's work models or informs may also have an anticipatory function, invoking what Agamben has called "the coming community": "Decisive here is the idea of an *inessential* commonality, a solidarity that in no way concerns an essence."[77]

As in all Neuhaus's work, the reception of a Moment work is indeterminate; every individual's experience is different, both from that of the artist and from those of the other listeners. Sought by Neuhaus was nothing other than a common being together in difference, a sense of communal belonging without predication on any *belonging to*—and, correlatively, free of any *exclusion from*. It is here that Neuhaus's last work connects back to and develops ideas proposed in his Op-Ed three decades earlier. In much the same way that Neuhaus refused to distinguish between those sounds that were proper and those that were improper within the urban environment, his instigation of community refuses any distinction between those who would be proper and those who would be improper to it: free of any structure of identification to which one must adhere, there are no criteria by which to be cast out. In Agamben's terms, Neuhaus's community would be one of singularities "mediated not by any condition of belonging" but merely "by belonging itself."[78] "Through this relation," writes Agamben,

> singularity borders all possibility and thus receives its *omnimoda determinatio* not from its participation in a determinate concept or some actual property ([for example] being red, Italian, Communist), but *only by means of this bordering*. It belongs to a whole, but without this belonging's being able to be represented by a real condition: Belonging, being-*such*, is here only the relation to an empty and indeterminate totality.[79]

Agamben's notion of coming community has been criticized as utopian, a term that might be equally applied to Neuhaus's politics with all pejorative associations removed. For at their most profound, Neuhaus's Moment pieces seek to bring into existence precisely such an "empty and indeterminate totality," a community united by adjacency rather than identification with whatever exclusionary ideal. Built around an empty and indeterminate *tonality*, Neuhaus's sound installations aim to engage in a coming politics, based on a disappearing sound that is always, also, to come.

Notes

1 Carter Ratcliff, "Max Neuhaus: Aural Spaces," *Art in America* 75, no. 10 (October 1987), p. 162.

2 One important exception being Brandon LaBelle, who has similarly noted "a certain criticism that keeps Neuhaus within a purely 'aesthetic' domain." (LaBelle, *Background Noise: Perspectives on Sound Art* [New York: Continuum, 2006], p. 159.)

3 Max Neuhaus, "BANG, BOOooom, ThumP, EEEK, tinkle," *New York Times*, December 6, 1974, p. 39.

4 Philip Wechsler, "State Calls on Railroad to Explain Freight Din," *New York Times*, January 13, 1974, p. 75.

5 "Turnpike Planning June 1 Crackdown on Noise Pollution," *New York Times*, March 27, 1974, p. 91; and Shawn G. Kennedy, "Final Federal Standards Issues Setting Noise Levels for Trucks," *New York Times*, October 23, 1974, p. 20.

6 Martin Tolchin, "U.S. Says Noise Level in City Bars Federal Funds for Housing," *New York Times*, June 23, 1974, p. 34. Roger Starr, New York City administrator of housing and development, lamented, "The whole environmental movement, no matter how nobly motivated, has provided opportunities for those who would challenge projects, to delay or abort housing under a glow of legitimacy although the fundamental objections are exclusionist, racially motivated or based on class prejudices."

7 ". . . and Less Noise," *New York Times*, June 17, 1974, p. 30.

8 David Bird, "City Environmental Body Is in Turmoil under Beame," *New York Times*, October 13, 1974, p. 1; and Eugene M. Friedman, "Letters to the Editor: Save Our Ears," *New York Times*, October 22, 1974, p. 40.

9 Neuhaus, "BANG," p. 39.

10 Nicholas Bergman, "What Noise Does to Us," *New York Times*, December 21, 1974, p. 26. Citizens for a Quieter City, which was founded in 1966 by Robert Alex Baron, seems to have folded in 1974 or shortly thereafter. Its records are located in the New York City Public Library. See http://www.nypl.org/research/chss/spe/rbk/faids/citizensforaquieter.pdf (accessed January 2, 2009).

11 Emily Thompson, *The Soundscape of Modernity: Architectural Acoustics and the Culture of Listening in America, 1900–1933* (Cambridge: MIT Press, 2002), pp. 121, 156–57.

12 Ibid., p. 131.

13 Ibid., p. 123.

14 The almost rote repetition within the literature on Neuhaus of the fact that he toured with Pierre Boulez and Karlheinz Stockhausen serves to occlude Neuhaus's connection, in person and in performance, to a much wider and more politicized array of composers, musicians, and artists that includes George Brecht, Sylvano Bussotti, Joseph Byrd, John Cage, Philip Corner, Morton Feldman, Mauricio Kagel, Alison Knowles, Jackson Mac Low, Bo Nilsson, Frederic Rzewski, James Tenney, David Tudor, Edgard Varèse, La Monte Young, and others.

15 John Cage, "Lecture on Nothing," in *Silence: Lectures and Writings* (Middletown, Conn.: Wesleyan University Press, 1961), p. 117.

16 On Cage's early invocations of jazz, which were always somewhat equivocal, see Cage, "The Future of Music: Credo" (1937), in *Silence*, p. 5; Cage, "Goal: New Music, New Dance" (1939), in *Silence*, p. 87; and Cage, "Grace and Clarity" (1944), in *Silence*, pp. 91–92.

17 Cage, "Forerunners of Modern Music," in *Silence*, p. 63, n. 3. On Cage's distancing of himself from jazz, see George E. Lewis, "Improvised Music after 1950: Afrological and Eurological Perspectives," *Black Music Research Journal* 16, no. 1 (spring 1996), pp. 91–122.

18 Raymond Ericson, "Showcase Offers Music of Germany," *New York Times*, April 30, 1964, p. 29.

19 Ibid.; and Harold C. Schonberg, "Music: Stockhausen's 'Originale' Given at Judson," *New York Times*, September 9, 1964, p. 46.

[20] See Cornelius Cardew, *Stockhausen Serves Imperialism and Other Articles* (London: Latimer, 1974). Neuhaus would later perform in Cardew's memorial concert. See John Rockwell, "In the Arts: Critics' Choices," *New York Times*, May 23, 1982, p. 103; and Rockwell, "Music: Cardew Benefit," *New York Times*, May 30, 1982, p. 46.

[21] Quoted from Neuhaus's poster, reproduced in Michael Nyman, *Experimental Music: Cage and Beyond*, 2nd ed. (Cambridge: Cambridge University Press, 1999), p. 105, and in this book, p. 103.

[22] Neuhaus, "Listen," in *Max Neuhaus: Elusive Sources and "Like" Spaces* (Turin: Giorgio Persano, 1990), p. 20.

[23] Ibid., p. 20. The text erroneously reports that the walk began on the geographically impossible corner of Avenue D and *West* Fourteenth Street.

[24] Israel Shenker, "Foundations Get Real and Unreal Pleas for Aid," *New York Times*, September 2, 1976, p. 66.

[25] Christina Kubisch, "Time into Space/Space into Time: New Sound Installations in New York," trans. Michael Moore, *Flash Art*, nos. 88–89 (March–April 1979), p. 16.

[26] Amy Hiffner, "Interview avec Max Neuhaus," *Artitudes International*, nos. 9–11 (April–June 1974), p. 70. ("Actuellement, il y a énormemément de possibilités pour rendre la musique disponible aux gens, et c'est d'autant plus ridicule d'être bloqué dans la situation des salles de concert.")

[27] "Vortrag Neuhaus," International Academy of Philosophy of Art, *End of Art—Endings in Art*, ed. Gerhard Seel (Basel: Schwabe Verlag, 2006); online at http://www.max-neuhaus.info/bibliography/IAPA.htm (accessed December 11, 2008).

[28] Kubisch, "Time into Space," p. 18.

[29] Neuhaus, *Max Neuhaus: Sound Works*, vol. 3, *Place* (Ostfildern-Ruit, Germany: Cantz, 1994), p. 20.

[30] Neuhaus's *Three Hours of Sound Construction* was announced in "Entertainment Events," *New York Times*, January 8, 1968, p. 32, and reviewed in Donal Henahan, "Electronic Music Hits Open Switch," *New York Times*, January 9, 1968, p. 35. The stairwell performance of *King of Denmark* was reported in Thomas Willis, "Just Like Space Age, Music Has Its Hardware," *Chicago Tribune*, April 10, 1966, pp. G9–10.

[31] Willis, "Just Like Space Age," p. G10.

[32] Karen Monson, "Neuhaus' Submerged Premiere," *Christian Science Monitor*, January 19, 1972, p. 6. The poster for Neuhaus's Water Whistles *XV*, *XVI*, and *XVII* also titled them "Underwater Music." See the reproduction in Richard H. Axsom and David Platzker, *Printed Stuff: Prints, Posters, and Ephemera by Claes Oldenburg, a Catalogue Raisonné 1958–1996* (New York: Hudson Hills Press, in association with Madison Art Center, Wisconsin, 1997), p. 244.

[33] Harold C. Schonberg, "Things You May Not Know You Missed—Until Now," *New York Times*, January 2, 1972, p. D11.

[34] Al Brunelle, "Deep Float: Neuhaus' 'Water Whistle,'" *Art in America* 62, no. 5 (September–October 1974), p. 91.

[35] Ibid., p. 91.

[36] "Max Neuhaus: 'Underground Music(s) II,'" *The Museum of Modern Art Members Calendar*, July 1978; and "Underground Music," *MoMA* 7 (Summer 1978), p. 7. *Underground Music(s) II* was the original title of Neuhaus's subsonic sound work in the sculpture garden of New York's Museum of Modern Art.

[37] Hal Foster, "Exhibition Reviews," *Artforum* 18, no. 5 (January 1980), p. 70.

[38] Brunelle, "Deep Float," p. 91.

[39] On the political implications of Robert Morris's Minimal sculpture, see Maurice Berger, *Labyrinths: Robert Morris, Minimalism, and the 1960s* (New York: Harper and Row, 1989) and my *Beyond the Dream Syndicate: Tony Conrad and the Arts after Cage* (New York: Zone Books, 2008).

[40] "The public works are all deliberately pitched at a threshold of perception, a point where people can notice them or not notice them. They're often disguised, almost hidden in their

environment." (Neuhaus, "Lecture at the Seibu Museum Tokyo" [1982], in *Max Neuhaus: Sound Works*, vol. 1, *Inscription* [Ostfildern-Ruit: Cantz, 1994], p. 64; online at http://www.max-neuhaus.info/bibliography/ [accessed December 11, 2008].)

41 Neuhaus, "Lecture at the University of Miami" (1984), in *Max Neuhaus: Sound Works*, vol. 1, *Inscription*, p. 75; online at http://www.max-neuhaus.info/bibliography/Miami.htm (accessed December 11, 2008).

42 Ibid.

43 Neuhaus, "Program Notes" (1974), in *Max Neuhaus: Sound Works*, vol. 1, *Inscription*, p. 34 (emphasis added). Also quoted in Kubisch, "Time into Space," pp. 16–17.

44 La Monte Young and Marian Zazeela, "Dream House," in *Selected Writings* (Munich: Heiner Friedrich, 1969), n.p.

45 Young, quoted in Richard Kostelanetz, *The Theatre of Mixed Means* (New York: RK Editions, 1980), pp. 217–18.

46 Richard Lorber, "Max Neuhaus, *Times Square*," *Artforum* 16, no. 5 (January 1978), p. 64. Lorber goes on to relate the experience to "meditation." See also John Rockwell, "Avant-Garde: Max Neuhaus' Sounds," *New York Times*, November 11, 1977, p. 74. Neuhaus has noted, "Some people call my work meditative because of this need to focus. I don't like the baggage the word carries. These works demand only attention." (Neuhaus, "Notes on Place and Moment" [1992], in *Max Neuhaus: Sound Works*, vol. 1, *Inscription*, p. 98.)

47 Neuhaus relates his aesthetic development to "the gradual insertion of everyday sound into the concert hall, from Russolo through Edgard Varèse and finally to John Cage," in Neuhaus, "Listen," p. 20. On the notion of "transparency," see my "John Cage and the Architecture of Silence," *October*, no. 81 (Summer 1997), pp. 80–104.

48 Neuhaus, "Notes on Place and Moment," p. 98.

49 Neuhaus, "Lecture at the Seibu Museum Tokyo," p. 61.

50 Jean-Christophe Ammann, "Notes on Max Neuhaus," trans. Catherine Schelbert, in *Max Neuhaus: Sound Installation* (Basel: Kunsthalle Basel, 1983), p. 14; reprinted in *Max Neuhaus: Sound Works*, vol. 1, *Inscription*, p. 21.

51 For a reception allied with metaphysical presence (which, in the end, is the same as transcendent mysticism), see, for instance, Denys Zacharopoulos, "Max Neuhaus," in *Max Neuhaus* (Locminé: Centre d'art contemporain, Domaine de Kerguéhennec, 1987), n.p. "The process is without end and this is how the work's permanence is to be understood; not as art's state but as an infinite transformation of reality. The work never becomes an object. It is never permanently fixed. It never stops and can never start again mechanically. As soon as a work is there, it becomes identical with a place. One could even venture to say that a work ends at the precise moment when it begins to exist, since it irreversibly merges with a place."

52 Giorgio Agamben, *The Coming Community*, trans. Michael Hardt (Minneapolis: University of Minnesota Press, 1993), p. 101 (emphasis in original).

53 Although *Max-Feed* could be considered Neuhaus's first art object, it could also be considered a composition, on the order of Gordon Mumma's *Hornpipe* (1967), a cybernetically modified horn. As Michael Nyman writes about the latter, "since it is designed specifically to bring about a particular kind of musical result—it is a particular kind of *composition* in effect." Nyman, *Experimental Music*, p. 102 (emphasis in original). Indeed, Neuhaus submitted the electronics schema of *Max-Feed* as his contribution to John Cage's collection of musical scores, *Notations*. (Cage, *Notations* [New York: Something Else Press, 1969], n.p.) As an artwork-composition hybrid, *Max-Feed* takes its place within what I have outlined elsewhere as the post-Cagean "theatrical" legacy. See my *Beyond the Dream Syndicate*, pp. 82–84. Another of Neuhaus's devices to follow in the art/musical lineage was *By-Product* (1966), which produced "bits of

paper tape with electronic drawings on them generated by the sounds of the concert." (Theodore Strongin, "Avant-Garde Music Switched on Here," *New York Times*, September 14, 1966, p. 54.)

[54] Grace Glueck, "If It's Art You Want, Try Your Supermarket," *New York Times*, August 6, 1967, p. 99.

[55] Alfred E. Clark, "And in the Park It's a Happening," *New York Times*, January 1, 1967, p. 40. Neuhaus's performances have been released as Max Neuhaus, *Fontana Mix—Feed: Six Realizations of John Cage 1965/1968*, Alga Marghen CD 18NMN.044, 2003. In a nod to the spatial implications of Neuhaus's realizations, the CD liner notes declare: "If you wish to come close to replicating these performances, move your loudspeakers to opposite sides of the listening room and turn the volume of your system up as high as you can stand it . . . but watch out for your ears" (ellipses in original).

[56] Theodore Strongin, "Artist 'Realizes' Taped Music and Plays Piano from Inside," *New York Times*, March 23, 1965, p. 34. It was likely to *Fontana Mix—Feed* that Nicholas Bergman, of Citizens for a Quieter City, referred when he wrote that "of course electronic percussionist Max Neuhaus does not like noise abatement. At one concert he added electronic amplification 'so that not only the initial impact tore at the ears, but the echoes as well.'" (Bergman, "What Noise Does to Us," p. 26.)

[57] Glueck, "If It's Art You Want," p. 99.

[58] In Neuhaus's *Public Supply* broadcasts, which took place in 1966, 1968, 1970, and 1973, sounds, expressions, and interjections of any sort called in by the public were mixed and broadcast live. The project developed into *Radio Net* (1977)—in which callers were invited to whistle, the result being like a Minimalist composition with an insistent feeling of intentionality that makes it hard to relegate to background listening—and, eventually, *Auracle*, which runs today at http://www.auracle.org. Like many broadcasting experiments of the 1960s and 1970s, such as those at Boston public-television station WGBH, Neuhaus's projects aspired to intervene in the broadcasting medium to create two-way, collective and collaborative, media works.

[59] John Rockwell has reported that Neuhaus "bitterly attacks" Muzak. (Rockwell, "Whistle While You Tune In to Avant-Garde Radio," *New York Times*, January 2, 1977, p. 73.)

[60] Although Cage proclaimed his acceptance of Muzak's sounds (though not Muzak itself) in 1956, he reiterated his distaste for it in 1961. (See Cage, "Letter to Paul Henry Lang," in *John Cage: An Anthology*, ed. Richard Kostelanetz [New York: Da Capo, 1970], p. 117; and John Cage, "Interview with Roger Reynolds," in *John Cage* [New York: C.F. Peters/Henmar Press, 1962], p. 46.)

[61] Cage, "A Composer's Confessions" (1948), in *John Cage: Writer*, ed. Richard Kostelanetz (New York: Limelight Editions, 1993), p. 43.

[62] http://music.muzak.com/why_muzak/ (accessed December 23, 2008).

[63] Neuhaus, "Lecture at the Seibu Museum Tokyo," p. 67.

[64] See, for instance, Neuhaus's remarks on "sound character," in Max Neuhaus, "Sound as a Medium," in *Three to One: Max Neuhaus* (Brussels: Encore, in association with La Lettre volée, 1997), n.p.

[65] Max Neuhaus, "Notes on Place and Moment," p. 97.

[66] Carter Ratcliff, "Space, Time and Silence: Max Neuhaus' Sound Installations," in *Max Neuhaus: Sound Installation*, p. 10.

[67] LaBelle, *Background Noise*, p. 164. See also the brief comments by Simon Shaw-Miller in "Sounding Out," *Oxford Art Journal* 20, no. 1 (1997), p. 107. LaBelle overstates the uniqueness of sound in this regard, as precisely the same comparison of perception and memory occurs in the experience of Robert Morris's Minimal sculpture. As Morris explained to Cage, "I feel that by reducing the stimulus to next to nothing . . . one turns the focus on the individual, as if to say, 'whatever you got in the past you brought along anyway, so now really work at it.'" (Morris, "Letters to John

Cage," *October*, no. 81 [Summer 1997], p. 73.)

[68] Guy Debord, *The Society of the Spectacle*, trans. Donald Nicholson-Smith (New York: Zone Books, 1995), p. 110.

[69] Many of Neuhaus's more recent sound-work series seem similarly vectored to avoid the reading of presence by which his production has been received. In his Elusive Source pieces, such as *Infinite Lines from Elusive Sources I* (1988–90), the sound is nearly unlocatable, presenting an experience more baffling and disorienting than centering. In a series of doubled or otherwise acoustically distinguished architectural installations, such as *Two Sides of the "Same" Room* (1990) and *Three "Similar" Rooms* (1990–present), Neuhaus instigates acoustic differences between two or more visually identical spaces, not only showing the capacity of sound to condition spatial experience but also instilling a difference that cannot be perceptually resolved.

[70] Neuhaus, "Time Piece Series," in *Max Neuhaus: Two Sound Works 1989* (Bern: Kunsthalle Bern and Kölnischer Kunstverein, 1989), p. 8.

[71] Ibid. p. 8.

[72] Walter Benjamin, "Surrealism: The Last Snapshot of the European Intelligentsia" (1929), in *Selected Writings*, vol. 2, 1927–1934, ed. Michael W. Jennings, Howard Eiland, and Gary Smith (Cambridge: Harvard University Press, 1999), p. 218.

[73] Neuhaus, "Moment," in *Max Neuhaus: Moment / Stund* (Reykjavik: Second Floor, 1997), n.p.

[74] Ratcliff, "Space, Time, and Silence," p. 11.

[75] Neuhaus, "Time Piece Series," pp. 9–10.

[76] Ibid., p. 8.

[77] Agamben, *The Coming Community*, pp. 18–19 (emphasis in original).

[78] Ibid., p. 85. Neuhaus's propositions on community take on greater force in those installations that can be heard by individuals in their daily environment than in those that must be visited within an art institution.

[79] Ibid., p. 67 (emphasis in original).

A Talk between Peter Pakesch and Ulrich Loock about Max Neuhaus's Time Pieces

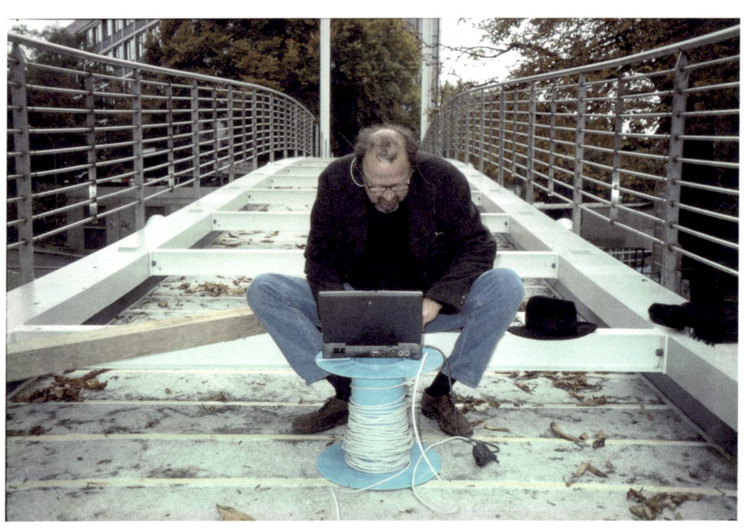

Max Neuhaus installing *Suspended Sound Line* (1999–present) in Bern, 1999.
Collection Kunst im öffentlichen Raum, Bern

Peter Pakesch and Ulrich Loock, long-time friends of Max Neuhaus, both worked with the artist on several occasions. They were each responsible for commissioning a Time Piece.

Peter Pakesch: For how long was *Time Piece Bern* up at the Kunsthalle Bern?

Ulrich Loock: It was up for approximately four years, starting in 1989. It was the first full-scale Time Piece Max Neuhaus made. As far as the equipment is concerned, however, it was actually a prototype. It was not made to be permanent.

PP: To us he said that he wasn't going to do it without a permanent installation, meaning a purchase.

UL: It is true that a work like that must be purchased and in principle dealt with like a large sculpture.

PP: The situation in Graz here at the Kunsthaus Graz was special and shaped the process in a thrilling way. There was an unusual new building, and the architects Peter Cook and Colin Fournier spontaneously came to treat Max's project as a complement to the architecture, as a congenial contribution. They gave Max's work their support in an artistically generous manner.

UL: In Bern, the piece was never formally announced to the public. It just began one day. You could hear the sound for more than two or three hundred yards from its source, all the way across the square where the Kunsthalle stands.

PP: Exactly the same as here in Graz.

UL: Inside the building, the sound was immediately perceived as an artwork. In fact I had thought it would be accepted as an element of the building, something like the noise a heating system makes. I remember an exhibition with Jean-Marc Bustamante, who was downright bothered by Max's work. He found it to be an intrusion into his exhibition space. I can't remember whether or not we turned off the piece during the exhibition.

PP: Max would never have accepted it.

UL: No.

PP: Here, each time the sound from the piece runs for the five minutes before each hour. Max runs an automatic check and receives a report by e-mail if something, such as a power outage, goes wrong. And he complains whenever there is a malfunction! *Time Piece Graz* [2003–present] is never felt to be a disruption. Max's sound here in the building is something perfectly obvious to everyone, an integral component of the environment. And then, unconsciously, you also begin to orient yourself to it, above all, the hourly rhythm; it's like the ringing of a bell, which is very much one of Max's intentions, that the whole thing be an orienting sound.

UL: It was like that for me, too. I could always hear the sound in my office, inside the building, and always kept my ear out for it. It was soothing, somehow. I didn't really connect to it in the sense of a chronometer, but it was a reliable presence, a sound that regularly recurred and indicated the passing of time. It was a gracious and affirming presence, inspiring trust in the passing of time.

PP: For me it went even further, from the temporal dimension to the spatial. It occurs to me there was once a very beautiful text by the Japanese architect Shin Nakagawa about the construction of the city of Kyoto according to sonic principles. Neuhaus's Time Pieces have something to do with urban architecture. I found your formulation of intimate presence illuminating: that a work like that can be an aid to orienting oneself. One mustn't underestimate the part of the aural with respect to spatial orientation.

UL: One could probably define that aspect of spatial orientation even more precisely. We could attempt to compare the Moment pieces (the Time Pieces) with the Place works. With the latter, it's more the place of a sound—and often a complex sound. (One should never underestimate this, for with Max it's never just one frequency.)

PP: No, the sounds are complex.

UL: Yes, they're very complex. And I have the feeling that the tones in the recent work have become more complex—let's say in quotes "more symphonic." I sometimes joke with Max, referring to the tonal "richness" of the sounds he has recently been creating. There has been development in the texture and tone of the sounds he has been deploying. In the beginning, he often worked with desiccated sound, simple clicks. As far as the spatial goes, with the Place works, like *Times Square* [1977–92; 2002–present] in New York, for example, the sound is inserted into an urban or natural or parklike setting, where it is more or less clearly demarcated. Neuhaus establishes a sound field or sound block.

PP: And it is much more continuous than with the Time Pieces . . .

UL: It is fully continuous. Each temporal cycle, each differential of time, is drawn out. The sound stands still, so to speak, even when it is rich in internal oscillation. That means that one either moves into the sound field or moves out of it. Max has worked intensively to create the technical prerequisites for these fields and blocks to be sharply demarcated. With a Time Piece it's quite different. Because they come on only at designated times, such as every hour or every half hour, there is no possibility for an active relation to the sound for us as "receivers."

PP: We don't know how to relate to it . . .

UL: We don't know how to relate to it. When it is time, we are immersed in this sound, washed over or surrounded.

PP: It breaks over us with clocklike regularity. Compare it with an indoor piece, like the untitled work [1979–89] that was part of the old Museum of Contemporary Art in Chicago but no longer exists in the new site. In the Place works, you can perceive yourself in your relation to the space.

UL: Exactly.

PP: And consciously you are aware of your own perception, which is not the case with the Time Pieces. There it is more subcutaneous, that slow swelling of the tone, one you only notice relatively late, and which, even when it is truly present, disappears again.

UL: Exactly. And with the differing degrees of involvement on the part of the receiver, the pieces take on a different social position. While it is true that the Time Pieces are comparable to bells or other civic signals, we should not forget that the sound in a Time

Piece is an individually invented sound. This distinguishes it from the sound of bells, which we owe to a long cultural development and which create a social bond.

PP: Here we have a clear issue of acceptance. Thus, in Graz, the question of getting a permit became quite a suspenseful one. Inherently, for a regional state institution like ours, it would be expedient to get one. Then again, the municipal bureaucracy was not able to find its way to issuing one. Now it is quasi-sanctioned by custom. That much one could agree on. But such an intervention into urban space, which today is highly regulated, would now be completely impossible. Noise-reduction ordinances have become quite rigid, which was not true to the same degree at the time of the work's inception. What we have here is arguably a remarkable transformation of public space. Public space changes with noise, especially traffic noise, which cannot be controlled. And the fact that sound cannot be easily located and identified arouses opposition. The public would like to protect itself against it, so there are consequently strict regulations. They are extremely difficult to get around, and even various traditional sounds would not be possible if suggested now. Of course there are various customary exceptions for churches and the like. But it is interesting that in our social fabric we treat only defensively qualities that, as Neuhaus's work teaches us, are essential for our orientation.

UL: It makes a difference whether an individually created work, an artwork, finds its place in museums or Kunsthalles, which today are created for things of that type, or whether such a work finds its site in public space. The difference lies in the fact that in public space we may not consciously choose whether we pass by just there, whether we allow ourselves to be affected by the work or not. With the museum, however, we make a choice either to go in or not to go in. We can also leave. But I cannot necessarily choose for myself whether I go to work over this bridge, or whether I cross Federal Plaza every morning in order to reach my office building. To this extent, it is proper that there be a permit procedure, which means a social consensus determines whether we as a society would like to be confronted by an artwork in public space or not. There is a delicate and awkward balance between the claims of the individual, or individual proposals, such as those of artists, and the claims of the collective.

PP: And here I believe that people in cities today, in comparison with earlier times, are more sensitive on the plane of the aural because of other acoustic stresses and the impossibility of withdrawing from them than they are to visual noise, which people are apparently prepared to accept much more.

UL: Yes, but with Richard Serra's *Tilted Arc* [1981], for example, and other cases, we saw that public visual work isn't always accepted either. As far as sculpture in public space goes, Max's work is particularly interesting. The Place works—and the Time Pieces also tend in this direction—do not impose themselves. Max leaves a relatively wide degree of freedom as to whether one engages with his work, even though it is publicly present. If someone is not prepared to consciously take in the sound that comes on every hour, and would rather offset it against some street sound—new street-cleaning equipment, for example—that person can easily do so. When one is ready or has a desire to engage with the work, one has a different experience. Thus this piece is an important example of work in that area of tension between the claim of the individual and the social claim.

PP: That corresponds to what we were able to observe in Graz. There were absolutely ambivalent reactions. A couple of people objected to the piece. Therefore we came to a slight compromise as far as its nighttime playing and stopped an hour earlier than planned. But at the same time we received extremely positive feedback. Actually we had a lucky launch. Graz was just then a Capital of Culture of Europe, and the Kunsthaus was built for the occasion. In the end, the inhabitants displayed a very open attitude to this distinctive architecture. The previously rather neglected neighborhood underwent a particular appreciation in its value from the building and running of the Kunsthaus. So the launch of Max's piece was borne with greater tolerance than could otherwise have been expected. The first objections came only a couple of months later, when normalcy set in.

UL: In any case, you can say that the sound and the placement of Max's works are never provocative in themselves.

PP: They are never offensive . . .

UL: They are never offensive, unlike *Tilted Arc*, which took a stand against its architectural situation, which the artist saw as impossible. This was an iron fist in the face of the generic architecture. This doesn't happen with Max.

PP: I would define the effect of those works as subcutaneous. Like an undertone, they go under the skin, without your being able in the first moment to clearly locate it.

UL: The sound is made on-site. Max always builds it in the situation in which it will occur. Each time he takes on elements of the sonic texture of the site and its surroundings.

PP: In Graz, he tried many different things all over the area. There he was, sitting at a café on the other side of the river, trying out things through a wireless network. Sometimes it was as if he were trying to tune the building.

UL: Yes, I also think he is seeking an exact balance (which can only be found experimentally) between sound that is to be expected in the situation, and therefore tends not to be distinguishable from the sonic texture of the surroundings, and sound that seems somehow strange and other. But even when his sounds relate to the sonic texture of the surroundings, and thus have something of the contextual —as we know it from the 1970s—they do not imply a straightforward analysis of the surroundings existing in reality.

PP: Absolutely not. They enrich, shape, and mold the environment.

UL: Yes, and change it in a certain way. How is the work to be situated aesthetically? Could one say, in order to be more precise, that it belongs with Abstract Expressionism?

PP: Well . . .

UL: With Pop art?

PP: I like very much Max's idea of describing his work as sculpture. Yet I am interested in understanding the work as coming from music. He was a percussionist, supposedly one of the best of his time. For me, in percussion there is something that sculpturally disrupts space. And this holds not only for so-called New Music. Even in pop music, you will remember, drummers have erected amazing spatial installations.

UL: Yes, in fact, while he was a percussionist he invented a new way of constructing arrays of percussion instruments, so he could play them as if they were one instrument. This was required by most of the works in his repertoire. Each work in his solo concerts had its own assemblage of metal, wood, membranes, etc. Yes, quite sculptural in the traditional sense, but all this is beside the point—here we are talking about his invisible sculpture.

PP: I think Max has quite concretely and consciously oriented his work with respect to Minimal sculpture. But he also sets himself apart from it to the extent he operates with notions of perception that are shared with Minimal music. And in this regard, one can certainly perceive a difference between the Time Pieces, or Moment works, and the Place works. One could consider the Place works as being much more in the context of Minimal sculpture. These pieces in and of themselves have something of the "theatrical" about them. They imply a "relating-to" and cannot be merely "perceived." Whereas with the Time Pieces, it is just this special "perceiving" that gives them their quality. It is a completely different form of perception, a questioning of perception, which we also know from Anthony Caro's sculpture, or more recently from artists like Liz Larner or Taft Green.

UL: I do agree with you that the work shares characteristics with certain examples of Minimal sculpture. Take Carl Andre, for example. When you look at one of his floor pieces as a place—"sculpture as place"—which changes the spatial conditions for the person standing or moving on it, or moving around it, and changes the conditions for sensation and perception, even when the physical transformation is minimal, the parallels are quite clearly drawn. In the Time Pieces, there is also the added moment of social convention, which we mentioned earlier. This is probably less strongly marked in Minimal art, which rather tends to single out the receiver, whereas with the Time Pieces others are quite obviously hearing the same thing I am hearing in the moment.

PP: But there is one thing we shouldn't overlook. When Max began making installations, there was already, in the milieu of Minimal art, or in what subsequently came to be called Process art, a confrontation with sound as sculptural material. As an example, one could mention certain works of Keith Sonnier. That was also a scene that was quite close to music, to Minimal music . . .

UL: . . . with the great activating figure of John Cage . . .

PP: Certainly, but it wasn't just John Cage. I think that in music Morton Feldman was of the greatest significance for Max. There was a milieu, one which didn't consist only of John Cage, even though Cage was, of course, an important figure, where artists kept really looking for material and testing its usefulness. In my eyes, Max was massively involved in this, too, and this constitutes an important aspect of his significance.

UL: Yes.

PP: In this regard, I would like once again to bring up the significance of Keith Sonnier's sound pieces. Unfortunately he didn't continue working with this form, but there was great ambition there, to work with sound in a completely different way, and much more with original sounds in the sense of musique concrète, also context related, both analytically and in the choice of material. Here the Minimalist takes on even other facets. This, I believe, must have continued to fascinate Max, and I think it would be interesting to discuss the significance French musique concrète had for him, and especially Luc Ferrari, who worked with ambient sounds very early on.

UL: Yes, but musique concrète is the manipulation of sounds that have actually been recorded, one might say sound "photographs," whereas Neuhaus never uses recordings. He creates sounds from scratch, from his imagination. These may resemble actual sounds, but this is precisely how he plays with "plausibility."

PP: There was an entire field, laid out in the 1960s, that favored the development of this work from many sides.

UL: I think we have to make sure not to construct incorrect lines of influence. We should remember that Neuhaus was quite well known even at an early stage, commingling with the art community as he did. It might be an interesting subject for research to find out at what point people like Sonnier, Bruce Nauman, and others in the visual arts became aware of Max's very active voice—the art and modern-dance communities were, in fact, all following his work during the period from 1963 when he was a performer. At this point, one should repeat that for the discourse around his work it was extraordinarily important to make a break with the concept of music.

PP: I think by now it is clear that we are not dealing with music here . . .

UL: Because sound is abstracted from the temporal dimension, one essential characteristic of music is lacking. Even when this sound—and this is why it is called Time Piece—periodically recurs and features a crescendo, which again implies a temporal moment, it is in its essence a static sound inserted into its surroundings. The repetition probably plays an important role. Sound is in and of itself a temporally structured element set on the space, even generating a place, as the case may be. To that extent, although it has this temporal dimension, it is more sculptural and site bound . . . Now here, as we have just heard the sound again, I would like to re-emphasize what I alluded to earlier, that the sound—despite all its ties to place, to the existing ambient sound, to the social convention of bells—is also very personal. The sound color Max creates, this sonorous hum, would be hard to attribute to either an animal or a human but could plausibly be attributed to some organic being rather than to a technical or technoid one . . .

PP: I find it quite comparable to techniques in painting, where ostensibly simple phenomena become charged through highly developed techniques and through which plainness is subjected to complex perception. One example of this is the many sophisticated glazes in the work of Barnett Newman. I know from Max how much he cares about the "building" of the sounds. He produces multilayered textures, which are important for the reception of the work to last.

UL: With a painter, one can speak of color sense or signature. The sound has a breadth and a depth, which are closely bonded to Max Neuhaus's sensibility. To that extent here we are dealing with the artist as auteur, and the traditional conception of the artist is maintained—which perhaps in a certain way stands in contradiction to the original desire of dissolving the opposition between performer and public into which Max was tied as a solo percussionist.

PP: Yes, I do think he is working to get at something specific. On one hand, what he uses as material is not at all interchangeable—which is different from the case of Minimal art. There, especially when it moves into the conceptual, as with Carl Andre or Sol LeWitt, someone else can also produce the work, or the industrial processing or fabrication is interchangeable. To this extent, Neuhaus is traditional. He is one of those sculptors or artists who consciously build. He builds not only space—which in the case of the Time Pieces consists of urban space—but sound itself, and one that is finely chiseled.

UL: But now we are getting close, it seems to me, to saying he is actually a traditional landscape painter.

PP: Yes, if sculptors could paint landscapes. One could draw out the genre idea to the point of absurdity.

UL: There was one important experience in Bern: at the moment when in the Time Piece the sound breaks off, all the other background noises return and are heard again, differently and—here I can confirm a formulation that comes from Max himself—"cleansed." As if they were cleansed. All of them. The standing noise of the city is once again there . . .

PP: But comes back differently . . .

UL: It comes back differently. Max contaminates the standing sound of the city with his own sound, which on the hour and the half hour swells and moves into the foreground, before breaking off. When Max removes the sound he has himself inserted, there is an effect of cleansing.

PP: For me it was of great significance that the Graz project first be presented in the framework of "Imagination," an exhibition project based on the shaping of perception. We approached our "naive" conception of "true" perception of the surrounding world as a theme to show how various individual forms of perception function and how our representation of homogeneous images in homogeneous space is constructed within a framework of complex cerebral and cultural processes. Max's contribution is important in this regard because he deceives our "naive" understanding. In the field of the visual, we know that images are composed from quite varied areas of brain activity and that here the eye is of rather secondary importance. It is different in the field of the aural. Here I am thinking of how selectively we listen and hear, how much the brain filters, suppresses the unnecessary, in order to very precisely condition everything we mean to perceive objectively. We would probably go crazy, or in any case be overwhelmed, were we to perceive the total range of a particular aural spectrum completely unfiltered. Here Max produces an interesting kind of irritation, and it is in that sense a cleansing, that he brings in sound that cannot be classified. One might say one's hearing is recalibrated. This is effected through an apparently quite simple manner by the crescendo, the slow rising of the sound, and then the sudden breaking off. In this way, Max steals up on passersby with sound. We can classify the bird that sings and filter the birdsong out for ourselves. We can classify the car that drives by and filter it out for ourselves. It is no different with visual perception. Max's sound is no known sound, and it is not music, either. The relevant part of the brain must itself be reoriented, so to speak.

UL: That's an interesting way of putting it.

PP: The sound also has no clearly defined location. We are used to linking sounds with one place, "siting" it, so to speak. There is nothing worse than sounds whose location we cannot determine. This is distinct from the Place works, where the location is much more clearly definable as a place to which one can relate.

UL: Though there, too, one doesn't know where the sound is coming from.

PP: But at least it has a location . . .

UL: It has a *localization*, but the source is of course hidden, which in itself is something rather seldom seen when one aligns oneself to the postulates of the modern, with its claims of truth to material and transparency in all the elements involved. But within the logic of Max's work it is correct to hide the sources.

PP: Nonetheless, for me the Place works much more concretely have a location, one I can relate to, while with the Time Pieces there is this "coming-upon-one" that intensifies the irritation and challenges the perception.

UL: Here I find that the Time Pieces bring something generous into Neuhaus's work, in the sense that he shares with us, as receivers, a stance that rests on accepting that which is there. Max does not exclude any particular sounds as being noise pollution. Indeed, these sounds, and we ourselves, are wrapped in the sound of Time Piece. Somehow—how shall I put it?—they are part of the beauty of the piece and of the beauty of this sound.

PP: They have the potential to produce, so to speak, the orchestration of the city. The idea is now to continue on, with the other buildings of the Landesmuseum Joanneum in the city. I would like to do more Time Pieces with the next big set of building plans, to create the urban constellation of a museum that is present in many sites.

Graz, Austria, 2006
Translated from the original German
by Warren Niesluchowski

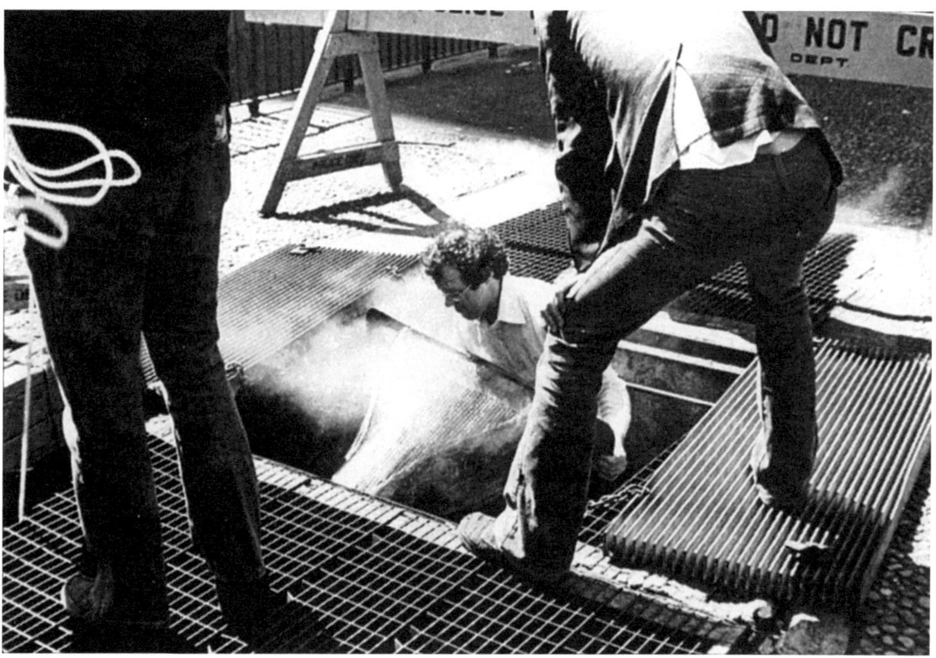

Max Neuhaus installing *Times Square*, 1977

Max Neuhaus: Sound into Space

Liz Kotz

One of the ironies of Max Neuhaus's sound installation *Times Square* (1977–92; 2002–present) is its siting in what must be one of the loudest places in the world. On a weekend afternoon, the traffic island where the piece is located teems with noise: taxi horns blare, tourists throng, traffic roars by, sirens blast, all kinds of announcers hawk their wares, and a steel band plays a block away. It is chaos, din. But, underneath this cacophony, another, quieter sound emerges: a rich, ringing drone, like a deep industrial hum. It is strangely unplaceable. As you walk over the steel grate, the sound fluctuates slightly, in loudness and tone. "Like the after-ring of a loud bell,"[1] it seems as though it has always been here, as though it will always be here: the sound of the city itself, a reverberation created from inside its very infrastructure, resonating underneath the roads and buildings and subway tunnels, the relics of centuries of urban life and machinery.

Using electronic sound generators, building up the sound by ear over a long period, Neuhaus constructed the tones to be "plausible," to seem as if they could be produced naturally by the subway ventilation shaft from which they emanate. The resonance of the underground vault and its tunnels transforms and modulates the dronelike tones: standing aboveground, on the grate, you hear "what the sound does to the chamber." And strangely, as you walk off the island, you can't really tell when you've gone out of range. The low, ringing hum triggers your sensitivity to these types of sounds, and you begin to hear it everywhere: this ring, this hum, the rumbling sound of the city.

Neuhaus has recalled that in 1974, when he first came upon the traffic island, Times Square was a no-man's-land, and a homeless guy was living on the grate in a cardboard box. Yet as Neuhaus has insisted, the piece works differently under different sound and social conditions, just as a piece of sculpture changes in different light. Returning to the site on a quiet and snowy winter night, when the massive square is

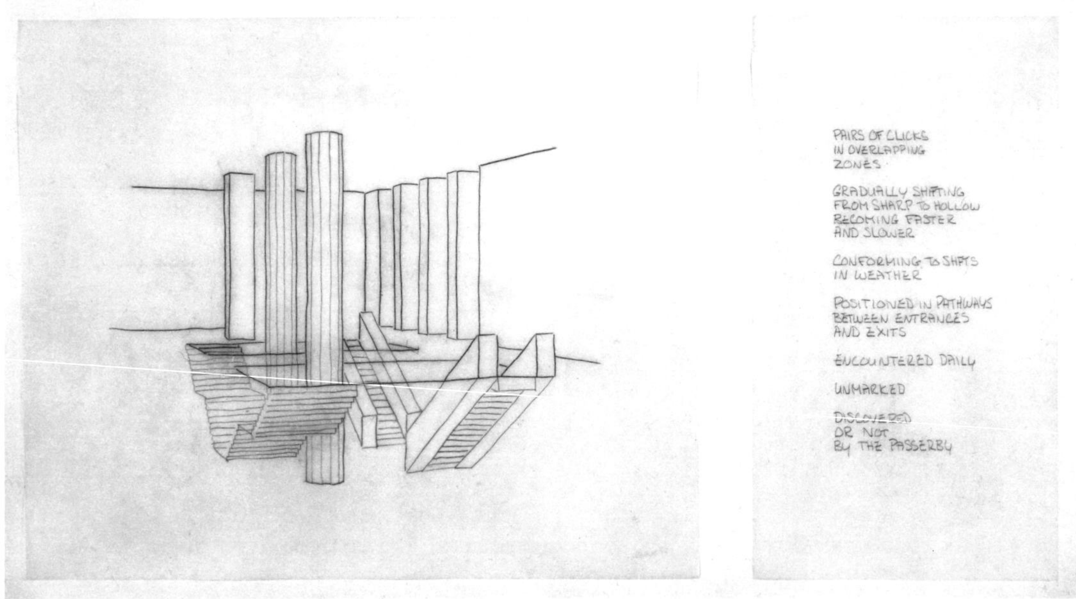

Max Neuhaus's Circumscription drawing for *Walkthrough* (1973–77), 1993. Pencil on paper; 2 parts, 23½ x 29½ inches, 23½ x 13⅜ inches (60 x 75 cm, 60 x 34 cm)

nearly deserted, you perhaps find it easier to take in the low, throbbing purr. In activating an inherently changing and chaotic urban site, Neuhaus's *Times Square* is designed to absorb such fluctuations.

It is no accident that *Times Square* was Neuhaus's first permanent piece, the project through which he fully conceived the idea of a lasting installation: a sound that was paradoxically not an "event," a temporal phenomenon, but a "place"—as if from this inconspicuous, inconsequential traffic island, you could listen in to the hum of the city. Neuhaus had made several temporary installations before, including *Walkthrough* (1973–77), which placed a series of overlapping clicking sounds in the subway entrance in the portico of the Metropolitan Transportation Authority building at Jay Street–Borough Hall in Brooklyn. In his effort to connect the work to its environment and to trigger an ongoing, active process, Neuhaus programmed the sounds to respond slightly to variations in temperature and humidity; physical shifts caused the speed of the clicks to change, altering how they interacted at different points in the large space. The work lasted for almost four years before it was destroyed by a custodian. However fraught, the project helped move Neuhaus toward what would become *Times Square*, the work that would crystallize a set of ideas about sound as a way to define a space.

* * *

After Neuhaus walked away in the late 1960s from a career as a percussionist of experimental music, his work began to trace out a number of options for dealing with sound. These represent both the extension and the transformation of what we might see as the legacy of the composer John Cage. Beginning in the late 1930s, Cage reconceived music as "organized sound" in a series of works for unorthodox percussion and electromechanical instruments. By the 1950s, Cage came to embrace what he termed "indeterminacy," renouncing the authority of the composer to create discrete works, in favor of the real-time generation of music through series of highly abstract graphic notations. Yet the work that most resonates with Neuhaus's project is Cage's legendary 1952 "silent" piece," *4'33"*, which directs a performer to remain silent for three time brackets. In its debut performance, the pianist David Tudor famously marked each of the three "movements" with a physical gesture, silently opening and closing the keyboard lid, as he sat at the instrument for the duration of the piece. Performed live in a formal concert setting, the composition invites the audience to hear ambient sound as music and throws the responsibility for the experience onto the perceptual capacities of its listeners. The work aims therefore to activate listening, to be sure, but also to trigger an attentiveness to space, to the site of the performance, and to the conventions and protocols that define the concert experience.

I

TACET

II

TACET

III

TACET

NOTE: The title of this work is the total length in minutes and seconds of its performance. At Woodstock, N.Y., August 29, 1952, the title was 4' 33" and the three parts were 33", 2' 40", and 1' 20". It was performed by David Tudor, pianist, who indicated the beginnings of parts by closing, the endings by opening, the keyboard lid. However, the work may be performed by any instrumentalist or combination of instrumentalists and last any length of time.

FOR IRWIN KREMEN JOHN CAGE

Copyright 1953 John Cage
All Rights Reserved Including the Right of Public Performance for Profit

John Cage, text score for *4'33"*, 1952

For post–World War II experimental music, *4'33"* represented a culmination but also a kind of endpoint, a provocation beyond which one could not go and still be creating "music."[2] As a result, few composers or musicians have taken its implications seriously, because doing so would require questioning the very boundaries of their field. Yet by using sound as a way to investigate a site in a series of works since the late 1960s, Neuhaus was able to embrace the deepest implications of Cage's work—and of post–World War II experimental music more generally—and push them into genuinely new and rich territories, moving in effect into the territory of visual art to help found a practice of what has been termed sound art or sound installation. In recent years, these terms have become quite vexed, as a flurry of exhibitions has turned them into catchalls for all manner of work with an auditory component. However, site-based work with sound grew out of two distinct trajectories: the investigation of site in Postminimalist visual art since the late 1960s, and the spatialization of music, a practice that has deep roots in the Western concert tradition but that reached a certain critical urgency in the immediate post–World War II era, as new technologies of electronic sound generation, sound mixing, loudspeakers, and amplification made it increasingly possible to control the distribution and modulation of sound in space.

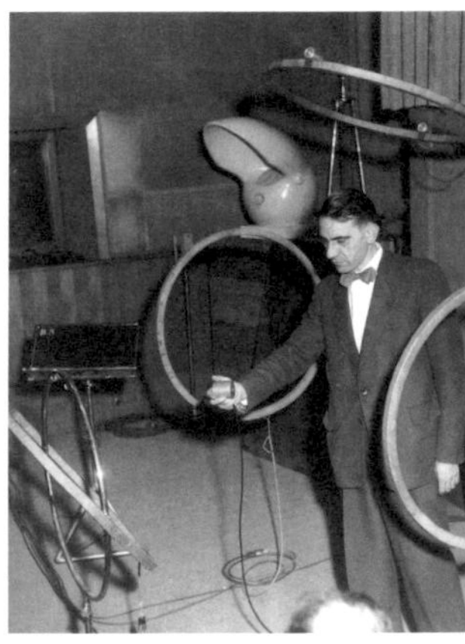

Pierre Henry, *pupitre d'espace*, a device utilizing induction coils, built by Jacques Poullin in 1951 at Pierre Schaeffer's suggestion

By 1951, the French musique concrète composer Pierre Schaeffer and his engineer Jacques Poullin had built a device Schaeffer called the *pupitre d'espace* (roughly, "space console" or "space desk"), which consisted of four electromagnetic induction coils that allowed the operator to gesturally manipulate and diffuse the spatial distribution of sounds. Schaeffer later established the Groupe de Recherches Musicales, a collective whose experimental designs eventually produced the Acousmonium, an "orchestra" of loudspeakers developed in 1974 by François Bayle. The device positions the composer as "a lonely conductor of an orchestra of loudspeakers, spatialising the sound from a control panel in the auditorium."[3] Installed in situations from formal concert halls to outdoor settings, the Acousmonium contains two mixing consoles and up to one hundred loudspeakers of different sizes distributed throughout a space, allowing a composer to control the sonic projection and directionality of a work. In Bayle's words, "It puts you inside the sound. It's like the interior of a sound universe."[4]

Spatialization is understood in this context as the distribution of sound within a listening environment—a concert hall, gallery, or home. It describes "the means by which loudspeakers are used to articulate or create a spatial musical experience for listeners in playback or performance," including specific technical formats (stereophonic, quadraphonic, etc.), and "the placement and movement of sounds in space in any number of listening situations."[5] The term appears in an online glossary compiled by the Ears: ElectroAcoustic Resource Site under the larger category of "Performance Practice and Presentation," and, in its French post–musique concrète manifestations, the spatialization of sound is indeed understood as a means to enhance the listening experience as it occurs in a concert setting. Such devices have a compensatory quality, designed to enliven concerts of electroacoustic music and restore a more robust spatial dimension to prerecorded sound materials, which, by their nature, are severed from their source. This understanding of spatialized sound as a device to structure or augment the concert experience of music also underlies works like Karlheinz Stockhausen's 1955–56, "Gesang der Jünglinge" (Song of the Youths), which is often credited as one of the first works to incorporate spatialization as a compositional element, as its five loudspeakers direct and move the sound around the space.[6]

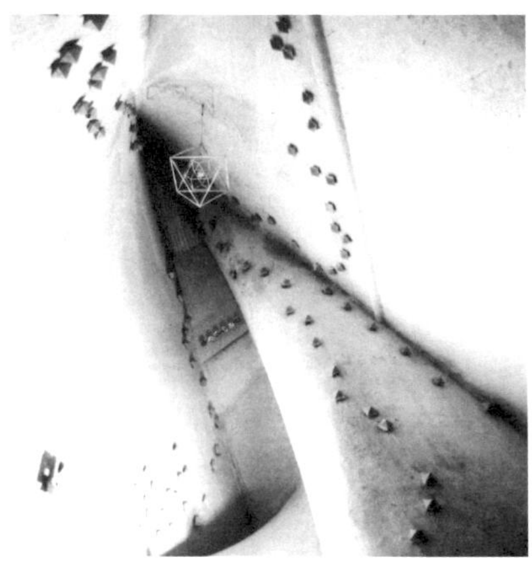

Le Corbusier, in collaboration with Edgar Varèse and Iannis Xenakis, curved interior walls with loudspeakers, Philips Pavilion, 1958. Research Library, The Getty Research Institute, Los Angeles (2002.R.41)

Such a concert-based project, it should be clear, could not be more different from the post-Cagean and Postminimalist activation of space that animates Neuhaus's work. Yet when composers and musicians refer to the "spatialization of sound," often what they are talking about is, at heart, an enhanced, multidirectional or immersive concert experience —whether or not it takes place in a traditional concert venue. The most celebrated example of this tendency is the 1958 Philips Pavilion, which was designed by the architect Le Corbusier and his then assistant, Iannis Xenakis, for the presentation of two pieces of prerecorded music, Edgard Varèse's eight-minute composition *Poème Électronique* and Xenakis's short *Concrèt PH*, at the Brussels World's Fair.[7] Le Corbusier conceived of the temporary exhibition as a total work of art, joining sound, images, light, and architectural container into an overpowering, immersive spectacle. While Xenakis composed the pavilion's mathematically generated parabolic form, which gave the building its striking look, it was Philips engineers who designed its sonic guts: the building's sound system comprised over three hundred loudspeakers that diffused the music throughout the space along "routes" of sound, employing stereophonic effects and reverberation to give the score direction and depth. A series of black-and-white still images was projected onto the building's curved interior walls, and a visual stream of projected stencils and colors accompanied the music to produce chance juxtapositions and superimpositions within the eight-minute matrix of the work.[8]

The Philips Pavilion was commissioned by the Dutch audio firm to publicize its newly developed technologies in stereophony and sound engineering. Despite this technologically advanced infrastructure, Le Corbusier's conception was ultimately aesthetically conservative, a grand fusion of collage aesthetics and humanistic images that surrounded visitors in a high-tech, late-Romantic theatrical spectacle that the architect imagined as a "celestial space." As Marc Treib notes, "The Philips Pavilion presented a collage liturgy for twentieth-century humankind, dependent on electricity instead of daylight and on virtual perspectives in place of terrestrial views."[9]

For Varèse, the exhibition provided a late-in-life chance to realize long-held ambitions for spatially orchestrating colliding sound masses. In a 1936 talk, he had outlined his vision of a new musical apparatus that would project compositions into three-dimensional space: "When new instruments will allow me to write music as I conceive it, the movement of sound-masses, of shifting planes, will be clearly perceived in my work, taking the place of linear counterpoint. . . . Today, with the technical means that exist and are easily adaptable, the differentiation of the various sound masses and different planes as well as these beams of sound, could be made discernable to the listener by means of certain acoustical arrangements."[10] Ultimately Varèse's project continues and intensifies the role of the composer: "I am sure that the time will come when the composer, after he has graphically realized the score, will see his score automatically put on a machine that will faithfully transmit the musical content to the listener."[11] This French modernist trajectory arguably reaches its logical outcome in the virtuoso technologies of sound projection, such as that of Bayle's Acousmonium, but its concert-based model is fundamentally opposed to the post-Cagean and Postminimalist site-oriented project that emerged out of the intersection of experimental music and the visual arts in the 1950s and 1960s.

By the time of Cage's legendary 1958–59 Experimental Composition class at the New School in New York City, artists trained as painters and sculptors were turning to sound to expand and disrupt an increasingly environmental visual-art experience. Happenings artists, such as Jim Dine, Allan Kaprow, and Claes Oldenburg, incorporated sound effects into their works, using voice and noise as expressive elements in a larger construction. Despite this introduction of sound into a visual-art context, these artists were not yet producing "sound art" or isolating the physical or expressive properties of sound as a potentially spatial material.

A fascinating precursor to the practice of sound installation comes from the work of the Japanese artist Atsuko Tanaka, who presented her installation *Bell* at the First Gutai Exhibition in Tokyo in 1955. Like many Gutai artists, Tanaka sought to extend the gestural automatism and expressionism of Surrealist and Art Informel practices into three-dimensional spaces that would breach the boundaries between art and life. Tanaka installed twenty electric bells throughout the exhibition space, connecting them to a switch and providing a card that cued visitors to press a button.[12] Tanaka describes the "acoustic composition" as follows: "The work consists of twenty electric bells connected by forty metres of cords that run all over the exhibition space. The bells will be turned on in sequence, regulated automatically by a motor, to ring one by one, the closest ones ringing loud and the farthest ones heard only faintly. It was my intention to create an acoustic composition with the differing loudness of bell sounds."[13]

The sequence of clanging bells mapped the exhibition hall temporally and spatially, using physical properties of sound to define the space. Like the New York–based Happenings artists, Tanaka saw her work as a bodily, temporal, and three-dimensional

MOTOR
VEHICLE
SUNDOWN
(EVENT)

(TO JOHN CAGE)
SPRING/SUMMER 1960
G. BRECHT

Any number of motor vehicles are arranged outdoors.

There are at least as many sets of instruction cards as vehicles.

All instruction card sets are shuffled collectively, and 22 cards are distributed to the single performer per vehicle.

At sundown (relatively dark, open area incident light 2 foot-candles or less) the performers leave a central location, simultaneously counting out (at an agreed-upon rate) a prearranged duration 1 1/2 times the maximum required for any performer to reach, and seat himself in, his vehicle. At the end of this count each performer starts the engine of his vehicle and subsequently acts according to the directions on his instruction cards, read consecutively as dealt. (An equivalent pause is to be substituted for an instruction referring to non-available equipment.) Having acted on all instructions, each performer turns off the engine of his vehicle and remains seated until all vehicles have ceased running.

A single value from each parenthetical series of values is to be chosen, by chance, for each card. Parenthetic numerals indicate duration in counts (at an agreed-upon rate). Special lights (8) means truck-body, safety, signal, warning lights, signs, displays, etc. Special equipment (22) means carousels, ladders, fire-hoses with truck-contained pumps and water supply, etc.

INSTRUCTION CARDS (44 per set):

1. Head lights (high beam, low beam) on (1-5), off.
2. Parking lights on (1-11), off.
3. Foot-brake lights on (1-3), off.
4. (Right, left) directional signals on (1-7), off.
5. Inside light on (1-5), off.
6. Glove-compartment light on. Open (or close) glove compartment (quickly, with moderate speed, slowly).
7. Spot-lamp on (1-11), move (vertically, horizontally, randomly), (quickly, with moderate speed, slowly), off.
8. Special lights on (1-9), off.
9. Sound horn (1-11).
10. Sound siren (1-15).
11. Sound bell(s) (1-7).
12. Accelerate motor (1-3).
13. Wind-shield wipers on (1-5), off.
14. Radio on, maximum volume, (1-7), off. Change tuning.
15. Strike hand on dashboard.
16. Strike a window with knuckles.
17. Fold a seat or seat-back (quickly, with moderate speed, slowly). Replace.
18. Open (or close) a window (quickly, with moderate speed, slowly).
19. Open (or close) a door (quickly, with moderate speed, slowly).
20. Open (or close) engine-hood, opening and closing vehicle door, if necessary.
21. Trunk light on. Open (or close) trunk lid (if a car), rear-panel (if a truck or station-wagon), or equivalent. Trunk light off.
22. Operate special equipment (1-15), off.

23–44. Pause (1-13).

George Brecht, instruction cards for *Motor Vehicle Sundown (Event)*, 1960

extension of painting, a practice that engaged the participation and perceptual capacities of its viewer-listener. The groundbreaking actions and exhibitions of the Gutai group, published in international magazines, inspired not only visual artists like Kaprow but also experimental dancers like Simone Forti, who recalled the striking effect of photographs of Gutai performances on her own practice as it emerged out of workshops with the choreographer Anna Halprin in northern California in the late 1950s. The Gutai emphasis on "one thing," Forti has recalled, helped her isolate a proto-Minimal action out of a larger stream—a simple action or gesture that she then crossed with a Duchampian focus on the conventionality of the art experience: "When you question a convention, you isolate it, and become aware of it, and then that becomes your topic."[14]

During the period 1959 to 1962, downtown New York was the scene of a genuinely interdisciplinary art world that propelled visual artists, dancers, poets, and composers to explore new durational and time-based forms. For Fluxus artists, such as George Brecht, Dick Higgins, Alison Knowles, and Yoko Ono, the perceptual frame and text-based score of *4′33″* provided a potent model for rethinking visual art as a kind of event structure. Brecht, in particular, devised an ongoing series of what he called "event scores" that reframed performed actions, assembled objects, and simple everyday occurrences as linguistic, notated "events." In the *Motor Vehicle Sundown (Event)*, of 1960 (dedicated to Cage), detailed instruction cards direct participants to assemble in automobiles at sundown at a central location. After starting their engines, each "performer" initiates randomly ordered series of actions: turning headlights and brake lights off and on, sounding siren and horn, accelerating motor, opening and closing doors, windows and hood, turning the radio on and changing its tuning, all to produce a visual and sonic cacophony.

The piece can be seen as both a precursor of and a contrast to Neuhaus's 1967 work *Drive-in Music*, first produced for the Albright-Knox Art Gallery in Buffalo. Considering this version as a prototype, Neuhaus described the piece as a potentially permanent work: "Drive In Music is a sound environment for people in automobiles. It consists of setting up areas of sound, which can only be heard thru an AM radio, along a mile of street or roadway. The piece is set up permanently or semi-permanently and is available twenty-four hours a day to anyone driving along that road."[15] As visitors navigated the space, with their radios tuned to a prescribed frequency, they passed through different combinations of sounds created by the system of low-power transmitters mounted along the roadway.[16] Neuhaus noted that "in the prototype version, the sound generators themselves were weather sensitive, i.e. they were composed with electronic circuitry which was sensitive to changes in temperature, humidity, and light, so that the sounds themselves were constantly changing with minute changes in the atmospheric environment."[17]

Although both works involve participatory explorations of sound (and vision) using automobiles, the differences between Brecht's 1960 "event" and Neuhaus's 1967 "environment" are striking: Brecht's piece is a performance, organized by a loose time structure; its chance juxtapositions and superimpositions occur in time as participants perform different actions according to the cards they are dealt. Neuhaus, however, envisioned his work as a physical installation of radio signals that individual participants realize in a temporal form as they navigate through overlapping areas of broadcast.[18] Both represent radical extensions of Cage's imperative to explore everyday and urban ambient sounds as material for art, yet while Brecht produces, in effect, an anarchic outdoor orchestra of performed automobile sounds, Neuhaus works with the electronic sound technology built into the car—the humble AM radio—to construct a sonically animated space.

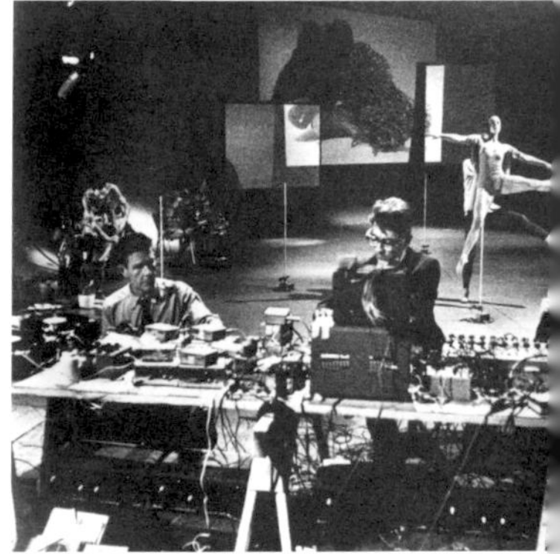

John Cage, *Variations V*, 1965, showing Cage at electronics table with David Tudor and Gordon Mumma (foreground), Carolyn Brown, Merce Cunningham, and Barbara Dilley (background)

To differentiate Neuhaus's project from even the most adventurous electroacoustic sound practices that came out of the Cage nexus, it is useful to juxtapose it with David Tudor's sustained work with electronic sound. By the early 1960s, Tudor's brilliant performances of piano music increasingly involved amplification and electronics. To perform Cage's 1961 *Variations II*, Tudor sought to transform the unorthodox graphic score—a collection of eleven tokens, drawn on sheets of transparent plastic, whose points indicate sound events and whose lines establish the parameters of frequency, duration, timbre, amplitude, and morphology. As musicologist James Pritchett insists, for Cage, "the openness of the graphic space was a way of exploring the total space of sounds. . . . The notation of *Variations II*, because it allows any configuration of dots and lines, can describe any sound."[19]

Tudor's interpretation of *Variations II* helped to trigger his own compositional voice and opened the door to his increasingly influential work as a "composer" of instruments, as a designer of elaborate sound-generating devices and electroacoustic mechanisms. In the 1960s and 1970s, Tudor developed many of these projects, including various versions of *Rainforest*, in his work for the Merce Cunningham Dance Company (collaborating since *Rainforest IV* with the group Composers Inside Electronics).[20] Tudor's decision to perform Cage's score using an amplified piano outfitted with contact microphones produced, in effect, "a unified electronic instrument with its own characteristics"[21]—a technical setup generating a number of feedback loops whose behavior and performance then took on a life of their own. Unlike Cage's sound world of discrete "sounds in themselves," in Tudor's version of *Variations II*, sounds "merge, overlap and run into one another in waves of feedback and reverb," largely independent of the composer's control or the design of the score.[22]

Despite Tudor's rigorous attention to the resonant qualities of found objects and electroacoustic devices, he consistently conceives of these as instruments, not spaces or sites. Tudor never really moved from exploring the object as a resonating body to treating the room itself as an instrument. As Neuhaus recalled, Tudor always insisted on performing—the assemblages of objects and circuits that would result in Tudor's *Rainforest* projects and installations were, in effect, instruments: "He was always building these things in the pit with Cunningham, activating them. . . . *Rainforest* was an exposure, a way to bring it out of the darkness of the pit."[23]

Ironically, the work Tudor retrospectively considered his first independent composition, the 1964 installation *Fluorescent Sound*, contains the seeds of a more explicitly site-based practice. To produce a sound accompaniment for a performance of Robert Rauschenberg's dance *Elgin Tie* at the Moderna Museet in Stockholm, Tudor devised a score for the museum's fluorescent-light switches, which he proceeded to perform on the switch panel. In a 1988 interview, he recalled, "One day I was in the room when someone was turning on the fluorescent lights and they didn't know which to turn on and all of a sudden there was the most beautiful music. I thought, 'OK, I'll put some contact microphones up there from the bulbs to see if the sound can be made really audible."[24] In his work using contact mics, Tudor in a sense extends the model of Cage's composition *Cartridge Music* (1960), which employed old-fashioned phonograph cartridges to amplify the "small sounds" produced by any number of objects: "in practice," Tudor explained, "it was found convenient to attach the cartridges to pieces of furniture (tables, ladders, moveable carts, chairs, etc.) to which are attached contact microphones."[25] Different performers each prepared their own parts, orchestrating interactions and contradictions between actions that helped to make *Cartridge Music* "one of the first successful theatrical pieces of live electronic music."[26]

Neither Tudor nor Cage would take up the latent spatial or environmental potential for amplifying sounds produced by everyday objects. This trajectory is evident, however, in the work of La Monte Young, whose 1958–60 compositions for sustained drones and assaultively loud frictive sounds—for example, *Poem for Chairs, Tables, Benches, Etc. (and other sound sources)* (1960)—implicitly used sound to activate spaces like lofts, where many performances were held.[27] By 1964, Young was envisioning his subsequent Dream House installations, which would use electronic instruments to generate perfectly proportioned frequency ratios for drawn-out periods. In a 1964 grant proposal to the Ingraham Marshall Foundation, Young outlined the project:

> It is true that in the plans for my *Dream Houses* I have desired a kind of spiritual retreat, a dwelling in which many musicians and students could live and execute a musical work which would last as long a time as there were enough performers interested in keeping the form alive . . . . Now the immediate advantage of machines/music boxes which can produce this music over a long period of time becomes more evident. The instruments which may operate on electricity or other types of energy cannot only be transported from one location to another, concert halls, museums, theatres, but they may be utilized to provide *Eternal Music* in the home, the office, on ocean liners and airplanes. It is important that it be understood that these instruments will not merely serve the simple function of reproduction found in a magnetic tape or disc recording, but that the design and concentration will be such that these highly intricate and delicate machines may be programmed by the composer or by a programmer from the composer's score to actually create new compositions and new realizations of compositions.[28]

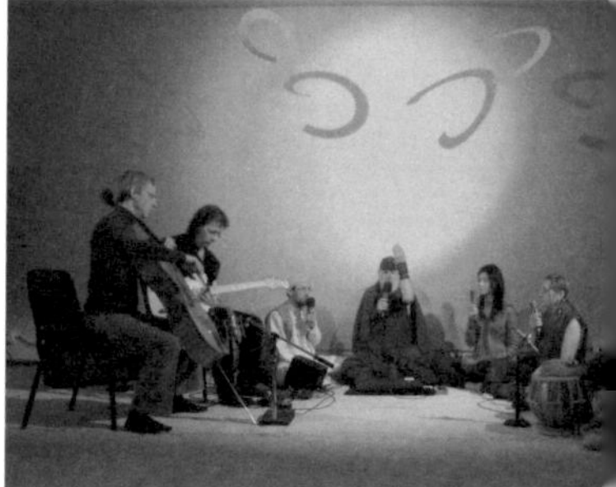

La Monte Young, Marian Zazeela, and the Just Alap Raga Ensemble performing *Raga Sundara, ektal vilampit khayal* in *Raga Yaman Kalyan* in a setting of *Imagic Light*, June 27, 2008. *Dream House: Seven + Eight Years of Sound and Light*, 275 Church Street, New York City. Charles Curtis, Jon Catler, Da'ud Constant, La Monte Young, Jung Hee Choi, Marian Zazeela, and Naren Budhkar (left to right)

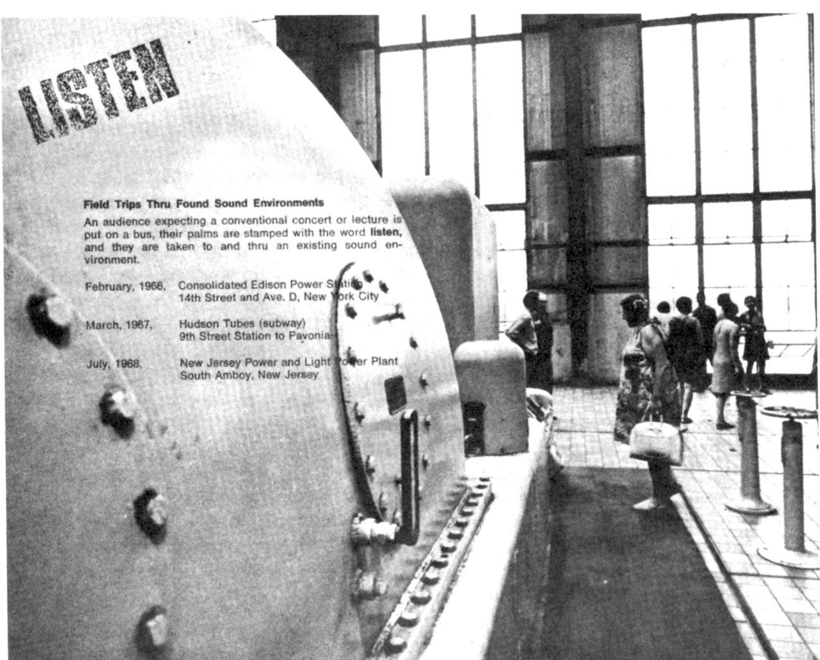

Max Neuhaus, *Listen* poster, with photo by Peter Moore

Young's description of the Dream House as a kind of "spiritual retreat" makes it clear that the focused experience of sound it entails is detached from everyday urban experience. The perceptual focusing and seclusion he describes conceptually lie closer to the light installations of Robert Irwin than to, say, the explicitly site-based projects of Richard Serra or Gordon Matta-Clark. Electronics provide a technical means to achieve durations beyond the capacities of human performers. As the Dream House project developed, Young would employ standing waves to construct a sound topography. By choosing frequencies that "fit" in a room, a composer or engineer can in effect physically shape sound waves, so that their reflections and interactions create series of nodes and antinodes. As listeners move through the space, they encounter different pockets of sound, giving them the impression they are "tuning" or "playing" the space with their own bodies and movements.[29] In a sense, Young's ongoing Dream House and Neuhaus's *Times Square* represent the polarities of post-Cagean uses of spatialized sound. As Young's early proposal suggests, his conception is closer to the French tradition of controlled diffusion of what is still a composed work. As Neuhaus once remarked, Young's Dream House is still music: in it, an installation is just "a very long piece of music."[30]

In contrast, Neuhaus's goal was not just to get outside the concert hall but to produce works that were no longer music: "Since the only category we had for artists who dealt with sound was musician, composer . . . I had to stop being that."[31] The first step was the series of sound walks he began in 1966 titled *Listen*. A listing on the concert program invited listeners outside the hall, where the word "listen" was stamped on their hands before they were taken on a tour of local urban soundscapes. In the first performance, Neuhaus recounts, he led a group of friends down Fourteenth Street toward the East River: "At that point the street bisects a power plant and, as I had noticed previously, one hears some spectacularly massive rumbling. We continued, crossing the highway and walking along the sound of its tire wash, down river for a few blocks, re-crossing over a pedestrian bridge, passing through the Puerto Rican street life of the lower east side to my studio, where I performed some percussion pieces for them."[32]

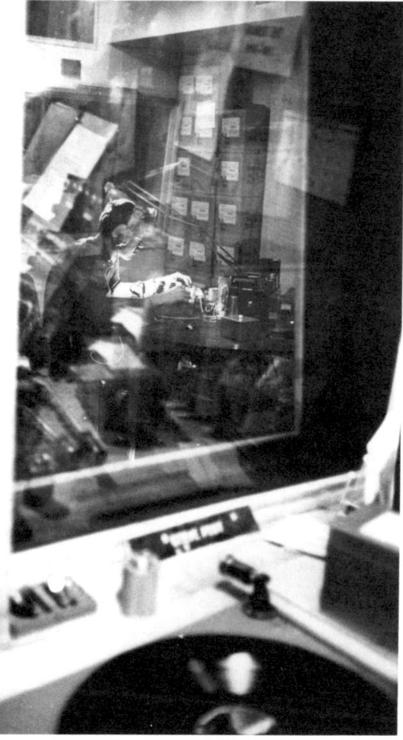

Photo by Peter Moore showing Max Neuhaus during *Public Supply* broadcast at WBAI studios, New York City, October 8, 1966

The sound walks inverted the modernist paradigm—from Luigi Russolo to Varèse to Cage—of bringing noise and everyday sounds into the concert setting.[33] Such works of noise music failed, in Neuhaus's view, because audience members seemed more impressed by the scandal effect than by the sounds themselves: "few were able to carry the experience over to a new perspective on the sounds of their daily lives. I became interested in going a step further. Why limit listening to the concert hall? Instead of bringing these sounds into the hall, why not simply take the audience outside?"[34] To investigate the aural properties of existing spaces, Neuhaus drew on his skills as a percussionist working with timbre, resonance, and timing: he would "sound out" a site, analyzing its patterns of resonance and ambient sound, and devise sonorities accordingly. As Neuhaus notes, since a concert hall is "a white space for sound," like the white box of the gallery, by definition "any sound outside the concert hall was site specific."[35]

In addition, Neuhaus systematically explored new sound-producing devices and systems—from his *Max-Feed* (1966), a feedback-producing gadget, to his extraordinary series of *Public Supply* (1966–73) and *Radio Net* concerts (1977), which used call-in telephones on live radio (initially, New York station WBAI) to produce a real-time continuous flow. Neuhaus saw the *Public Supply* pieces as extensions of his practice as a performer: "I was interested in the challenge of making a live work from unknown materials, enlisting the aid of anyone who wanted to telephone into this station as the producers of that material."[36] Neuhaus's role was one of designing the system, then switching and mixing while on air.

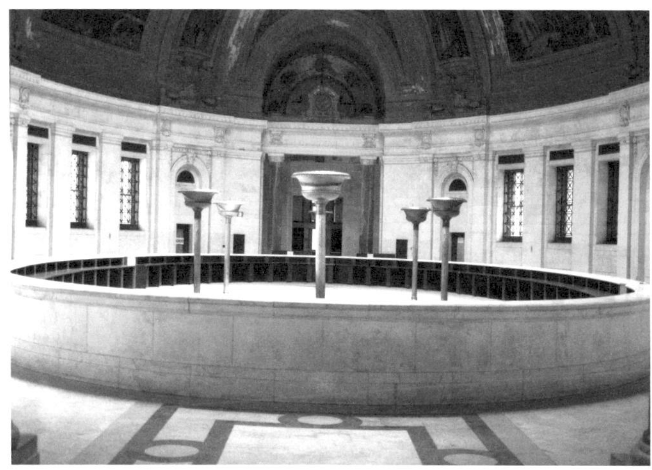

Site of Max Neuhaus, *Round*, November 19–21, 1976, sponsored by Creative Time, U.S. Custom House, New York City

At a time when critics of "site-specific" and "public" art continue to belabor relatively anodyne object-based sculptural models, Neuhaus's early broadcast works have received relatively little attention from art historians, even though they are part of a movement toward publication-based and broadcast forms that intervened in public space in challenging and unpredictable ways. While Neuhaus frequently compared his work to the sculptures of Richard Serra, his approach shares certain tendencies with Lawrence Weiner's work. Although Weiner's linguistically notated "statements" are discrete pieces, their placement in public and private settings insinuate them into the fabric of everyday urban life in a subtle and usually nonconfrontational manner that recalls Neuhaus's deliberate unobtrusiveness.[37]

Like Cage's famous exploration of the anechoic chamber and work with amplified "small sounds," many of Neuhaus's pieces straddle the boundaries of what is audible—liminal conditions of audibility and perception that various Fluxus projects also explored.[38] Within the music tradition, a historical precedent for this deliberate unobtrusiveness is Erik Satie's *Furniture Music* (1917), proto-ambient compositions that were designed to be played, for example, in the lobby, not the concert hall, as background music. Similarly, the extreme temporal extension of Satie's *Vexations* (circa 1893)—a short piece of piano music appended with the direction that it should be played 840 times at a very slow tempo—heralded the possibility of very long pieces of music whose durational experience would introduce a sitelike dimension. When performed for the first time in 1963 at the Pocket Theatre in New York, by a group of pianists organized by Cage and Tudor, the concert lasted more than twenty-five hours, suggesting a scale at which even performed sound becomes less an event and more a situation or even a place.[39] Though no doubt informed by these experiments, Neuhaus's project crucially diverges as it endeavors not only to make the sound permanent but also to resituate this durational experience to public, mostly outdoor spaces—locations that are, by nature, unbounded and are, for the most part, visually unmarked. While some of his sound installations have been placed in gallery or museum interiors, Neuhaus prefers liminal spaces—for instance, a stairwell of Chicago's Museum of Contemporary Art was the home of a now-destroyed untitled sound piece from 1979. Although you can find *Times Square* by going to the correct traffic island—an unremarkable little triangle on Broadway between Forty-fifth and Forty-sixth streets in Manhattan—its sound completely bleeds into the surrounding aural landscape and vice versa. In keeping with this unmarked condition, Neuhaus located works like *Times Square* in anonymous places. There is no placard or marker: you find it for yourself, by ear.

Paradoxically, although sound was a common element in the intermedia, assemblage, and Neo-Dada practices of the early 1960s, aural phenomena largely drop from the lexicon of 1960s Minimalist sculpture, despite that movement's emphasis on the physical and phenomenological encounter with the viewer. A crucial exception can be found in some of Bruce Nauman's early works, which use sound as a central structuring mechanism; produced in the period 1967–70, they are roughly contemporaneous with Neuhaus's early sound installations. Nauman's influential *Studio Films* of 1967–68 are also sound pieces, and his 1968 exhibition *Six Sound Problems for Konrad Fischer* comprised six short sound pieces on tape loops designed for a gallery space.[40] Neuhaus tended to differentiate his project from works by Nauman, Vito Acconci, and other artists who used prerecorded sound and the voice. Though it's true that some of Nauman's works, such as *Get Out of My Mind, Get Out of This Room*, presented in 1969 at Nicholas Wilder Gallery, Los Angeles, rely on prerecorded voice, other installations, such as the *Sound Breaking Wall* (1969) and *Diagonal Wall (Acoustic Wall)* (1970), used dampened sound to create a spatial and bodily situation; and Nauman's *Touch and Sound Walls* (1969) used microphones and time delay to explore the spatial properties of sound in a manner analogous to his better-known video corridors. While Neuhaus has a tendency to define site-based work in a way that precludes the use of prerecorded sound, Alvin Lucier's celebrated work *I Am Sitting in a Room* (1969) would precisely combine these two structures, as the accumulation of room tone and audio distortion gradually dismantles the continually rerecorded spoken text. Instead, what perhaps differentiates Neuhaus's use of sound from that of artists like Acconci and Nauman is their interest in building a psychological space. Even in works that do not use language, Nauman deployed operations like sound delay, silence, and out-of-sync or out-of-phase sound to trigger disconcerting emotional or psychological states or associations in the viewer. Likewise, his sound-dampening walls and video corridors generate complex emotional and even cognitive responses because they attempt to mimic or mirror interior states of mind. This sense of psychic displacement is largely absent from Neuhaus's works, which can be seen as almost classically Minimalist in their emphasis on a present-tense confrontation with the physical and material properties of the work.

Yet the fact that Neuhaus uses sound as an autonomous material will always complicate this encounter. In the Moment works, the sudden absence of a sound that has been almost imperceptibly building up over time leaves listeners with a wrenching sense of loss and emptiness. The very experience of sound topographies is almost inherently uncanny. As Neuhaus notes, part of the difficulty of site-based work with sound, and with any delineation of a sound space, is that the properties of sound run counter to containment: sound dissipates, disperses evenly with distance. By its nature, sound produces perceptual effects in its listeners that seem to exceed physical presence: *Times Square*'s ringing reverberates long after one has left the pedestrian island and gone out of earshot of the piece. Perhaps because most of us are far less skilled at listening than at seeing, and at sorting out confusing and conflicting auditory cues than visual ones, the boundary between the subject and object in hearing seems more fluid than in vision. It is the spatial and perceptual instability of sound that makes it such a rich territory for Neuhaus.

Notes

1 Unless otherwise indicated, quotations from Max Neuhaus come from my extended interview with him, conducted in Santa Monica and Pasadena, California, on January 26, 2005.

2 As Douglas Kahn cogently argues, by "shifting the production of music from the site of utterance to that of audition," *4'33"* "opened music up into an emancipatory endgame" that paradoxically performed its own gesture of silencing. (Douglas Kahn, *Noise, Water, Meat: A History of Sound in the Arts* [Cambridge, Mass.: MIT Press, 1999], pp. 158, 164.)

3 Goran Vejvod and Rob Young, "My Concrete Life: Pierre Schaeffer," *The Wire*, no. 258 (August 2005), p. 48.

4 "The Acousmonium," http://emfinstitute.emf.org/exhibits/acousmonium.html (accessed March 31, 2005).

5 "Spatialisation," Ears: ElectroAcoustic Resource Site, http://www.ears.dmu.ac.uk/rubrique.php3?id_rubrique=240 (accessed March 31, 2005).

6 Many other examples or precedents for such spatialized composition could be cited, such as the physically dispersed orchestras by American composer Charles Ives and Cage's 1952 tape composition *Williams Mix*, which was designed to be played by eight loudspeakers distributed around a room.

7 While Edgard Varèse's score combined electronically generated tones and altered piano chords and voices, Iannis Xenakis's short interstitial music—designed for the period during which the audience was filing in and out—was composed at the Groupe de Recherches Musicales studios in Paris using electronically processed sounds of amplified burning charcoal.

8 See Marc Treib, *Space Calculated in Seconds* (Princeton, N.J.: Princeton University Press, 1996).

9 Ibid., p. 3.

10 Varèse, "The Liberation of Sound" (1936), in *Contemporary Composers on Contemporary Music*, ed. Elliott Schwartz and Barney Childs (New York: Da Capo Press, 1998), p. 197.

11 Ibid., p. 198.

12 Ming Tiampo, "Electrifying Painting," in *Electrifying Art: Atsuko Tanaka 1954–1968* (Vancouver: Belkia Art Gallery and Grey Art Gallery, New York, 2004). See also *Scream Against the Sky: Japanese Art after 1945*, ed. Alexandra Monroe (New York: Harry N. Abrams, 1994); and Shin'ichiro Osaki, "Action in Post-war Japan," in Paul Schimmel, *Out of Actions: Between Performance and the Object 1949–1979* (Los Angeles: Museum of Contemporary Art, 1998).

13 Atsuko Tanaka, in a 1955 press interview, cited in Tiampo, p. 68.

14 Simone Forti, interviewed by the author, Los Angeles, October 26, 2000.

15 Max Neuhaus, "Drive In Music," undated typescript.

16 As Neuhaus notes, "The composite sound the listener hears at any one moment is a product of his distance, at that moment, from each of the transmitters in the general area." (Neuhaus, in conversation with the author, January 26, 2005.)

17 Neuhaus, "Drive In Music." This effort to incorporate atmospheric conditions prefigures Neuhaus's use of such elements in *Walkthrough*, and it is perhaps evident of a struggle to incorporate process-based structures into his site-based works.

18 As Neuhaus retrospectively observed: "The Passage works are situated in spaces where the physical movement of the listener through the space to reach a destination is inherent. They imply an active role on the part of listeners, who set a static sound structure into motion for themselves by passing through it. My first work with an aural topography, *Drive In Music* in 1967, falls within this vector." (Max Neuhaus, "Passage," http://www.max-neuhaus.info/soundworks/vectors/passage/, accessed March 31, 2005).

19 James Pritchett, "David Tudor as Composer/Performer in Cage's *Variations II*," *Leonardo Music Journal*, no. 14 (2004) pp. 11–12.

20 *Rainforest* was the name Tudor gave to a series of large-scale performed installations of hybrid

loudspeaker objects. The first version was commissioned for a 1968 Merce Cunningham dance concert, but the project has deeper roots in Cage's 1960 *Cartridge Music* and Tudor's 1966 work *Bandoneon*, created for 9 Evenings of Theatre and Engineering, a series of performances at the New York Armory in October 1966, organized by Experiments in Art and Technology (EAT). For more information, see John Driscoll and Matt Rogalsky, "David Tudor's *Rainforest*: An Evolving Exploration of Resonance," *Leonardo Music Journal*, no. 14 (2004), pp. 25–30.

21 Pritchett, p. 14.

22 Ibid., p. 15.

23 Neuhaus, conversation with the author, January 26, 2005.

24 David Tudor, "I smile when the sound is singing through the space," interview by Teddy Hultberg, Düsseldorf, May 17–18, 1988, http://www.emf.org/tudor/Articles/hultberg.html (accessed January 15, 2001).

25 David Tudor, description of *Cartridge Music* (circa 1988), draft of liner notes for the CD *John Cage, Vol. 4: Music for Merce Cunningham* (Mode 24), David Tudor papers, Getty Research Institute.

26 Ibid. As Kahn notes, *Cartridge Music* represents part of a larger shift in Cage's work toward "silence [and] small and barely audible sounds" that required amplification to be heard. Reading Cage's famous experience in an anechoic chamber as a defining event, Kahn proposes that thereafter he "would increasingly employ technology as a discursive means for musical listening and not just for practical musical production" (Kahn, *Noise, Water, Meat*, p. 192). As a result, "Percussion was replaced by amplification as the means to listen to objects" (p. 197).

27 Composed in January 1960, *Poem* consists of detailed verbal instructions to performers to drag or scrape heavy pieces of furniture across a floor; random numbers determine the duration of the piece, the number of events, and their entry and exit points. The work was performed by Tudor several times in 1960 and 1961.

28 La Monte Young, Dream House proposal to the Ingraham Marshall Foundation, 1964; David Tudor Papers, Getty Research Institute. See also the description of a Dream House in La Monte Young and Marian Zazeela, *Selected Writings* (Munich: Heiner Friedrich, 1969) and the Ubu Classics edition reissued in 2004 online at ubu.com.

29 As Kahn reminds us, many artists and musicians of the time were interested in the physicality of loud sounds—understood "as the establishment of a palpably saturated acoustic space, as the experience of the intensity of vibrations on the whole body as well as within it" (Kahn, *Noise, Water, Meat*, p. 227). Seen in these terms, the ways that amplified sounds envelop and immerse their listeners in a manufactured sonic environment have inherent spatial effects: "With enough amplification any performance space could be turned into a resonant chamber, much like a body of a very large instrument in which humans are played" (p. 233).

30 Neuhaus, January 26, 2005.

31 Neuhaus, lecture, Art Center College of Design, Pasadena, January 26, 2005.

32 Neuhaus, "Listen," in *Max Neuhaus: Elusive Sources and "Like" Spaces* (Turin: Giorgio Persano, 1990), p. 20.

33 Of course, by the time his collection *Silence* was published (Middletown, Conn.: Wesleyan University Press, 1961), Cage himself had shifted his understanding of *4'33"* as a formal composition performed in a concert setting to an experience of activated listening that could be performed anywhere.

34 Neuhaus, "Listen," p. 20.

35 This explicitly site-based orientation thus differentiates Neuhaus's project from, for instance, the work of Tony Conrad, Young, and other members of the Theatre of Eternal Music, a group that played loud sounds for extended durations to activate listening in the creation of sound—as Conrad retrospectively proclaims, the "route out of the modernist crisis was to move away from composing to LISTENING" (liner notes, *Four Violins,* Table of the Elements CD #17, 1996). As Kahn notes,

"Apart from the Theatre of Eternal Music, a number of artists and composers in the early 1960s combined sustained sound and repeated sounds with loudness and amplification to hear features of sound masked in a momentary or singular incidence of the sound. The phasing involved in a sound might reveal itself only when that sound is sustained for a long time, as might the way a sound interacts with the acoustic properties of a particular site" (Kahn, *Noise, Water, Meat*, pp. 231–32).

36 Neuhaus, interview by William Duckworth (1982), in *Max Neuhaus: Sound Works*, vol. 1, *Inscription* (Osfildern-Ruit, Germany: Cantz, 1994), p. 45; also at http://www.max-neuhaus.info/bibliography/Duckworth.pdf.

37 See my essay "In the Stream of Life," in *Lawrence Weiner: Until It Is* (Columbus: Wexner Center for the Arts, 2002).

38. For a detailed history of these projects, see Douglas Kahn, "The Latest: Fluxus and Music," in Elizabeth Armstrong and Joan Rothfuss, *In the Spirit of Fluxus* (Minneapolis: Walker Art Center, 1993), pp. 100–20.

39 Although it would be tempting to read the durational model of the 1963 concert as arising from, for instance, Young's systematic exploration of long sounds, archival records show that Cage was attempting to produce Satie's piece soon after he received a copy of the manuscript in 1948.

40 In a quite different manner, the programmed light-sound environments of the Pulsa group, done in the period 1967–72, emerged partly out of a visual-art context and partly in relation to experimental music and performance. Beginning at sunset each day, the *Programmed Environment* at the boat pool at the Boston Public Gardens in October 1968 used underwater strobe lights and Poly-Planar speakers placed at water level to distribute sound and light waves around the site. For more information, see Lucy R. Lippard, "Pulsa," *Arts Canada* 25, no. 124/125 (December 1968), and Patrick Clancy, "Tape Transcription (3-25-92)," http://www.vasulka.org/archive/Interviews/53Clancy.pdf.

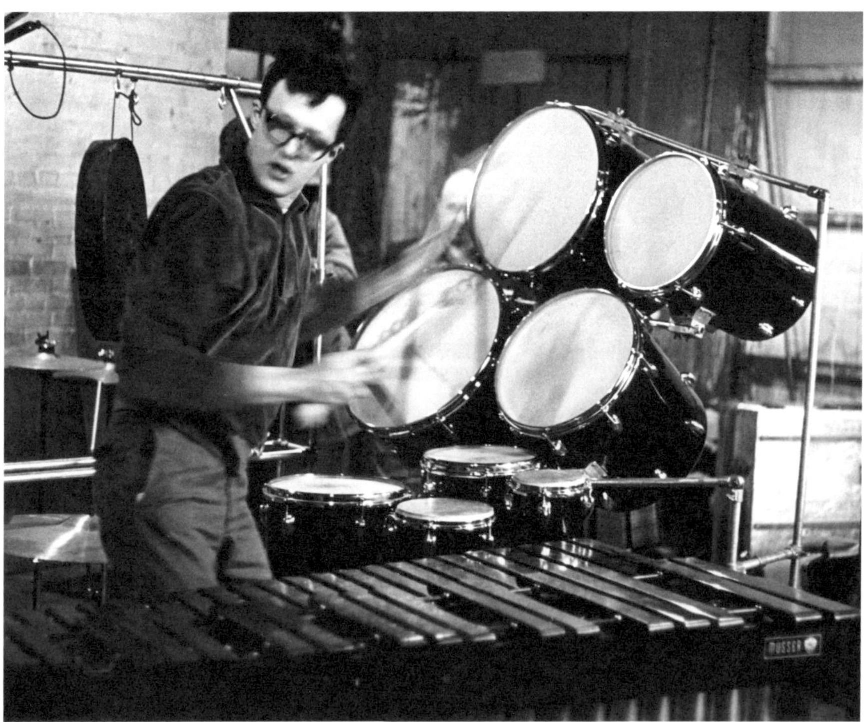

Max Neuhaus during *Listen*, March 27, 1966, photo by Peter Moore

Installing Duration: Time in the Sound Works of Max Neuhaus

Christoph Cox

It was a fascination with time that drew Max Neuhaus into the world of music, and time that led him out of it. "Intoxicated" by Gene Krupa's sense of time and by the drummer's role in "building time," Neuhaus decided to become a percussionist.[1] By the age of nineteen, in 1958, he was working with some of America's foremost musical experimentalists: Henry Cowell, Harry Partch, John Cage, Morton Feldman, and Earle Brown. A few years later, Neuhaus was touring Europe with Pierre Boulez and Karlheinz Stockhausen and giving solo recitals at Carnegie Hall. After recording his repertoire on an LP for Columbia Masterworks in 1968, Neuhaus promptly ended his career as a musician and began to devote himself to what he was the first to call "sound installation." Such works eschewed live performance in favor of electronic transmission, the concert hall in favor of public spaces and institutions, and metrical music in favor of meterless drones.

Neuhaus consistently articulated this career change as a move from time to space, a shift of interest from the *time of music* to the *space of sound*. In a program note from 1974, he wrote:

> Traditionally composers have located the elements of a composition in time. One idea which I am interested in is locating them, instead, in space, and letting the listener place them in his own time. I am not interested in making music exclusively for musicians or musically initiated audiences. I am interested in making music for people.[2]

This idea is echoed in Neuhaus's 1994 introduction to his collection of Place works:

> Communion with sound has always been bound by time. Meaning in speech and music appears only as their sound events unfold word by word, phrase by phrase, from moment to moment. The works collected in this volume share a different fundamental idea—that of removing sound from time, and setting it, instead, in place.[3]

In 2002, reflecting on his permanent sound installations, Neuhaus told an interviewer: "The important idea about this kind of work is that it's not music. It doesn't exist in time. I've taken sound out of time and made it into an entity."[4]

Neuhaus casts the music/sound art dichotomy in terms of time/space—a distinction embraced by younger sound artists such as Stephen Vitiello.[5] Yet the time/space distinction is a red herring, for the real distinction concerns different conceptions of time. To see this, we need to situate Neuhaus's sound work within the general shift in temporal thinking that took place during the 1950s and 1960s and was manifest in both the Cagean tradition in experimental music and Postminimalism in the visual arts.

Beyond the Musical Object: From Being to Becoming, from Time to Duration

John Cage's work of the 1950s launched an attack on the musical object and, along with it, initiated a refiguration of musical time. Cage articulated this most clearly in a series of lectures, collectively titled "Composition as Process," delivered in Darmstadt in 1958. He notes that the essential formal aspect of European art music is the production of "time-objects": "the presentation of a whole as an object in time having a beginning, a middle, and an ending, progressive rather than static in character, which is to say possessed of a climax or climaxes and in contrast a point or points of rest."[6] Such time-objects bind musical flow within definite temporal limits and tend to give it the narrative shape characteristic of traditional conceptions of time and history. Against this notion, Cage sought a different conception of time, one that transcends human construction. Hence, Cage endorsed a theory of music as "a process essentially purposeless," "a process the beginning and ending of which are irrelevant to its nature." In place of the bounded, narrative conception of time characteristic of the traditional musical work, Cage affirmed duration and simultaneity. He wanted his music to mirror and to become part of the open, ateleological flux of the world—"art," he was fond of saying, "must imitate nature in her manner of operation"[7]—and he affirmed that this flux is not singular but multiple, a conjunction of many different flows.

The two notions of time contrasted by Cage—that of the time-object and that of the purposeless process—match the terms of an opposition made by the twentieth century's greatest philosopher of time, Henri Bergson, who, after a long period of neglect, has become a central figure in recent philosophical and cultural debates. Bergson famously contrasted two different experiences of time. The first is exemplified by the figure of the clock, on which moments—discrete, present entities—are laid out side by side in spatial succession. This is the concept of time that has dominated our thinking since at least the seventeenth century: time as an objective, quantitative measure of events, as something that is not part of events, movement, or change but that measures them from the outside. The concept of *number*, as discrete, discontinuous, and infinitely divisible, is inherently spatial, and the notion of time as a quantitative measure subordinates time to space. Insofar as it treats time as a matter of discrete moments, clock time cannot account for the *passage* of time, without which time is nothing at all. This key feature of passage points to a more fundamental experience of time that Bergson calls *duration*: time as a qualitative process, a flow in which past, present, and future permeate one another to form a genuine continuum.[8]

Cage's compatriot Morton Feldman drew just this distinction. Feldman objected to Stockhausen's idea that the composer could "reduce . . . [Time] to so much a square foot" and to Stockhausen's view that "Time was something he could handle and even parcel out, pretty much as he pleased." "Frankly this approach bores me," Feldman bluntly declared. Alluding to Bergson, he continued: "I am not a clockmaker. I am interested in getting to Time in its unstructured existence." "I feel that the idea is more to let Time be, than to treat it as a compositional element. No — even to construct with Time won't do. Time simply has to be left alone." Recalling Cage, he concluded: "Not how to make an object, not how this object exists by way of Time, *in* Time, or *about* Time, but how this object exists *as* Time. Time regained, as Proust referred to his work."[9] This interest in time as duration, in making music that would not control time but would flow *with* it and *as* it, led Feldman, late in his career, to compose works of immense length, for example, the four-hour *For Philip Guston* (1984) and the five-and-a-half-hour *String Quartet II* (1983). "Up to one hour you think about form," he wrote, "but after an hour it's scale. Form is easy—just the division of things into parts. But scale is another matter. Before my pieces were like objects; now they're like evolving things."[10]

These two conceptions of time are also directly at issue in Cage's most famous composition, *4′33″* (1952), which Cage himself felt to be his most successful and important piece.[11] *4′33″* sets up a confrontation between measured time and limitless duration. The title of the piece explicitly refers to the spatialized time of the clock—a fact Cage underscores by noting that the title could also be read "four feet, thirty-three inches."[12] And, of course, the performance of the piece is regulated by a stopwatch. Yet the arbitrariness of this temporal scope (compositionally determined through chance procedures) and the sonic experience it discloses indicate that *4′33″* aims to engage another experience of time—the time of duration, a time that does not parse out musical events but bears witness to the general acoustic flux of the world.

A year before composing *4′33″*, Cage wrote a piece called *Imaginary Landscape No. 4 (March No. 2)*, scored for twelve radios. For Cage, the radio was a tool of indeterminacy, since the composer and the performers had to submit themselves to whatever happened to be on the air at the time. Radio is also a perfect model for acoustic flow: it is always there, a perpetual transmission, but we tap into it only periodically. Moreover, the simultaneous activation of twelve radio transmissions acknowledges the multiple layers, streams, and speeds of flow that make up the general acoustic flux of the world. Indeed, *4′33″* functions like a radio. For a brief window in time, it tunes us into the infinite and continuously unfolding domain of worldly sound. As Cage once put it: "Music is permanent; only listening is intermittent."[13]

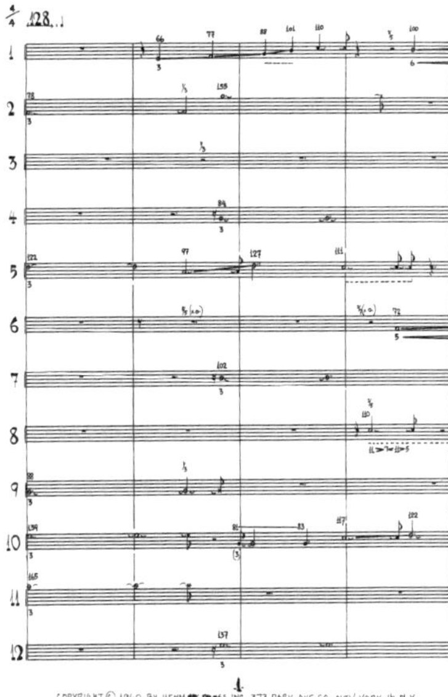

John Cage, page from the score for *Imaginary Landscape No. 4 (March No. 2)*, 1951

The sequel to this work, *0′00″* (1962), intensifies this argument about temporality. The piece calls for "nothing but the continuation of one's daily work, whatever it is . . . done with contact microphones, without any notion of concert or theater or the public." "What the piece tries to say," remarked Cage, "is that everything we do is music, or can become music through the use of microphones; so that everything I'm doing, apart from what I'm saying, produces sound." Again, Cage includes the temporal marker. But, at the same time, he reduces it to zero, puts it under erasure. "I'm trying to find a way to make music that does not depend on time," he said of the piece. "It is precisely this capacity for measurement that I want to be free of."[14]

The aim of *4′33″* and *0′00″*, then, is to open time to the experience of duration and to open musical experience to the domain of worldly sound. It is also to open human experience to something beyond it: the nonhuman, impersonal flow that precedes and exceeds it. "I think music should be free of the feelings and ideas of the composer," Cage famously remarked. "I have felt and hoped to have led other people to feel that the sounds of their environment constitute a music which is more interesting than the music which they would hear if they went into a concert hall."[15] To this end, Cage urges the composer "to give up the desire to control sound, clear his mind of music, and set about discovering means to let sounds be themselves rather than vehicles for man-made theories or expressions of human sentiments."[16]

Chance and silence were Cage's transports into this domain. These two strategies allowed the composer to bypass his subjective preferences and habits in order to make way for sonic conjunctions and assemblages that are not his own. And "silence," for

Cage, names not the absence of sound (an impossibility, he points out) but the absence of *intentional* sound and discloses the sonic life of the world or nature. *4'33"* remains Cage's most elegant attempt along these lines. But so much of his work reveals that he conceived of sound (natural and cultural alike) as a ceaseless flow and of composition as the act of drawing attention to or accessing it.

Cage's understanding of an open, purposeless process affirms duration, affirms a post-theological, ateleological universe that is without origin, end, or purpose. Musical Minimalism affirmed a similar conception of time. Composers such as La Monte Young, Tony Conrad, Steve Reich, Philip Glass, Pauline Oliveros, and Charlemagne Palestine explored what Gilles Deleuze calls "nonpulsed time," as opposed to the "pulsed time" of classical composition. Pulsed time has nothing to do with regular, even repetitive, pulses (a key feature of musical Minimalism). Rather, it is the time of narrative development that organizes the musical piece into identifiable sections and landmarks, allowing the listener to know where he or she is and is going. It sets up conflicts to be resolved that actively solicit the listener's sense of narrative time. Hence, Deleuze tells us, pulsed time is the time of the bildungsroman, the novel of education, which "measures, or scans, the formation of a subject."[17]

The nonpulsed time of the Minimalists is something else entirely. Minimalist compositions dispense with narrative and teleology and show no interest in charting the progress of a hero, whether it is the composer, the solo instrument, or the listening subject. Rather, as Belgian Minimalist composer Wim Mertens notes, "the music exists for itself and has nothing to do with the subjectivity of the listener . . . the subject no longer determines the music, as it did in the past, but the music now determines the subject."[18] Reich notes that his early Minimalist compositions "participate in a particular liberating and impersonal kind of ritual. Focusing in on the musical process makes possible that shift of attention away from *he* and *she* and *you* and *me* outwards towards *it*."[19] That is, the nonpulsed time of Minimalist composition places composer, performer, and listener on a wave of becoming that flows, shifts, and changes, but extremely gradually so that one loses any clear sense of chronological time (what Deleuze calls Chronos) and instead is immersed in a floating, indefinite time, a pure stationary process (Deleuze's Aion).[20]

Installing Duration: Postminimalism in the Visual Arts

Cage was content to call this sonic flux "music" and remained more or less satisfied with the role of composer, even if he vastly expanded the scope of the term and relinquished a great deal of compositional authority. Yet his work had a profound effect on

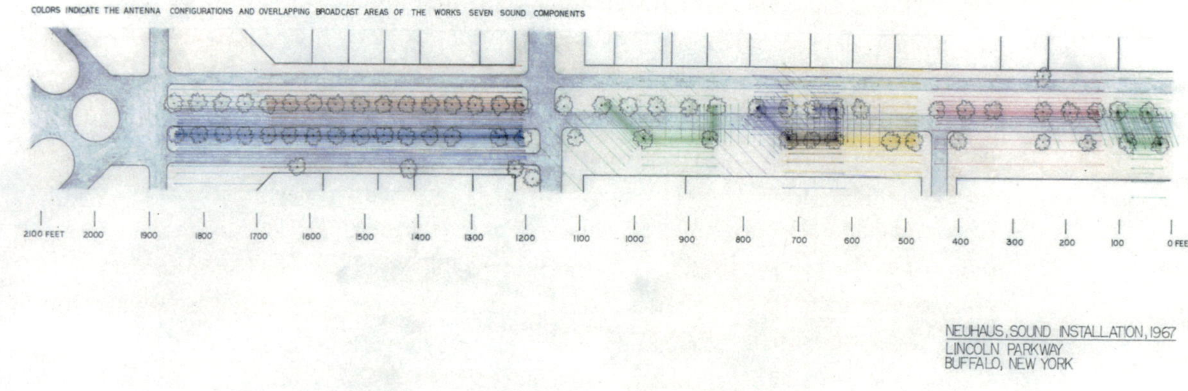

Plan of antenna configurations for Max Neuhaus's *Drive-in Music*, 1967, Lincoln Parkway, Buffalo, New York

artists interested in exploring sound outside the musical context. Neuhaus's first work as a sound artist,[21] his project *Listen*, begun in 1966, for example, carried *4'33"* beyond the concert hall. Hands stamped with the word *listen*, audience members were taken on a tour past a nearby power plant, a highway overpass, and other sites that were to be experienced aesthetically as sound environments. At the same time, Neuhaus extended Cage's work with radios. *Public Supply I* (1966) used the radio studio to perform a live mix of sounds phoned in by listeners, while *Drive-in Music* (1967) employed short-range transmitters to sculpt a sequence of sound fields received by the radios of passing cars.

Drive-in Music marks Neuhaus's break with music and the inception of his sound installation practice. Installing sound allowed Neuhaus to dispense with live performance and thus to remove what he called "the onus of entertainment" that burdened music but of which, Neuhaus felt, the visual arts were largely free.[22] Indeed, for Neuhaus, the concerns of sound installation are shared more fully by the visual arts than by music. "In terms of classification," he told William Duckworth in 1982,

> I'd move the installations into the purview of the visual arts even though they have no visual component, because the visual arts, in the plastic sense, have dealt with space. Sculptors define and transform spaces. I create, transform, and change spaces by

> adding sound. This spatial concept is one which music doesn't include; music is supposed to be completely transportable.[23]

This interest in site-specificity was just one of the concerns that Neuhaus shared with visual artists of the time. Indeed, while the impetus for Neuhaus's sound installations came, in part, from the Cagean tradition in experimental music, it was equally due to the emergence, at the same time, of installation practices in the visual arts. Not coincidentally, these practices shared Cage's dismissal of clock time and discrete artistic objects in favor of works that engaged the temporality of process, becoming, and duration.

Michael Fried's enormously influential 1967 essay "Art and Objecthood" took aim at these installation practices, drawing a fundamental distinction between, on the one hand, autonomous works of art that suspend time and absorb the spectator's attention and, on the other hand, "theatrical" or "literalist" works that engage the spectator's physical presence in space and time and thereby short-circuit the achievement of an epiphanic aesthetic experience.[24] Much has been written about Fried's essay, and I have no wish to rehearse those critical polemics here; I want simply to show that, despite its utter silence about sound (a silence characteristic of contemporary art history and criticism), "Art and Objecthood" helpfully illuminates the importance and radicality of the sound art that emerged concurrently with Minimalism and "expanded field" practices in the visual arts, and that it does so via an examination of aesthetic temporality.

In the essay, Fried espouses a formalist modernism, according to which art is essentially self-sufficient and self-aware, concerned with its own nature and medium. The modernist paintings and sculptures Fried champions have, he argues, an interior, syntactic unity. They are whole and complete and, as such, possess a magisterial presence that absorbs the spectator in a peculiarly aesthetic experience that transcends the banality of everyday life. By contrast, the theatrical works Fried decries are heteronomous. They offer not self-sufficient unities but instead essentially incomplete or open situations that solicit the spectator's presence and draw attention to the material conditions of their exhibition. As Fried's major target Robert Morris famously put it, sculptural installations such as his own "take . . . relationships out of the work and make . . . them a function of space, light, and the viewer's field of vision."[25] That is, such works do not absorb the viewer into a contemplation of their interior formal relationships but rather explore the temporal and spatial relationships that obtain *between* the work and the viewer's mobile body. This betweenness, these relationships, this distance between beholder and artwork, Fried writes, "make . . . the beholder a subject and the piece in question . . . an object."[26] Literalist or theatrical work, then, threatens to collapse the distinction between works of art and mere ordinary objects in all their dumb obstinacy. "Whereas literalist work aimed to project and hypostatize objecthood," Fried writes in a retrospective essay, "the abstract painting and sculpture I admired sought to undo or neutralize objecthood in one way or another."[27]

Yet, despite the title of the essay and the attention it gives to the topic, "objecthood" plays a secondary role in Fried's analysis. For Fried's true concern lies elsewhere.[28] That concern emerges in Fried's notorious discussion of Tony Smith's revelatory night drive on the unfinished New Jersey Turnpike. Fried quotes Smith's recounting of this anecdote:

> It was a dark night and there were no lights or shoulder markers, lines, railings, or anything at all except the dark pavement moving through the landscape of the flats, rimmed by hills in the distance, punctuated by stacks, towers, fumes, and colored lights. . . . The road and much of the landscape was artificial, and yet it couldn't be called a work of art. On the other hand, it did something for me that art had never done. . . . [Its] effect was to liberate me from many of the views I had had about art. It seemed that there had been a reality there that had not had any expression in art. The experience on the road was something mapped out but not socially recognized. I thought to myself, it ought to be clear that's the end of art. Most painting looks pretty pictorial after that. There's no way you can frame it, you just have to experience it.[29]

Smith's experience is not one of objects but, as Fried notes, of "empty, or 'abandoned,' *situations*." "What replaces the object," Fried continues, "—what does the same job of distancing or isolating the beholder, of making him a subject, that the object did in a closed room—is above all the endlessness, or objectlessness, of the approach or onrush of perspective."[30] Indeed, what vexes Fried about Minimalism and installation practices generally is not really objecthood at all, since such works may be void of objects. What aggravates him is something else, namely, the conception of *time* affirmed in such work, namely, the experience of temporal "endlessness," "inexhaustibility," "persistence in time"—in a word, "duration." "The literalist preoccupation with time," Fried writes,

> —more precisely with the *duration of the experience*—is, I suggest, paradigmatically theatrical, as though theater confronts the beholder, and thereby isolates him, with the endlessness not just of objecthood but of *time*; or as though the sense which, at bottom, theater addresses is a sense of temporality, of time both passing and to come, *simultaneously approaching and receding*, as if apprehended in an infinite perspective.[31]

Minimalism and installation, then, affirm a conception of time in its unlimited flow, its interminable fluid duration. And this Fried finds intolerable, for, following a modernist trajectory that extends back to Roger Fry and, ultimately, to Kant's metaphysics, Fried enlists art in the project of escaping this temporal flux. For Fried, art is, or ought to be, metaphysical. With "modernist painting and sculpture," Fried remarks,

> it is as though one's experience . . . *has no* duration . . . because *at every moment the work itself is wholly manifest*. . . . It is this continuous and entire *presentness*, amounting, as it were, to the perpetual creation of itself, that one experiences as a kind of *instantaneousness*, as though if one were infinitely more acute, a single infinitely brief instant would be long enough to see everything, to experience the work in all its depth and fullness, to be forever convinced by it.[32]

Such has been the dream of metaphysics and theology from Plato through Kant, Hegel, and Laplace, the dream of transcending time altogether, the fantasy of a God's-eye view to which all time and history would be present at once and in which becoming would be annulled by pure, simple, present being.[33] Nietzsche relentlessly criticized such metaphysical and theological fantasies, revealing them to be symptoms of a profound contempt for nature, life, and the sensuousness that is at the heart of aesthetic experience. Fried acknowledges the "overtly theological" cast of "Art and Objecthood," which, after all, opens with a quotation from the Calvinist theologian Jonathan Edwards and famously closes with the salvific couplet "We are all literalists most or all of our lives. Presentness is grace."[34]

As Fried rightly noted, the new generation of artists in the sixties rejected this conception of time and its underlying theology, asserting instead an antimetaphysical notion of time as duration. In a text published in *Artforum* a year after the appearance of Fried's essay in that same magazine, Robert Smithson explicitly countered Fried with a celebration of the artist's immersion in the Dionysian flux of time and matter that dissolves all objects and subjects. Art critics and the art market, Smithson noted, fasten on "art objects" and assign them "commodity values." Yet such objects are merely souvenirs from the artist's plunge into the "dedifferentiated," "oceanic" flux that constitutes the real aesthetic experience. "When a *thing* is seen through the consciousness of temporality, it is changed into something that is nothing," he wrote. "Separate 'things,' 'forms, 'objects, 'shapes,' etc. with beginnings and endings are mere convenient fictions: there is only an uncertain disintegrating order that transcends the limits of rational separations. The fictions erected in the eroding time stream are apt to be swamped at any moment."[35]

A year later, and once again in *Artforum*, Morris concurred with Smithson, celebrating "the detachment of art's energy from the craft of tedious object production" and favoring an art composed of "mutable stuff which need not arrive at the point of being finalized with respect to either time or space."[36] In this final installment of his "Notes on Sculpture," Morris criticized early Minimalist three-dimensional work (his own included) as still too objectlike and instead championed installations (for example, those of Barry Le Va) composed of "fields of stuff which have no central contained focus and extend into or beyond the peripheral vision." In his 1967 project *Steam*, Morris had already given up the use of solid objects in favor of that most ephemeral, intangible, and amorphous of visible entities. Two years later, he exhibited his *Continuous Project Altered Daily*. Over the course of its three-week exhibition, the artist made daily changes to the installation, which concluded with an almost empty space that simply presented a set of photographs and a tape recorder that played back the sounds of Morris's cleanup.[37] Such installations, Morris argued, shift the viewer's focus from "figure" to "ground," affirming a "dedifferentiated" mode of vision that implies "constant change" and encounters "chance, contingency, indeterminacy—in short, the entire area of process."[38] Morris's words echo those of Cage, who a decade earlier had called for a shift from musical objects to sonic processes, and precisely by means of chance, contingency, and indeterminacy.[39]

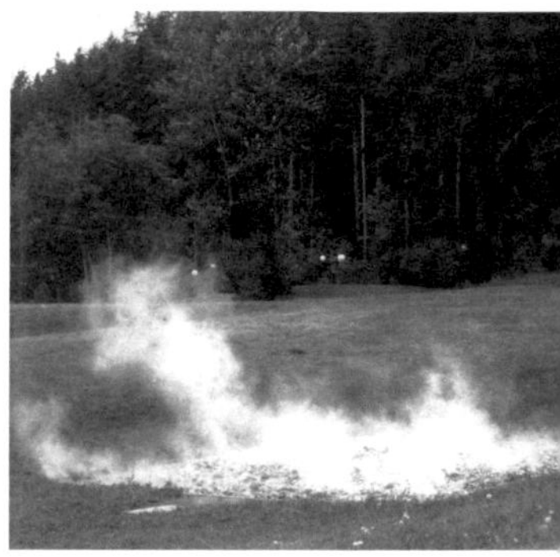

Robert Morris, *Steam*, 1974 refabrication of the 1967 original. Western Washington University, Bellingham

Sound art grew out of this artistic milieu, emerging via a radicalization of musical Minimalism, on the one hand, and Postminimalist sculptural installation, on the other. Sound was better suited than other media to satisfy Smithson's and Morris's desire for artworks that resisted reification and modeled Dionysian flux. The temporality and ephemerality of sound allow it to bypass objecthood and the instantaneity of opticality. Combined with the often site-specific nature of sound installation, these qualities make sound art resistant to commodification and, instead, encourage experience and participation. In this respect, early sound art joined forces with Conceptualism, which aimed at what Lucy Lippard famously called "the dematerialization of the art object."[40] Yet while Conceptualists, such as Lawrence Weiner, Joseph Kosuth, and the Art & Language group, tended to abandon the production of objects or to declare that physical objects are only indices of art's true content, namely, ideas,[41] the medium of sound allowed artists to find common ground between this austere idealism and a powerful physicality. For sound is at once thoroughly material and also invisible and intangible, made of ephemeral movements of air. A sound installation could be at once empty and full: void of objects but replete with sensory material.

Sound is the most immersive of sensory qualities, and at low frequencies it is non-directional. As such, it draws attention to the total field or situation rather than directing it to a thing or set of things. Much in the way that Morris, Le Va, and others sought a dedifferentiated form of installation that shifted focus from figure to ground, sound art shifted perception from the rarefied cultural domain of music, with its selection of discrete tones and timbres, to the engulfing field of environmental sound.

Time's Square

Both the Cagean tradition in experimental music and Postminimalist installation practices in the visual arts, then, presented critiques of aesthetic temporality. Though not identical, both critiques were directed at a notion of time that has held sway in European culture, a conception of time that accords with the metaphysical and theological privilege of being over becoming and for which the only genuine temporal

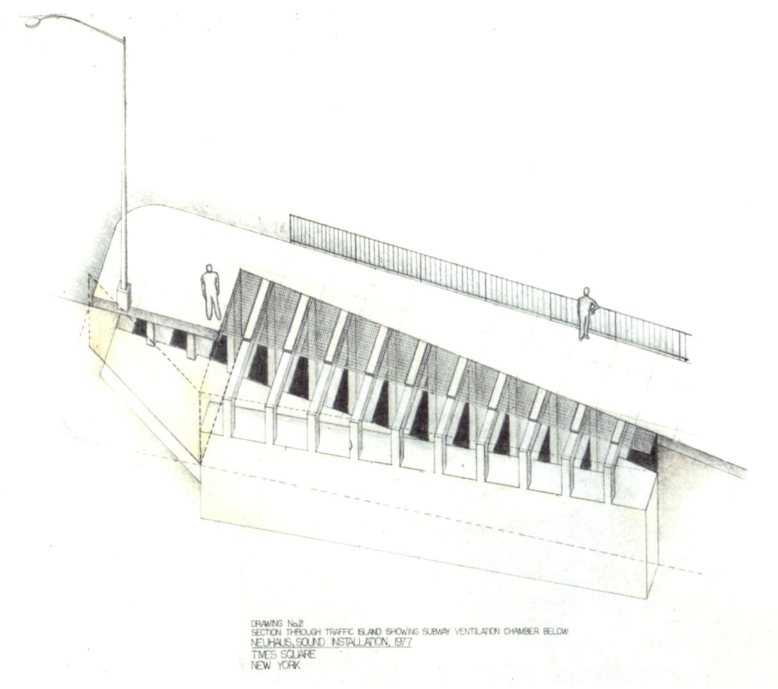

Rendering showing underground ventilation chamber for Max Neuhaus's *Times Square*, 1977

modality is the present.[42] The ideal, autonomous musical work of European modernity attempts to master time's elusive flow by making it a measured, closed, integral totality—an entity or time-object. Likewise, the ideal work of visual art is an integral, autonomous whole that, at each moment, is fully present. In both cases, the auditor or spectator is placed at the center of this aesthetic experience—or, rather, like Laplace's God, he or she is placed at its transcendent apex, able to survey the whole and dominate the temporal field. Against this conception of time, Cage and the Postminimalists posed a notion of time as duration and proposed an infinite, open process in which presence and completeness are forever deferred, a boundless flow that engulfs the auditor or spectator in a field he or she can never totalize.

Neuhaus's recurrent rejections of *musical time* in favor of *sonic space* must be read in this context. For, via sound installation, Neuhaus did not escape or reject time itself (surely an impossibility, particularly given the irreducibly temporal medium of sound). Rather, he rejected a particular conception of time: the measured, bounded temporality of the musical time-object. By the same token, Neuhaus's sound installations affirm duration. They are, in his words, "sound continuums," "sound works without a beginning or an end."[43] Indeed, from early to late, Neuhaus's "permanent" installations took time as their explicit subject. In the earliest of these, *Times Square* (1977–92; 2002–present), the titular reference to time is not incidental, not merely a designation of the work's location. Rather, the piece is a profound invitation to duration. Twenty-four hours a day, the installation has broadcast a stream of rich metallic drones from deep inside a subway vent on a pedestrian island in New York's busiest district. Audible but unobtrusive, the drones blend with and subtly alter the bustling sonic environment. This sonic stream is continuous, but it is experienced by visitors and passersby at particular moments within this temporal continuum. Such moments of conscious or unconscious apprehension serve as openings onto a flow of duration of which we are a part but that also surpasses us.

To some degree, of course, this is true of any work of art, which, though durable, is experienced in temporal slices. But, as Nietzsche and Schopenhauer pointed out, sound is fundamentally durational. It draws us out of the *principium individuationis* affirmed by the plastic arts and, instead, plunges us into the flux of time.[44] It is not a *thing* that *undergoes change* but change, flow itself. Bergson describes duration as a "qualitative multiplicity," a temporal flow that is heterogeneous and continuous, composed of different elements or states that are inextricably fused.[45] One could hardly find a better description of the drone: a complex, fluid mass composed of myriad tones, microtones, overtones, and combination tones that interpenetrate one another. Indeed, in a rich passage on sound, Bergson seems to point to the drone as the ideal sensuous presentation of duration. "A melody to which we listen with our eyes closed, heeding it alone," he writes,

> comes close to coinciding with this time, which is the very fluidity of our inner life; but it still has too many qualities, too much definition, and we must first efface the difference among the sounds, then do away with the distinctive features of sound itself, retaining of it only the continuation of what precedes into what follows and the uninterrupted transition, multiplicity without divisibility and succession without separation, in order to rediscover basic time. Such is immediately perceived duration, without which we would have no idea of time.[46]

A melody—a series of overlapping pitches that we draw together in memory—provides a fine first approximation of duration. Yet these pitches are still too discrete, distinct, and defined, and the whole composed by these pitches—the melody or phrase—is itself too bounded. So Bergson suggests that we melt these pitches together into a continuous, fluid mass—in short, a rich drone. To grasp duration, perhaps we need to go a step further, generalizing this flux beyond sound. Even so, the drone provides the richest sensuous manifestation of duration.

The drone has always been a figure of temporal continuity and endlessness. To emphasize this aspect, the Theatre of Eternal Music often began its drone performances before the arrival of the audience and continued to play for hours, reaching the point where, as Feldman noted, form gives way to scale.[47] Regardless, a musical performance is always temporally bounded. And so, in pursuit of duration, La Monte Young eventually moved to electronic sound generation and long-term installation. Nevertheless Young's installations remain carefully controlled environments, refuges from their sonic and temporal surroundings. By contrast, Neuhaus's *Times Square* is an open system comprising not only the tones broadcast by the artist but also the ever-changing cacophony of its environment; sounds that color one another and blend. It thus richly figures the open-ended, differential flow of duration.

Just as the title of Cage's *4'33"* implicates both space and time,[48] so, too, does Neuhaus's title: *Times Square*. Indeed, the two works are fundamentally akin, though the latter performs a sort of spatiotemporal inversion of the former. *4'33"*, as noted above, explicitly engages two conceptions of time: the chronometric time of its title, which provides a determinate temporal opening, and the durational flux of sound onto which it opens. For the temporal marker in Cage's title, *Times Square* substitutes a spatial, geographic reference. This is apt, for what is fixed in Neuhaus's piece is not the temporal window but the spatial region. *Times Square* (which we might read as "time's square") also offers an opening onto duration: a kind of spatial chasm through which a temporal flux emerges. In Cage's piece, what performs this opening is a period of silence; in Neuhaus's, it is a zone of continuous sound. Through Cage's silence, we hear the particular sonic field that fills the space and time of the performance—a synecdoche for the vast flux of time and sound that stretches beyond us. Neuhaus's unobtrusive drone draws the ambient flux into it, implicating the vibrational field of Times Square and, by extension, the vibrational flux of the world.

Time Pieces

The relationship between sound and time is even more explicitly at issue in the series of Moment works, or Time Pieces, that Neuhaus installed in various public contexts from the mid-eighties on. In each of these works, a regular temporal interval is marked by a slow sonic crescendo that abruptly ceases, leaving what Neuhaus describes as an "aural afterimage."[49]

This series was inaugurated by Neuhaus's contribution to the 1983 Whitney Biennial, a piece he later titled *Time Piece "Archetype."* It deployed a live electronic-processing system that collected street sounds from the stretch of Madison Avenue outside the museum, sent these through a computer program, and then broadcast the result into the Whitney's courtyard sculpture garden. Over the course of fifteen minutes, the computer program increasingly altered the pitch and timbre of the sampled sounds and layered this over the live material. Every quarter hour, the cumulative coloration of the street sounds was suddenly wiped away, leaving an undistorted sonic reflection.

For subsequent realizations of this idea, Neuhaus abandoned live processing in favor of using the recorded electronic drones that have become his signature, sounds that he describes as "resembling the after ring of large bells."[50] These later Time Pieces retain the basic form of *Time Piece "Archetype"*: the sonic material gradually increases in volume and culminates in an abrupt break. Yet their crescendos are reduced to five minutes and appear only once an hour on the half hour in the installation at Kunsthalle Bern (1989–93), five minutes before the hour in the version at Graz (installed in 2003), on the hour in the installation at Dia:Beacon (installed in 2005), and on the halachic hours of the Jewish ritual day in the version at Stommeln-Pulheim (installed in 2007).

These Time Pieces, then, would seem to be just that—timepieces, clocks—and Neuhaus would seem to have acceded to the circumscription of sound by measured time. Yet in fact, these installations resonate with a different practice of marking time: the liturgical, ceremonial, and civic practice of bell ringing that preceded the mechanical clock by centuries.[51] In his magnificent history of this practice, cultural historian Alain Corbin notes that bell ringing not only preceded the quantitative, homogeneous time ushered in by the mechanical clock but was, in many respects, at odds with clock time and with the scientific and economic rationalism that mandated it.[52] Where the clock marks a sequence of equidistant, equivalent, indifferent, and interchangeable instants, village bells announced privileged moments: births, baptisms, marriages, funerals, festivals, liturgical hours, holidays, etc. In the ordinary flow of time, such events were singularities, remarkable moments of change where what followed differed fundamentally from what preceded. Peals of bells thus referred not to the abstract, indifferent time of scientific measure, but to the concrete life of the community and to its collective rhythms.

Neuhaus's Time Pieces engage both conceptions of time at once. Their regular sonic signals accommodate the time of the clock. Yet they simultaneously force an opening within clock time that resonates with the very different, qualitative time of the bell. This opening is achieved by reversing the natural envelope of the bell stroke, which begins with an abrupt, loud attack and is followed by a slow, steady decay. By contrast, Neuhaus's installations build amplitude over the course of five minutes, and the sudden end to his harmonic drone heightens the listener's awareness of the ambient sound that had mixed with it. The effect is similar to that generated by dub-reggae producers, whose remixes of reggae singles suddenly drop out vocal or guitar tracks to open up cavernous, ghostly spaces and provoke vertiginous, hallucinatory experiences. Rather than dubbing music, Neuhaus dubs environmental sound. Precisely tuned to their sonic sites, Neuhaus's drones slowly insinuate themselves into the environment, drawing ambient sounds into their flow. They then swiftly withdraw the leading sound, effectively amplifying the ambient elements in the mix while producing a psychoacoustic after-ring, a symmetrical sound envelope that doubles (dubs) the sounding drone and colors the ensuing "silence."

In the courtyard at Dia:Beacon, for example, the low rumble of institutional HVAC units is overlaid with the clatter of silverware and bits of conversation from the museum café and punctuated by the occasional rattle and howl of a passing train, the flutter and chirp of a bird, or the muted moan of a distant airplane. Invisibly and inconspicuously, a low, dense chord emerges from within this sonic field—a wavering drone in which various tones and partials seem to quiver and bounce, emerge or withdraw. Present but unobtrusive, the drone could easily escape conscious awareness, except at its peak, when the courtyard is bathed in a rich, consonant sonority. No sooner is it fully audible than it disappears. Suddenly, voices and birdsong seem louder and crisper, and the hush of air vents more aesthetically appealing. Neither present nor fully absent, the after-ring recedes slowly from auditory memory. As it does, ambient sound is gradually drawn down to its ordinary amplitude.

Like Neuhaus's other Moment pieces, *Time Piece Beacon* marks time. But it also marks a temporary rift in time akin to the spatial breach encountered in *Times Square*. It presents a temporal and sonic singularity that alters ordinary experience: an opening onto a different time, a nonchronological time. I have noted that chronological time subordinates time to space, such that time becomes what Bergson calls "the fourth dimension of space."[53] Discrete moments are laid out side by side, and time is conceived as the quantitative measure of movement or change. What chronology cannot account for is the most crucial aspect of time: *that it passes*. For, if moments are discrete entities, how can the present pass? Where does one moment end and the next begin? How can one moment dislodge another and send it into the past? And does the past come into being *after* the present has passed? If so, into what could the present pass and what sort of existence would it then have? Bergson and Deleuze solve these puzzles by positing a deeper, nonchronological, nonspatial conception of time: what Bergson calls duration, and Deleuze nonpulsed time or Aion. In order for the present to pass, they argue, it must not be a discrete entity but a continuity inextricably bound with moments past and to come. Moreover, in order for the present to pass, there must exist a *domain* of the past into which it can pass. That is, the past must coexist with the present whose past it is. It must exist (or subsist) as a (virtual) field into which the (actual) present can pass. Memory shows us that this is the case, for when I am prompted to remember some event or idea, I do so by drawing it from a reservoir of the past that coexists with my actual, present experience but that remains, for the most part, latent or virtual. What this argument reveals, Deleuze notes,

> is the most fundamental operation of time: since the past is constituted not after the present that it was but at the same time, time has to split itself in two at each moment as present and past, which differ from each other in nature, or, what amounts to the same thing, it has to split the present in two heterogeneous directions, one of which is launched towards the future while the other falls into the past. Time has to split at the same time as it sets itself out or unrolls itself: it splits in two dissymmetrical jets, one of which makes all the present pass on, while the other preserves all the past. Time consists of this split . . . [which reveals] the perpetual foundation of time, non-chronological time.[54]

For Deleuze, this conception of time flashes forth in the "crystal-images" of post–World War II cinema. It equally emerges in Neuhaus's Time Pieces. In place of the bell stroke that marks chronological time, the sudden disappearance of the drone creates a caesura, a gap or break, in chronological time. In this gap, the drone lingers, but virtually, in memory. This virtual domain of the past, ignored or suppressed by ordinary experience, becomes suddenly sensuous and evident. At the same time, the ambient flux amplified by the drone presses into the future. Though the drone will return again an hour later, this ambient flux will not be the same but ever new. We witness, here, the splitting of time that is the condition of time's passage, the division of the present into a simultaneous past and future. Rather than marking the instants of the clock, then, Neuhaus highlights temporal passage, becoming itself. Here, time does not measure anything. It is not external to the movements and changes it charts. It is that movement and change itself, the fluid element in which all entities are borne along, from which they emerge and into which they recede.

Like *4'33"* and *Times Square*, the Time Pieces reveal temporal passage or duration by way of sonic flux. And this connection between sound and time is not incidental, for the sonic flux is, as we have seen, the privileged sensuous modality of duration. It is not surprising, then, that time has become the explicit subject of recent sound art, from Christina Kubisch's *Clocktower Project* (1997), which rewires a nineteenth-century bell tower to respond to varying conditions of light rather than clock time, and David Grubbs's *Between a Raven and a Writing Desk* (1999), a repeating, hour-long composition that at once marks and slackens clock time, to Jem Finer's *Longplayer* (1999), a thousand-year-long composition broadcast from a London lighthouse, and R. Luke Dubois's *SSB* (2008), which digitally stretches *The Star-Spangled Banner* across the four-year span of the American electoral cycle. The founding father of sound installation, Neuhaus investigated this relationship between sound and time for more than twenty-five years. From *Times Square* to the Time Pieces, his installations set sound into space not to circumvent time but to reveal its most fundamental dimension.

Notes

1 Max Neuhaus, "Background," http://www.max-neuhaus.info/soundworks/vectors/performance/background. Originally published in liner notes for the CD *Max Neuhaus: The New York School—Nine Realizations of Cage, Feldman, Brown*, Alga Marghen plana-N 22NMN.052, 2004.

2 Neuhaus, "Program Notes" (1974), in *Max Neuhaus: Sound Works*, vol. 1, *Inscription* (Ostfildern-Ruit, Germany: Cantz, 1994), p. 34. Neuhaus repeated this claim in interviews during the 1980s and 1990s. See, for example, the 1982 interview by William Duckworth, in *Max Neuhaus: Sound Works*, vol. 1, *Inscription*, pp. 42–49; the 1990 interview with Ulrich Loock, in *Max Neuhaus: Sound Works*, vol. 1, *Inscription*, pp. 122–35; and the interview with Michael Tarantino, quoted in Tarantino's "Two Passages," all available at http://www.max-neuhaus.info/bibliography.

3 Neuhaus, introduction to *Max Neuhaus: Sound Works,* vol. 3, *Place* (Ostfildern-Ruit, Germany: Cantz, 1994). See also http://www.max-neuhaus.info/soundworks/vectors/place.

4 Neuhaus, quoted in Alicia Zuckerman, "Max Neuhaus: Times Square," *Arts Electric* (2002), http://www.arts-electric.org/stories2002/020530_neuhaus.html.

5 See the conversation between Stephen Vitiello and Marina Rosenfeld, *NewMusicBox*, March 1, 2004, http://www.newmusicbox.org/article.nmbx?id=2414, and "Audio Files: Sound Art Now: An Online Symposium," April–May 2004, http://artforum.com/index.php?pn=symposium &id=6682.

6 John Cage, "Composition as Process II: Indeterminacy," in *Silence: Lectures and Writings* (Middletown, Conn.: Wesleyan University Press, 1961), p. 36; reprinted in *Audio Culture: Readings in Modern Music*, ed. Christoph Cox and Daniel Warner (New York: Continuum, 2004), p. 178.

7 See, for example, Cage's introduction to his *Themes & Variations* (Barrytown, N.Y.: Station Hill Press, 1982); reprinted in *Audio Culture*, pp. 221–25.

8 These arguments run throughout Henri Bergson's work but receive their most sustained formulation in *Time and Free Will: An Essay on the Immediate Data of Consciousness* (1888), "Memory of the Present and False Recognition" (1908), and *Duration and Simultaneity* (1922). See the selections from these texts in *Henri Bergson: Key Writings*, ed. Keith Ansell Pearson and John Mullarkey (New York: Continuum, 2002), pp. 49–77, 141–56, 205–19. I return to these arguments in the final section of this essay.

9 Morton Feldman, "Between Categories," in *Give My Regards to Eighth Street: Collected Writings of Morton Feldman*, ed. B. H. Friedman (Cambridge, Mass.: Exact Change, 2000), pp. 85–87.

10 *Morton Feldman: List of Works* (London: Universal Edition, 1998), p. 3.

11 See *Conversing with Cage*, ed. Richard Kostelanetz (New York: Limelight, 1988), p. 65.

12 Cage, in *Conversing with Cage*, pp. 70, 81.

13 See Cage, introduction to *Themes & Variations*; reprinted in *Audio Culture*, p. 224.

14 Cage, in *Conversing with Cage*, p. 69.

15 Ibid., p. 65.

16 Cage, "Experimental Music," in *Silence*, p. 10.

17 Gilles Deleuze, "Vincennes Seminar Session, May 3, 1977: On Music," trans. Timothy S. Murphy, *Discourse* 20, no. 3 (fall 1998), p. 211.

18 Wim Mertens, *American Minimal Music* (London: Kahn & Averill, 1983), p. 90. The relevant portion of this text is reprinted in *Audio Culture*, pp. 307–12.

19 Steve Reich, "Music as a Gradual Process," in *Writings about Music* (New York: New York University Press, 1974), reprinted in *Audio Culture*, pp. 304–6.

20 On Chronos and Aion and their relationship to music, see the "Vincennes Seminar," pp. 209ff, and *A Thousand Plateaus: Capitalism and Schizophrenia* (Minneapolis: University of Minnesota Press, 1987), p. 262. Deleuze first

introduces the Stoic distinction between Chronos and Aion in *The Logic of Sense*, ed. Constantin Boundas, trans. Mark Lester and Charles Stivale (New York: Columbia University Press, 1990). Deleuze and Guattari discuss the difference between Goethe's bildungsroman and Kleist's "pure 'stationary process'" in *A Thousand Plateaus*, pp. 268–69.

21 In a short essay from 2000, Neuhaus rejects the term *sound art* as a legitimate aesthetic category. See Neuhaus, "Sound Art?," http://www.max-neuhaus.info/soundworks/soundart. Nevertheless, I find the term to be helpful in distinguishing musical sound from other aesthetic uses of sound. For more on this, see my "Sound Art and the Sonic Unconscious," *Organised Sound* 14, no. 1 (2009), pp. 19–26.

22 Neuhaus, "Situation Esthetics: Impermanent Art and the Seventies Audience," *Artforum* 18, no. 5 (January 1980), pp. 27–29, reprinted as "Modus Operandi," in *Max Neuhaus: Sound Works*, vol. 1, *Inscription*, p. 18; and at http://www.max-neuhaus.info/ soundworks/vectors/passage/modusoperandi.

23 Neuhaus, interview by Duckworth, p. 45.

24 See Michael Fried, "Art and Objecthood" (1967), in *Art and Objecthood: Essays and Reviews* (Chicago: University of Chicago Press, 1998), pp. 148–72.

25 Robert Morris, quoted in Fried, "Art and Objecthood," p. 153.

26 Fried, "Art and Objecthood," p. 154.

27 Fried, "An Introduction to My Art Criticism," in *Art and Objecthood*, p. 41.

28 This concern is discussed in detail by Pamela M. Lee in *Chronophobia: On Time in the Art of the 1960s* (Cambridge, Mass.: MIT Press, 2004), pp. 36–81.

29 Tony Smith, quoted in Fried, "Art and Objecthood," pp. 157–58.

30 Fried, "Art and Objecthood," p. 159.

31 Ibid., pp. 166–67.

32 Ibid., p. 167.

33 Compare Laplace: "We ought then to regard the present state of the universe as the effect of its anterior state and the cause of the one which is to follow. Given for one instant an intelligence which could comprehend all the forces by which nature is animated and the respective situation of the beings who compose it—an intelligence sufficiently vast to submit these data to analysis—it would embrace in the same formula the movements of the greatest bodies of the universe and those of the lightest atom; for it, nothing would be uncertain and the future, as the past, would be present to its eyes." Pierre-Simon, marquis de Laplace, *A Philosophical Essay on Probabilities* (1814), trans. Frederick Wilson Truscott and Frederick Lincoln Emery (New York: Dover, 1951), p. 4.

34 Fried, "An Introduction to My Art Criticism," p. 46; "Art and Objecthood," p. 168.

35 Robert Smithson, "A Sedimentation of the Mind: Earth Projects," *Artforum* 7, no. 1 (September 1968), p. 50; reprinted in *Robert Smithson: The Collected Writings*, ed. Jack Flam (Berkeley: University of California Press, 1996), p. 112.

36 Robert Morris,"Notes on Sculpture, Part 4: Beyond Objects," *Artforum* 7, no. 8 (April 1969), p. 54; reprinted in *Continuous Project Altered Daily: The Writings of Robert Morris* (Cambridge, Mass.: MIT Press, 1993), p. 68.

37 Morris had earlier used sound as a way of de-reifying objects, notably in his *Box with the Sound of Its Own Making* (1961).

38 Morris, "Notes on Sculpture, Part 4," pp. 59, 61, 67.

39 On the relationship between Cage and Morris, see Branden W. Joseph, "Robert Morris and John Cage: Reconstructing a Dialogue," *October*, no. 81 (Summer 1997), pp. 59–69. Joseph discusses Cage's reception by Fried in "The Tower and the Line: Toward a Genealogy of Minimalism," *Grey Room*, no. 27 (Spring 2007), pp. 58–81, a version of which appears in Joseph's *Beyond the Dream Syndicate: Tony Conrad and the Arts after Cage* (New York: Zone Books, 2008), pp. 109–51.

40 See Lippard, "The Dematerialization of Art," in *Changing: Essays in Art Criticism* (New York: Dutton, 1971), pp. 255–76.

[41] See, for example, Lawrence Weiner, "Statements," Sol LeWitt, "Paragraphs on Conceptual Art," and Joseph Kosuth, "Art After Philosophy," in *Art in Theory, 1900–2000: An Anthology of Changing Ideas*, ed. Charles Harrison and Paul Wood (Malden, Mass.: Blackwell, 2003), pp. 846–49, 852–61, 893–94.

[42] Philosophical critiques of this conception of time have been offered by Nietzsche, Bergson, Derrida, and Deleuze.

[43] Neuhaus, cited in Tarantino, "Two Passages"; Neuhaus, interview by Duckworth.

[44] Nietzsche presents this argument most fully in *The Birth of Tragedy*. For a reading of *The Birth of Tragedy* along these lines, see my "Nietzsche, Dionysus, and the Ontology of Music," in *A Companion to Nietzsche*, ed. Keith Ansell Pearson (Malden, Mass.: Blackwell, 2005), pp. 495–513.

[45] See, for example, chapter 2 of Bergson's *Time and Free Will: An Essay on the Immediate Data of Consciousness*, trans. F. L. Pogson (New York: Harper & Row, 1960), p. 100; and the opening section of his *Creative Evolution* (1907), trans. Arthur Mitchell (New York: Henry Holt, 1931).

[46] Bergson, *Duration and Simultaneity*, in *Key Writings*, p. 205. Bergson goes on to extend interior, psychological intuition of duration, this "inner time," to "the time of things," "the duration of the universe." This passage is clearly a revision of his earlier view, according to which melody is presented as the best figure of duration. See Bergson, *Time and Free Will*, p. 100.

[47] For a rich, Bergsonian meditation on drones and duration, see a recent text by Theatre of Eternal Music member Tony Conrad, "Duration" (October 2004), http://tonyconrad.net/duration.htm.

[48] Recall Cage's suggestion that his title might be read "four feet, thirty-three inches."

[49] See the text panel in Neuhaus's drawing for "Time Piece Beacon," which is reproduced on the back endpapers in this book, see also the introduction to his Moment works, http://www.max-neuhaus.info/soundworks/vectors/moment/intro, and "Notes on Place and Moment" (1992), in *Max Neuhaus: Sound Works*, vol. 1, *Inscription*, pp. 100–1; also at http://www.max-neuhaus.info/soundworks/vectors/moment/notes.

[50] See the text panel in Neuhaus's drawing for *Times Square*, which is reproduced on the front endpapers in this book.

[51] Neuhaus himself associates his Time Pieces with the history of bell ringing. See his introduction to the Moment works and his "Notes on Place and Moment."

[52] See Alain Corbin, *Village Bells: Sound and Meaning in the 19th-Century French Countryside*, trans. Martin Thom (New York: Columbia University Press, 1998), pp. 110–12.

[53] See Bergson, *Time and Free Will*, p. 109, and *Duration and Simultaneity*, in *Key Writings*, pp. 214–15.

[54] Deleuze, *Cinema 2: The Time-Image*, trans. Hugh Tomlinson and Robert Galeta (Minneapolis: University of Minnesota Press, 1989), p. 81. This passage largely summarizes the conclusions of Bergson's 1908 essay "Memory of the Present and False Recognition," in *Mind-Energy: Lectures and Essays*, trans. H. Wilden Carr (London: Macmillan, 1920), pp. 172–85, to which Deleuze alludes throughout his corpus. See, for example, Deleuze's *Nietzsche and Philosophy*, trans. Hugh Tomlinson (New York: Columbia University Press, 1983), pp. 47–49; *Bergsonism*, trans. Hugh Tomlinson and Barbara Habberjam (New York: Zone Books, 1988), pp. 54–62; and *Difference and Repetition*, trans. Paul Patton (New York: Columbia University Press, 1994), pp. 79–80.

Biography

1939
Born in Beaumont, Texas (August 9)

1942
Family moves to Fishkill, New York

1954
Decides to become a musician
First work with various jazz, rock and roll, and dance bands

1955
Family moves to Houston

1957–61
Studies with Paul Prince at Manhattan School of Music

1958
Meets John Cage

1961
Meets Karlheinz Stockhausen and Pierre Boulez

1962
Completes Darmstadt International Summer Courses for New Music with Master of Music degree

1962–63
Tours with Pierre Boulez's Contemporary Chamber Ensemble

1963–64
Solo recital, Carnegie Recital Hall, New York
Tours United States and Canada as percussion soloist with Karlheinz Stockhausen

1965
Second solo recital, Carnegie Recital Hall, New York
Gives concerts in major European cities on solo tour

1966
Initiates *Listen*, first independent work as an artist and first in a series of fifteen works, 1966–76
Realizes first broadcast work, *Public Supply I*
Realizes *Max-Feed*, an editioned sound object produced with MassArt

1966–67
Realizes *American Can*, sound-event series, New York

1967
Realizes first sound installation, *Drive-in Music*
Realizes *Fan Music* on the rooftops of 137–141 Bowery, New York

1968
Records *Electronics and Percussion: Five Realizations by Max Neuhaus*, percussion repertoire produced by Columbia Masterworks
Decides to cease performing as a musician
Artist-in-residence at Bell Laboratories in Murray Hill, New Jersey, where he experiments with acoustics and electronics

1969
Lives on a boat journeying along Eastern Seaboard, studying underwater acoustics

1971
Realizes *Water Whistle I* at New York University's pool, first in a series of seventeen works, 1971–74

1973
Music Fellow, National Endowment for the Arts
Conceives *Times Square* and Paris Metro project
Installs *Walkthrough* at Jay Street–Borough Hall subway station, New York, extant until 1977

1974
Returns to live in New York
Preliminary studies for *Radio Net*
Incorporation of HEAR Inc.

1976
Installs *Round* at the U.S. Custom House, New York
Realizes *Underwater Music I*,

Radio Bremen, and *Underwater Music II*, Institute for Art and Urban Resources, New York

1977
Installs *Times Square* in New York, where it remains until 1992, to be reinstalled in 2002 as a permanent piece in the collection of Dia Art Foundation
Participates in Documenta 6
Radio Net realized on National Public Radio
Realizes *Underwater Music III*, Institute for Art and Urban Resources, New York
Begins to split his time between New York and Paris

1977–78
Fellow, DAAD, Berlin

1978
Begins development and construction of first computer-controlled multisynthesizer sound system
Conceives Sirens project, new designs and techniques for emergency sounds
Installs an untitled work in the Abby Aldrich Rockefeller Sculpture Garden at the Museum of Modern Art, New York

1979
First accession of a sound installation by an institution, an untitled work by Museum of Contemporary Art, Chicago
Realizes *Five Russians (A Tuned Room)* at the Clocktower Gallery, Institute for Art and Urban Resources, New York

1981
Conducts first outdoor experiments for Sirens project
Lecture tour through California

1982
Lecture tour through Japan
Visual Arts Fellow, National Endowment for the Arts

1983
Creates first works for European museums
Participates in Whitney Biennial at the Whitney Museum of American Art with a piece he would later title *Time Piece "Archetype"*

1986
Gives up New York residence to live full-time in Paris

1988–89
Continues tests for Sirens project in California desert

1989
Installs *A Bell for St. Cäcilien*, commissioned by Kölnischer Kunstverein, Cologne, extant until 1991
Installs first full-scale Time Piece, *Time Piece Bern*, commissioned by Kunsthalle Bern, extant until 1993

1991
Award of U.S. patent for siren sound design, first patent ever issued for a sound

1992
Participates in Documenta 9, contributing *Three to One*, a work that would become a permanent installation in the AOK Building in Kassel, Germany
Begins research for *Audium Model*

1994
Max Neuhaus: Sound Works, retrospective book series in three volumes, is published by Cantz Verlag, Ostfildern, Germany

1995
"Evoking the Aural," a retrospective exhibition of drawings from the Place works, organized by Villa Arson, Nice, and Museo d'Arte Contemporanea, Castello di Rivoli, Turin

1996
Moves to Italy
Installs an untitled permanent sound work in the entrance to the Castello di Rivoli, Museo d'Arte Contemporanea, Turin

1999
First freestanding sound-field work, *Intersection I*, at Venice Biennale
Installs *Suspended Sound Line*, commissioned by Kunst im öffentlichen Raum Bern

2002
Reinstallation of *Times Square*, which enters the collection of Dia Art Foundation
Installs *Promenade du Pin*, commissioned by Fonds Cantonale d'Art Contemporain, Geneva

2003
Installs *Time Piece Graz* at Kunsthaus Graz, Landesmuseum Joanneum, Graz, a permanent installation

2004
Launches Auracle at http://www.auracle.org, a networked sound instrument, controlled by the voice and played over the Internet
Network recordings made available on internet

2005
Installs *Time Piece Beacon* a permanent sound work at Dia:Beacon, Beacon, New York

2007
Installs *Eybesfeld* in Lebring, Austria
Installs *Time Piece Stommeln*, a permanent sound work in the town square of Stommeln-Pulheim, Germany

2008
Installs *Sound Figure* at the Menil Collection, Houston

2009
Dies in Maratea, Italy (February 3)

Selected Bibliography

Organized chronologically

Many of the articles, reviews, essays, and interviews listed below, as well as additional writings by Max Neuhaus and others, can be found in full at http://www.max-neuhaus.info. Where noted, texts can be found in the collection *Max Neuhaus: Sound Works*, vol. 1, *Inscription*. Ostfildern-Ruit, Germany: Cantz, 1994.

WRITINGS AND RECORDINGS BY THE ARTIST

Zyklus for One Percussionist. Wergo WER 60010 (LP), 1963.

Electronics and Percussion: Five Realizations by Max Neuhaus. Columbia Masterworks MS 7139 (LP), 1968. Liner notes by Max Neuhaus.

Cycle for One Percussionist (In Two Different Versions). Heliodor 2549 016, 1970. Featuring Christoph Caskel, Max Neuhaus, Frederic Rzewski, Karlheinz Stockhausen. Liner notes by Hanspeter Krellman.

"BANG, BOOooom, ThumP, EEEK, tinkle." *New York Times*, December 6, 1974, p. 39.

Program Notes. Toronto: York University, 1974. Excerpted in *Max Neuhaus: Sound Works*, vol. 1, *Inscription*.

"Situation Esthetics: Impermanent Art and the Seventies Audience: Max Neuhaus." *Artforum* 18, no. 5 (January 1980), pp. 27–29. Reprinted as "Modus Operandi," in *Max Neuhaus: Sound Works*, vol. 1, *Inscription*, 1994.

"Lecture at Seibu Museum Tokyo," 1982. In *Max Neuhaus: Sound Works*, vol. 1, *Inscription*. Full text at http://www.max-neuhaus.info/bibliography/Tokyo.htm.

"Lecture at University of Miami," 1984. In *Max Neuhaus: Sound Works*, vol. 1, *Inscription*. Full text at http://www.max-neuhaus.info/bibliography/Miami.htm.

"Audium, Projekt für eine Welt als Hör-Raum." In *Vom Verschwinden der Ferne: Telekommunikation und Kunst*. Cologne: DuMont, 1990, pp. 119–28.

"Listen." In *Max Neuhaus: Elusive Sources and "Like" Spaces*. Turin: Giorgio Persano, 1990.

"Notes on Place and Moment," 1992. In *Max Neuhaus: Sound Works*, vol. 1, *Inscription*. Full text at http://www.max-neuhaus.info/soundworks/vectors/moment/notes/.

"Siren—Aural Design." *Kunst & Museumjournaal* 4, no. 6 (1993), pp. 12–18.

"The Broadcast Works and Audium." In *Zeitgleich: The Symposium, the Seminar, the Exhibition*. Vienna: Triton, 1994.

"The Institutional Beast," 1994. In *Max Neuhaus: Sound Works*, vol. 1, *Inscription*. Full text at http://www.max-neuhaus.info/bibliography/InstitutionalBeast.htm.

"Sound Design." In *Zeitgleich: the Symposium, the Seminar, the Exhibition*. Vienna: Triton, 1994.

"Sound Art?" Liner notes for *Volume: Bed of Sound*. P.S. 1 Contemporary Art Center, New York, July 2000. Audio CD.

Fontana Mix–Feed: Six Realizations of John Cage 1965/1968. Alga Marghen, Milan, plana-P 18NMN.044, 2003. Liner notes by Donald J. Henahan, Max Neuhaus, and Theodore Strongin.

The New York School: Nine Realizations of Cage, Feldman, Brown. Alga Marghen, Milan, plana-N 22NMN.052, 2004. Liner notes by Malcolm Goldstein, Max Neuhaus, John Rockwell, and Theodore Strongin.

Zyklus: Stockhausen, Neuhaus. Alga Marghen, Milan, plana-P 23NMN.054, 2004. Liner notes by Max Neuhaus and John Rockwell.

"Netzwerke." *Neue Zeitschrift für Musik*, no. 5 (September–October 2004).

"Vortrag Neuhaus." In *End of Art –Endings in Art*. Ed. Gerhard Seel. Basel: Schwabe Verlag, 2006. Online at http://www.max-neuhaus.info/bibliography/IAPA.htm.

BOOKS AND CATALOGUES

Max Neuhaus: Sound Installation. Basel: Kunsthalle Basel, 1983. Texts by Jean-Christophe Ammann, Max Neuhaus, and Carter Ratcliff. Ammann and Ratcliff texts reprinted in *Max Neuhaus: Sound Works*, vol. 1, *Inscription*.

Max Neuhaus: Sound Installation. Providence, R.I.: Bell Gallery, Brown University, 1983.

Max Neuhaus: Installations Sonores. Geneva: Marie-Louise Jeanneret Art Moderne, 1984. Text by Pierre Restany.

Max Neuhaus. Locminé: Centre d'art contemporain, Domaine de Kerguéhennec, 1987. Text by Denys Zacharopoulos.

Max Neuhaus: Sound Line. Grenoble: Magasin, Centre National d'Art Contemporain, 1988. Text by Franz Keiser reprinted in *Max Neuhaus: Sound Works*, vol. 1, *Inscription*.

Max Neuhaus: Two Sound Works 1989. Bern: Kunsthalle Bern and Kölnischer Kunstverein, 1989. Texts by Wulf Herzogenrath, Ulrich Loock, and Max Neuhaus.

Max Neuhaus: Elusive Sources and "Like" Spaces. Turin: Giorgio Persano, 1990. Text by Denys Zacharopoulos; conversation with Ulrich Loock reprinted in *Max Neuhaus: Sound Works*, vol. 1, *Inscription*.

Max Neuhaus: Two Side of the "Same" Room. Dallas: Dallas Museum of Art, 1990. Text by Sue Graze.

Max Neuhaus: Sound Works, vol. 1, *Inscription*. Ostfildern-Ruit, Germany: Cantz, 1994. Original interview with William Duckworth; text by Wulf Herzogenrath, translated from the German by Margret Joss; text by Denys Zacharopoulos translated from the French by Charles Penwarden; text by Germano Celant, translated from the Italian by Brian Holmes.

Max Neuhaus: Sound Works, vol. 2, *Drawings*. Ostfildern-Ruit, Germany: Cantz, 1994. Texts by Yehuda Safran and Max Neuhaus.

Max Neuhaus: Sound Works, vol. 3, *Place*. Ostfildern-Ruit, Germany: Cantz, 1994.

Max Neuhaus: Zeichnungen. Heilbronn: Kunstverein Heilbronn, 1994.

Max Neuhaus: Evocare l'udibile. Milan: Charta, 1995. Texts by Ida Gianelli, Gregory des Jardins, Stuart Morgan, et al.

Max Neuhaus: La Collezione, The Collection. Milan: Charta, in association with Castello di Rivoli, Museo d'Arte Contemporanea, 1997. Texts by Max Neuhaus and Pier Luigi Tazzi.
Max Neuhaus: Moment / Stund. Reykjavik: Second Floor, 1997.
Three to One: Max Neuhaus. Brussels: Encore, in association with La Lettre Volée, 1997. Texts by Zsuzsanna Gahse, Max Neuhaus, and Yehuda Safran.
Max Neuhaus: Ears. Paris: Onestar Press, 2001.
Max Neuhaus: Time Piece Stommeln. Pulheim: Der Bürgermeister, 2007. Texts by Max Neuhaus and Ulrich Loock.

ARTICLES AND REVIEWS

Strongin, Theodore. "Concert Is Given By Percussionist." *New York Times*, June 3, 1964, p. 36.
Goldstein, Malcolm. "Neuhaus Realizations." *Village Voice*, June 1964.
Strongin, Theodore. "Artist 'Realizes' Taped Music and Plays Piano from Inside." *New York Times*, March 23, 1965, p. 34.
Saltzman, Eric. "Max Neuhaus's Electronics and Percussion." *HiFi Stereo Review* (November 1968).
Monson, Karen. "Neuhaus's Submerged Premiere." *Christian Science Monitor*, January 19, 1972, p. 6.
Hiffner, Amy. "Interview avec Max Neuhaus." *Artitudes International*, nos. 9–11 (April–June 1974), p. 70.
Brunelle, Al. "Deep Float: Neuhaus' 'Water Whistle.'" *Art in America* 62, no. 5 (September–October 1974), p. 91.
Johnson, Tom. "Creating the Context: Max Neuhaus." *Village Voice*, December 6, 1976. Reprinted in *Max Neuhaus: Sound Works*, vol. 1, *Inscription*.
Rockwell, John. "Whistle While You Tune In to Avant-Garde Radio." *New York Times*, January 2, 1977, p. 73.
La Barbara, Joan. "Max Neuhaus: New Sounds in Natural Settings." *Musical America* (October 1977). Reprinted in *Max Neuhaus: Sound Works*, vol. 1, *Inscription*.
Lorber, Richard. "Max Neuhaus, *Times Square*." *Artforum* 16, no. 5 (January 1978), p. 64.
Foster, Hal. "Exhibition Reviews." *Artforum* 18, no. 5 (January 1980), p. 70.
Princenthal, Nancy. "Sounds of Violence: Max Neuhaus' Siren Project." *Artforum* 20, no. 9 (May 1982), pp. 70–71.
Rockwell, John. "Environmental Composers & Ambient Music: Max Neuhaus." In *All American Music*. New York: Knopf, 1983. Reprinted in *Max Neuhaus: Sound Works*, vol. 1, *Inscription*.
Javault, Patrick. "Max Neuhaus: Noises in the Corridor." *Art Press*, no. 100 (February 1986), p. 55.
Restany, Pierre. "Max Neuhaus: concetto e metodo di una architettura Sonora." *Domus*, no. 684 (June 1987), p. 3.
Ratcliff, Carter. "Max Neuhaus: Aural Spaces." *Art in America* 75, no. 10 (October 1987), pp. 154–63.
Cueff, Alain. "Max Neuhaus: The Space of Sound." *Artscribe International*, no. 71 (September–October 1988), pp. 66–67. Reprinted in *Max Neuhaus: Sound Works*, vol. 1, *Inscription*.
Tomkins, Calvin. "HEAR." *New Yorker* (October 24, 1988), p. 110. Reprinted in *Max Neuhaus: Sound Works*, vol. 1, *Inscription*.
Danto, Arthur. "Max Neuhaus: Sound Works." *Nation* 252, no. 8 (March 4, 1991), pp. 281–84. Reprinted in *Max Neuhaus: Sound Works*, vol. 1, *Inscription*.
Weingarten, Susanne. "Brummen vor dem Tor." *Der Spiegel* (September 7, 1992), pp. 276–79. Reprinted in *Max Neuhaus: Sound Works*, vol. 1, *Inscription*.
von Drathen, Doris. "Max Neuhaus: Invisible Sculpture—Molded Sound." *Parkett*, no. 35 (March 1993), pp. 18–29. Reprinted in *Max Neuhaus: Sound Works*, vol. 1, *Inscription*.
Szeemann, Harald. "Max Neuhaus." *Kunstforum International*, no. 127 (July–September 1994), pp. 176–77. Reprinted in *Max Neuhaus: Sound Works*, vol. 1, *Inscription*.
Schwarze, Dirk. "Max Neuhaus und Karel Malich." *Kunstforum International*, no. 131 (August–October 1995), pp. 404–6.
Tazzi, Pier Luigi. "Constructed Sound: Max Neuhaus." *Carte d'Arte Internazionale* (November 1997).
Tarantino, Michael. "Two Passages." http://www.max-neuhaus.info/soundworks/vectors/passage/twopassages/, 1998.
von Drathen, Doris. "Gebaute Töne." *Künstler: Kritisches Lexikon der Gegenwartskunst* 41, no. 5 (1998).
Leffingwell, Edward. "Max Neuhaus at Christine Burgin and P.S. 1." *Art in America* 89, no. 4 (April 2001), p. 136.
Zuckerman, Alicia. "Max Neuhaus: Times Square." *Arts Electric*. http://www.arts-electric.org/stories/2002/020530_neuhaus.html. May 30, 2002.
Ryan, David. "Max Neuhaus." *Art Monthly*, no. 275 (April 2004), p. 42.
Safran, Yehuda. "Shaping Sound." *Domus*, no. 876 (December 2004): pp. 72–77.
Cascella, Daniela. "Max Neuhaus." *Contemporary*, no. 75 (2005), pp. 38–39.
Loock, Ulrich. "Times Square, Max Neuhaus's Sound Work in New York City." *Open: Cahier on Art in the Public Domain* 4, no. 9 (2005).
Traub, Peter. "Auracle." http://www.max-neuhaus.info/bibliography/PeterTraub.pdf, 2005.
LaBelle, Brandon. "Tuning Space: Max Neuhaus and Site-Specific Sound." In *Background Noise, Perspectives on Sound Art*, pp. 154–66. New York: Continuum, 2006.
Davila, Thierry. "Max Neuhaus, Times Square." *Art Press* 2, no. 5 (June 2007).
Reust, Hans Rudolf. "While Walking." http://www.max-neuhaus.info/bibliography/HansRudolfReust.pdf, 2007.
Carter, Kabir. "Houston; New York; and Beacon, New York." *Modern Painters* 20, no. 6 (July–August 2008), pp. 82–83.
Cox, Christoph. "Enduring Work: On Max Neuhaus (1939–2009)." *Artforum* 47, no. 9 (May 2009), pp. 49–50, 52.

Contributors

LYNNE COOKE was appointed curator at Dia Art Foundation, New York, in 1991, and in 2009 was named Dia's curator-at-large. In 2008, she became chief curator and deputy director at the Museo Nacional Centro de Arte Reina Sofia, Madrid. Co-curator of the 1991 Carnegie International and artistic director of the 1996 Sydney Biennale, she has also curated exhibitions in numerous venues in North America, Europe, and elsewhere. She has been on the faculty for curatorial studies at Bard College, in addition to teaching as a visiting scholar in the graduate fine art departments of several universities, including Yale University and Columbia University. In 2000, she was awarded the Independent Curators International Agnes Gund Curatorial Award and in 2006 she received the Award for Curatorial Excellence from the Center for Curatorial Studies at Bard College. Among her numerous publications are recent essays on the works of Rodney Graham, Jorge Pardo, Francis Alÿs, Richard Serra, Agnes Martin, and Zoe Leonard.

CHRISTOPH COX is professor of philosophy at Hampshire College and a member of the faculty at the Center for Curatorial Studies, Bard College. He is the author of *Nietzsche: Naturalism and Interpretation* (University of California Press, 1999) and coeditor of *Audio Culture: Readings in Modern Music* (Continuum, 2004). His essays on philosophy, art, and music have appeared in *Artforum*, *Cabinet*, *The Wire*, *Organised Sound*, *The Journal of the History of Philosophy*, *Review of Metaphysics*, and other magazines and journals. Cox has curated exhibitions at the Contemporary Arts Museum, Houston; The Kitchen, New York; New Langton Arts, San Francisco; and G Fine Art Gallery, Washington, D.C. He has written catalogue essays for exhibitions at the New Museum of Contemporary Art, New York; Mass MoCA, North Adams, Massachusetts; and Akademie der Künste, Berlin; among others. He is currently at work on a philosophical book about sound art and experimental music.

BRANDEN W. JOSEPH is Frank Gallipoli Professor of Modern and Contemporary Art in the Department of Art History and Archaeology at Columbia University. He is the author of *Random Order: Robert Rauschenberg and the Neo-Avant-Garde* (MIT Press, 2003), *Anthony McCall: The Solid Light Films and Related Works* (edited by Christopher Eamon for Northwestern University Press/Steidl, 2005), and, most recently, *Beyond the Dream Syndicate: Tony Conrad and the Arts after Cage* (Zone

Books, 2008). His writings have also appeared in *Artforum*, *Bookforum*, *Art Journal*, *Critical Inquiry*, *October*, *Texte zur Kunst*, *Parkett*, and *Les Cahiers du Musée national d'art moderne*, as well as in such catalogues as *CTRL [SPACE]: Rhetorics of Surveillance from Bentham to Big Brother* (2002), *X-Screen: Film Installations and Actions in the 1960s and 1970s* (2003), and *Robert Rauschenberg: Combines* (2005). He is also a founding editor of *Grey Room*, a journal of architecture, art, media, and politics, published quarterly by MIT Press since 2000.

LIZ KOTZ is a Los Angeles–based art critic and historian. She is the author of *Words to Be Looked At: Language in 1960s Art* (MIT Press, 2007) and coeditor, with Eileen Myles, of *The New Fuck You* (Semiotexte, 1994). She writes on contemporary art and interdisciplinary avant-gardes of the postwar era and has published essays on artists including Amy Adler, Lutz Bacher, Phil Collins, and Lawrence Weiner. She teaches modern and contemporary art history at the University of California, Riverside.

ULRICH LOOCK was born in 1953 in Braunschweig, Germany. After having served as the director of the Kunsthalle Bern and the Kunstmuseum Luzern, both in Switzerland, he has been the deputy director of Museu Serralves in Porto, Portugal, since 2003. He has written on several occasions on the work of Max Neuhaus and was responsible for the first installation of a Time Piece by Neuhaus at the Kunsthalle Bern in 1989.

PETER PAKESCH was born in 1955 in Graz, Austria, where he studied architecture. He was a member of the artist cooperative Forum Stadtpark and curated shows for this institution, as well as for the festival Steirischer Herbst. From 1980 to 1993, he ran a gallery in Vienna, where he showed such artists as Günther Förg, Mike Kelley, Albert Oehlen, Franz West, Christopher Wool, and Heimo Zobernig. He also published several magazines between 1986 and 1993, including *Durch* and *Fama & Fortune Bulletin*. After curating exhibitions at the National Gallery in Prague from 1993 to 1996, he became director of the Kunsthalle Basel, where he worked until 2003, showing the work of Franz Ackermann, Pawel Althamer, Olafur Eliasson, and Jason Rhoades, among others. He has served on the advisory boards of Soros International; the Sigmund Freud Museum, Vienna; the Akademie Schloß Solitude, Stuttgart; and the TBA 21, Vienna. Currently, he is the head of the Kunsthaus Graz and the Landesmuseum Joanneum in Graz, Austria. His recent exhibitions at the Kunsthaus include the overview exhibition "China Welcomes You" and the monographic shows "Modell Martin Kippenberger" and "Diana Thater—gorillagorillagorilla." He also commissioned Max Neuhaus's *Time Piece Graz* in 2003 for the Kunsthaus Graz.

ALEX POTTS is Max Loehr Collegiate Professor in the Department of History of Art at the University of Michigan, Ann Arbor. He is author of the books *Flesh and the Ideal: Winckelmann and the Origins of Art History* (Yale University Press, 1994 and 2000) and *The Sculptural Imagination: Figurative, Modernist, Minimalist* (Yale University Press, 2000) and coeditor of an anthology of texts on modern sculpture, *The Modern Sculpture Reader* (Henry Moore Institute, 2007). He is currently writing a book on experimental forms of realism in postwar European and American art, *Experiments in Modern Realism c. 1945–1965*.

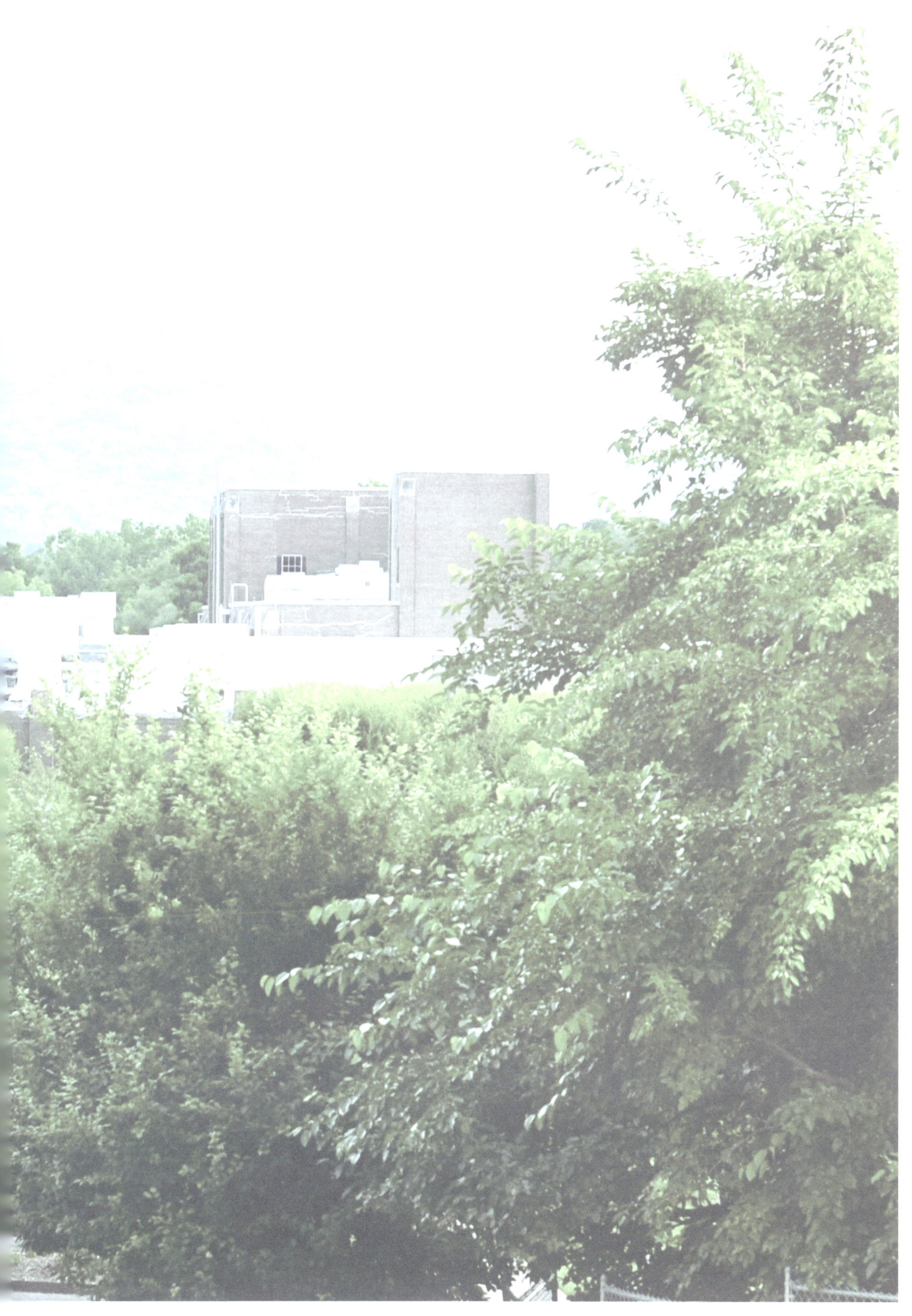

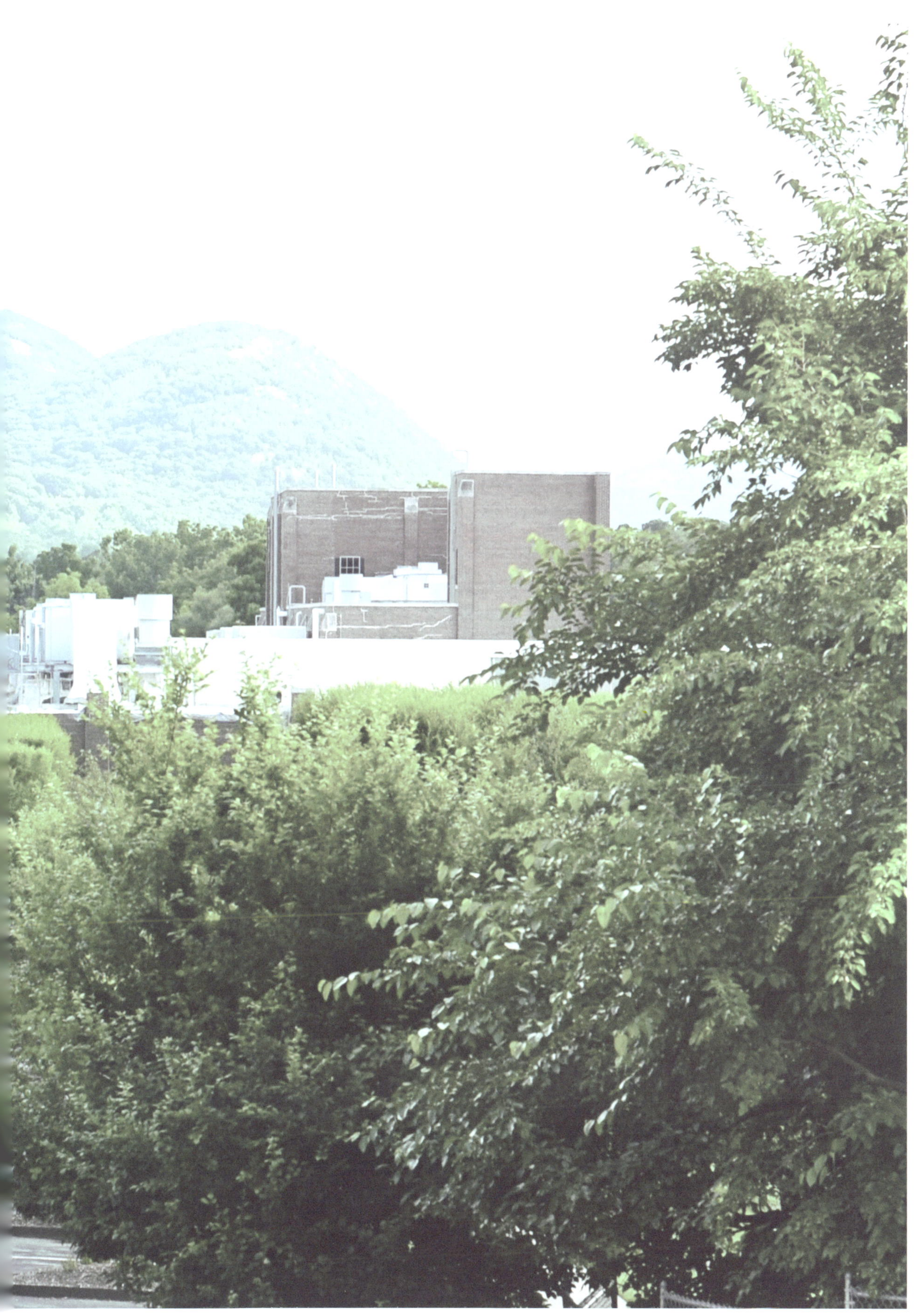

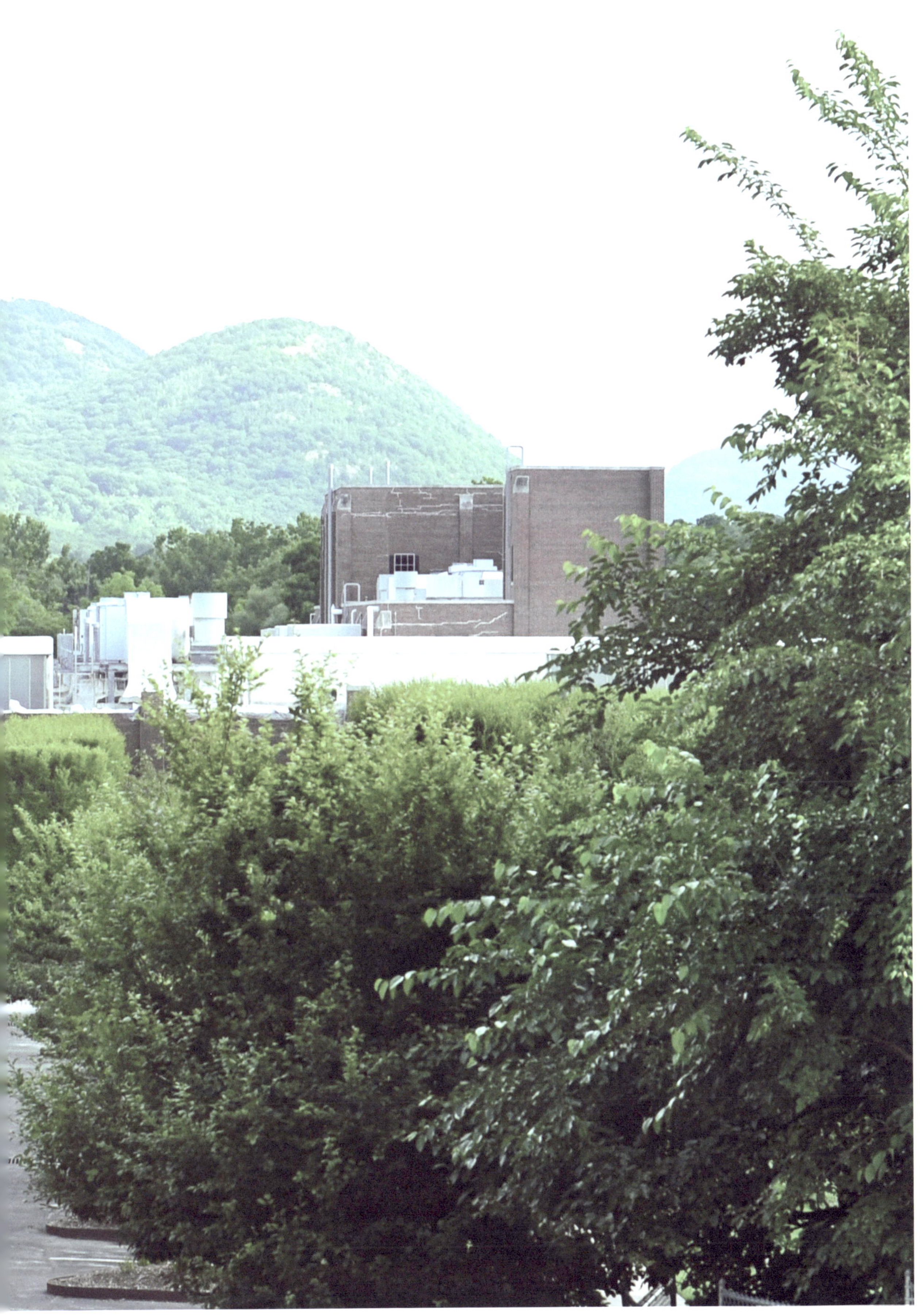

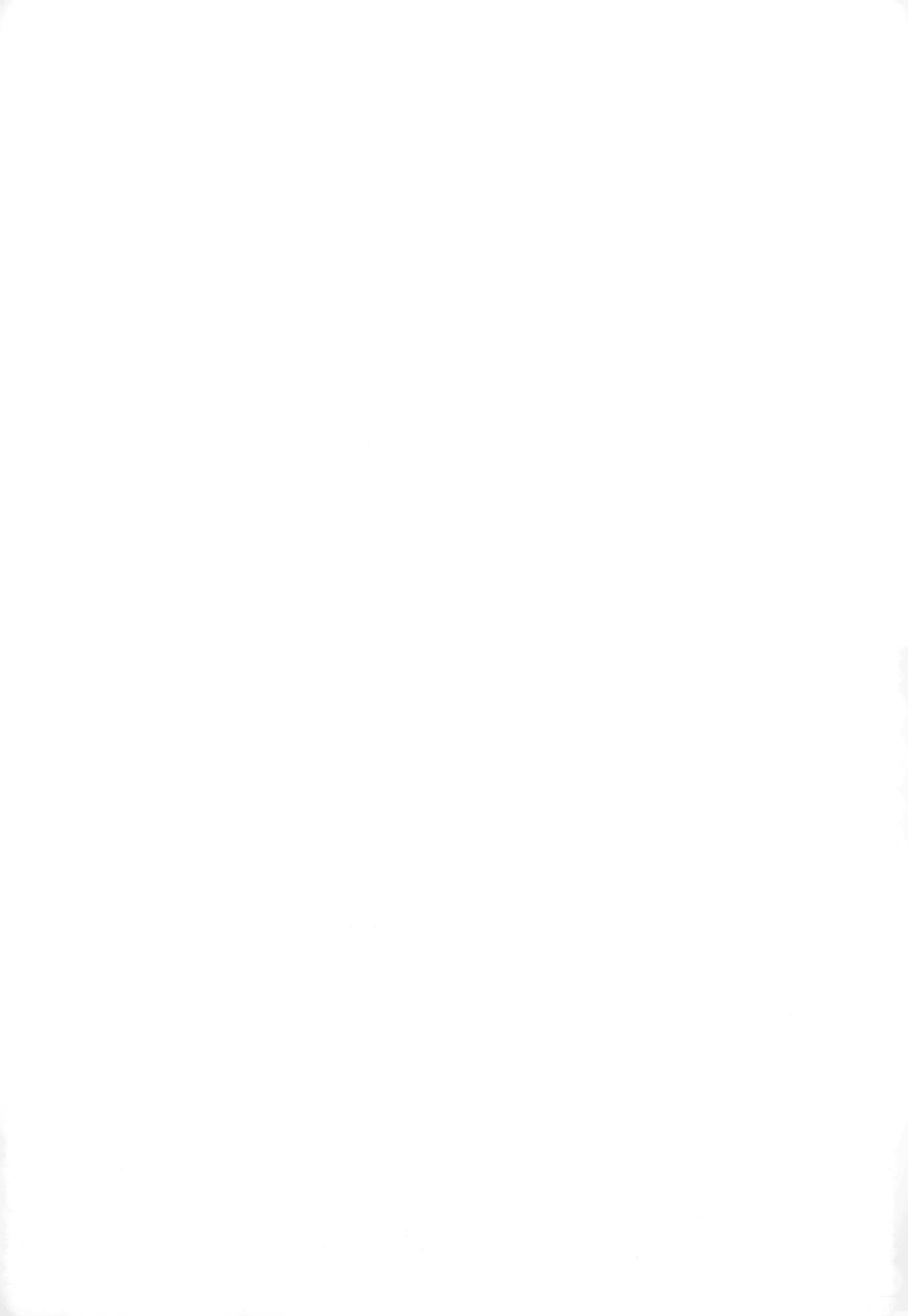

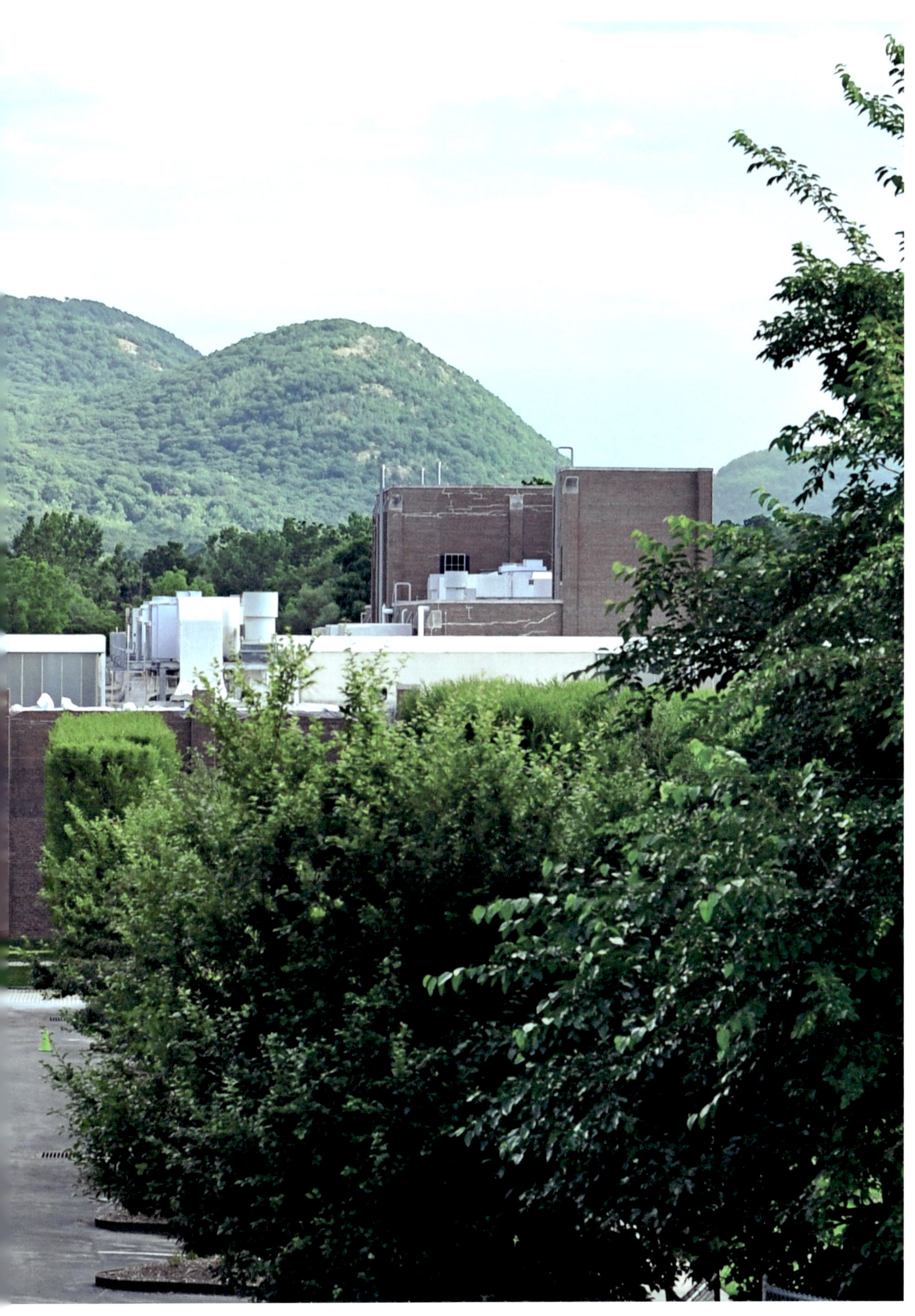

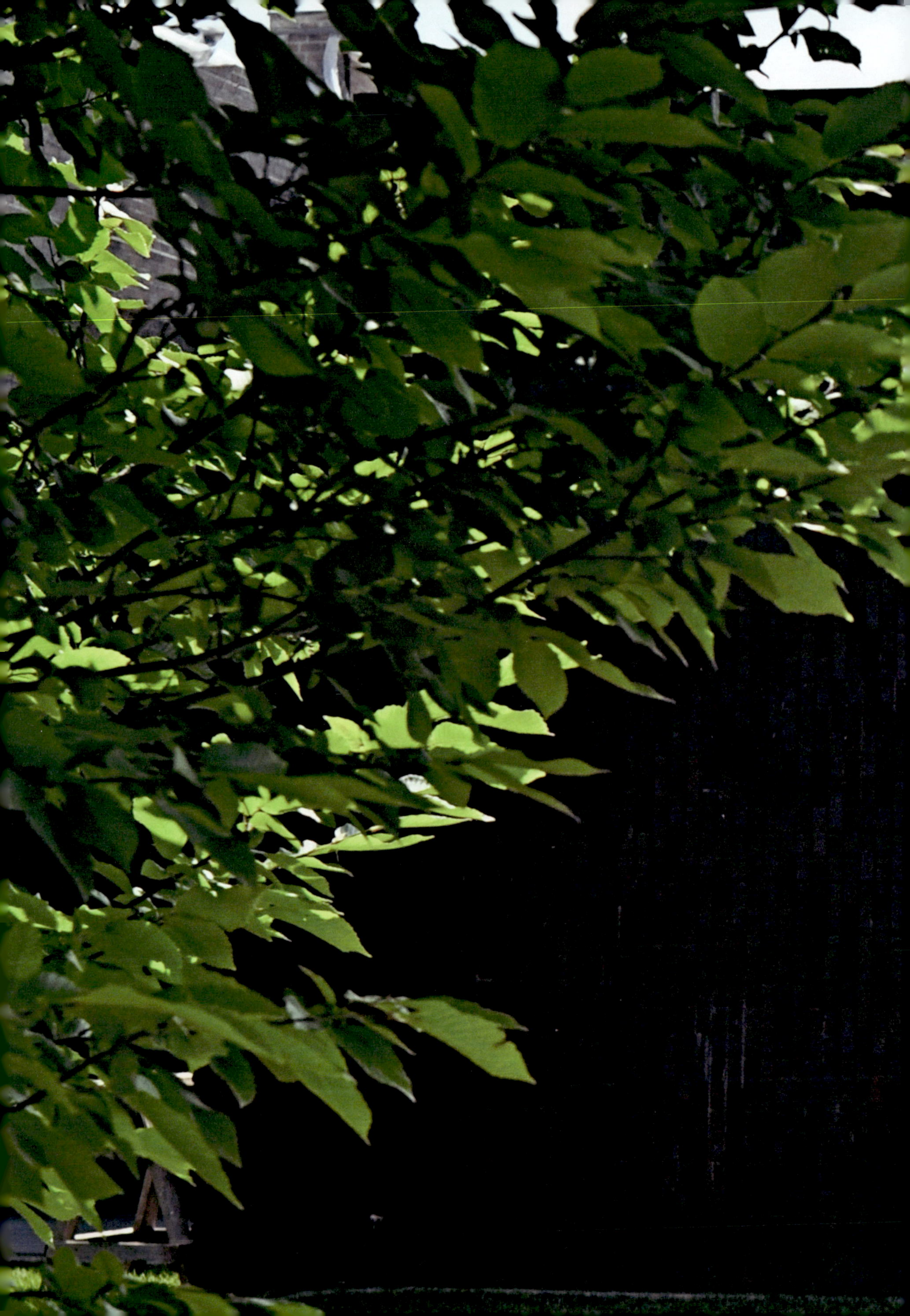

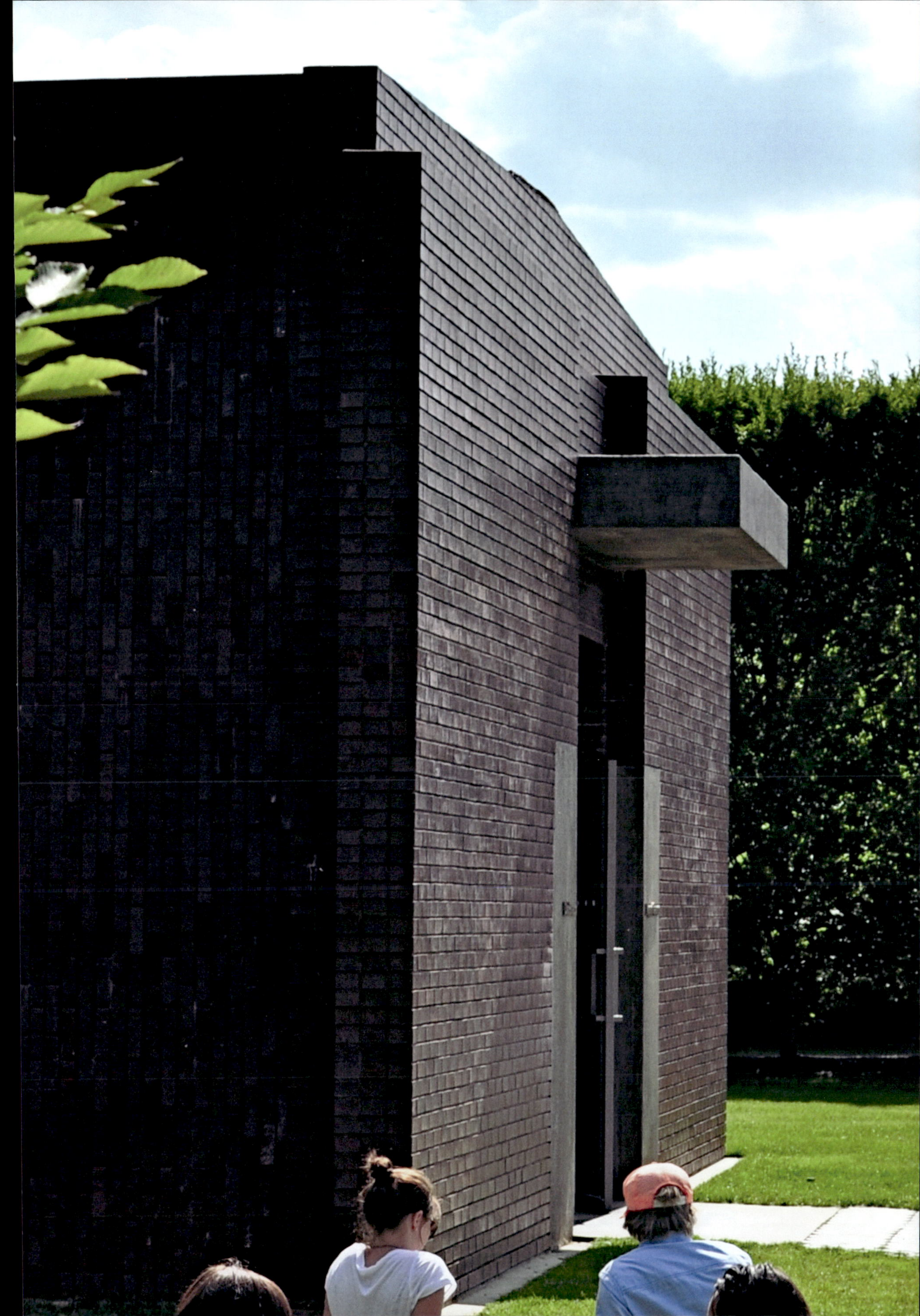

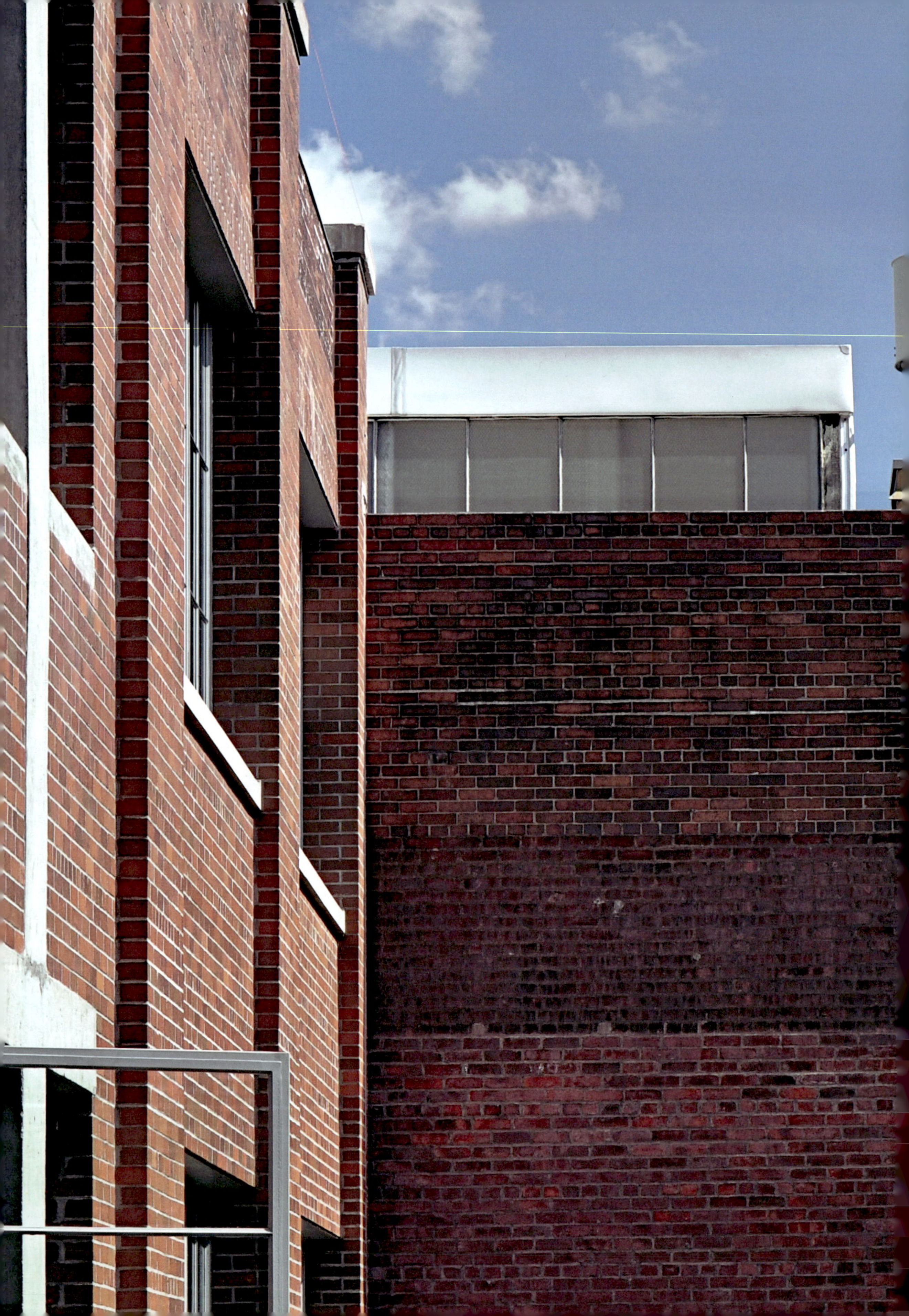

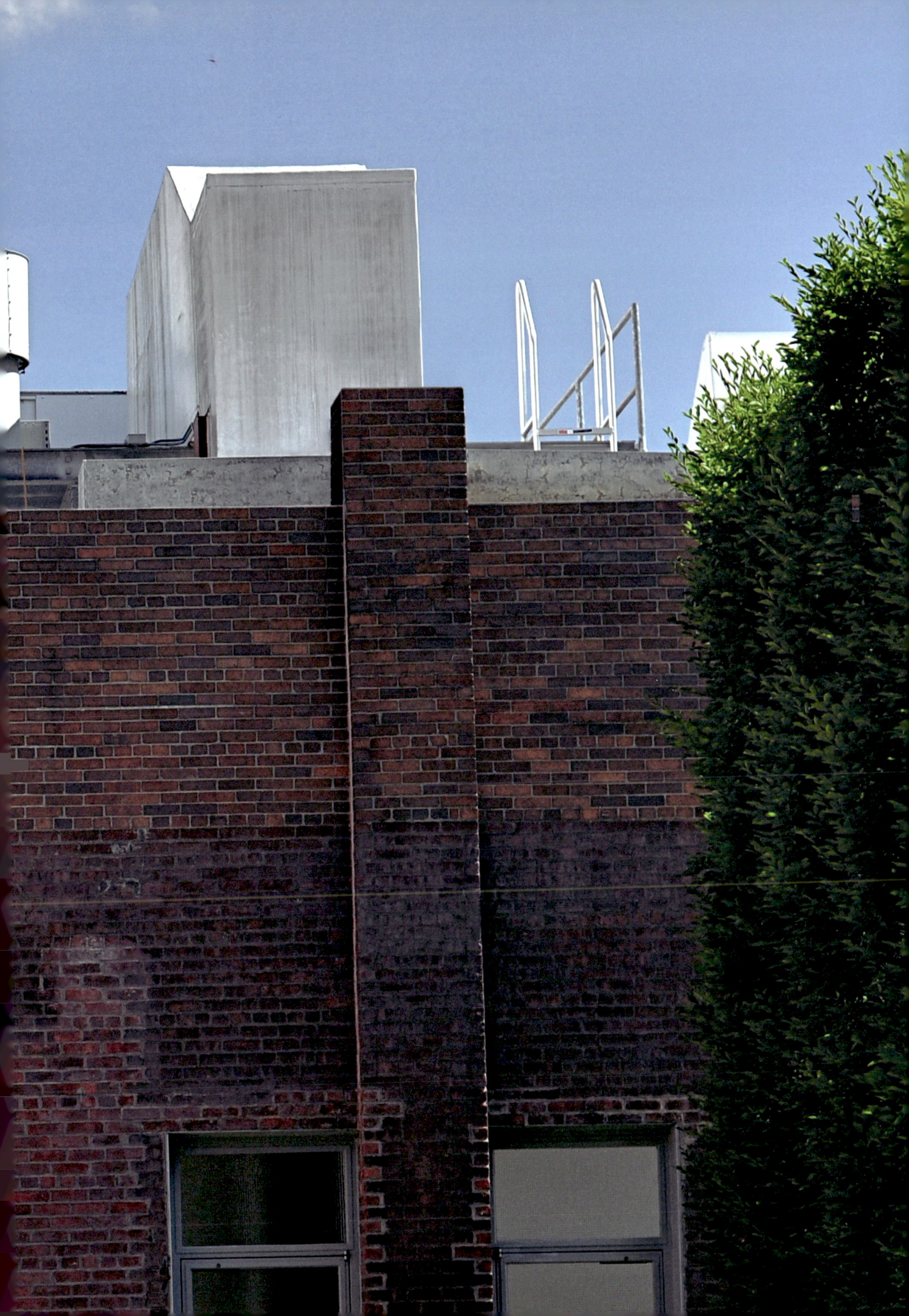

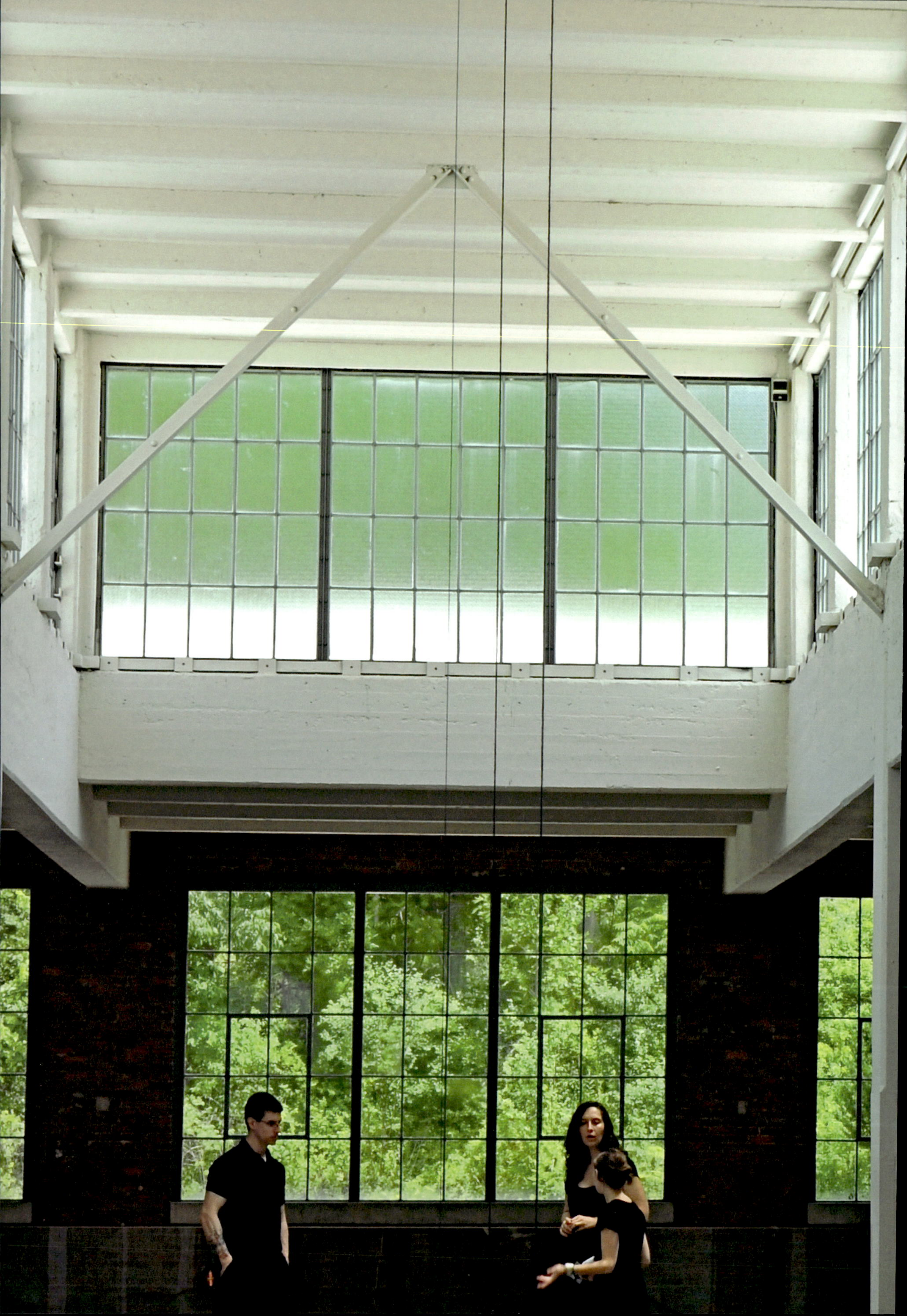

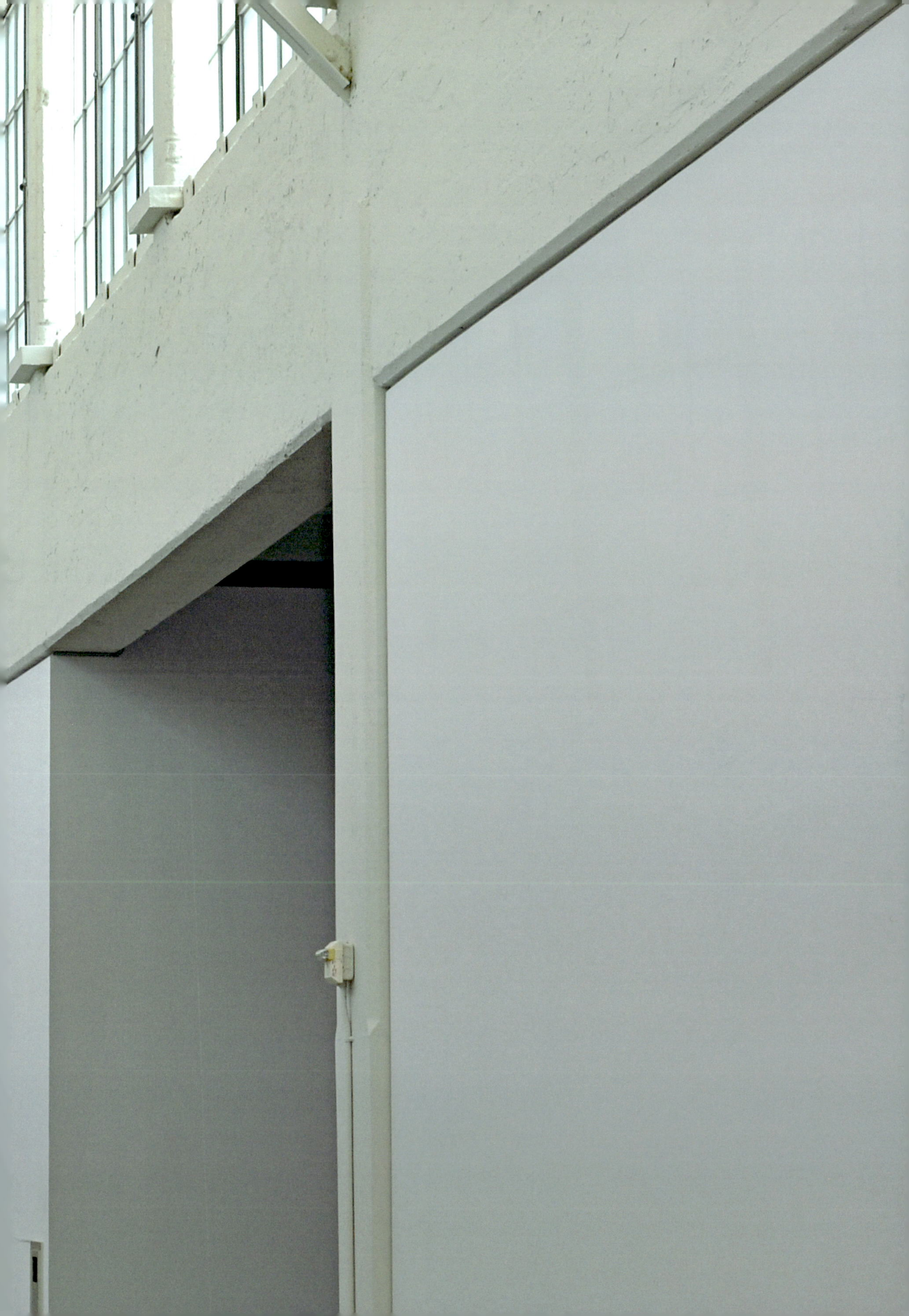

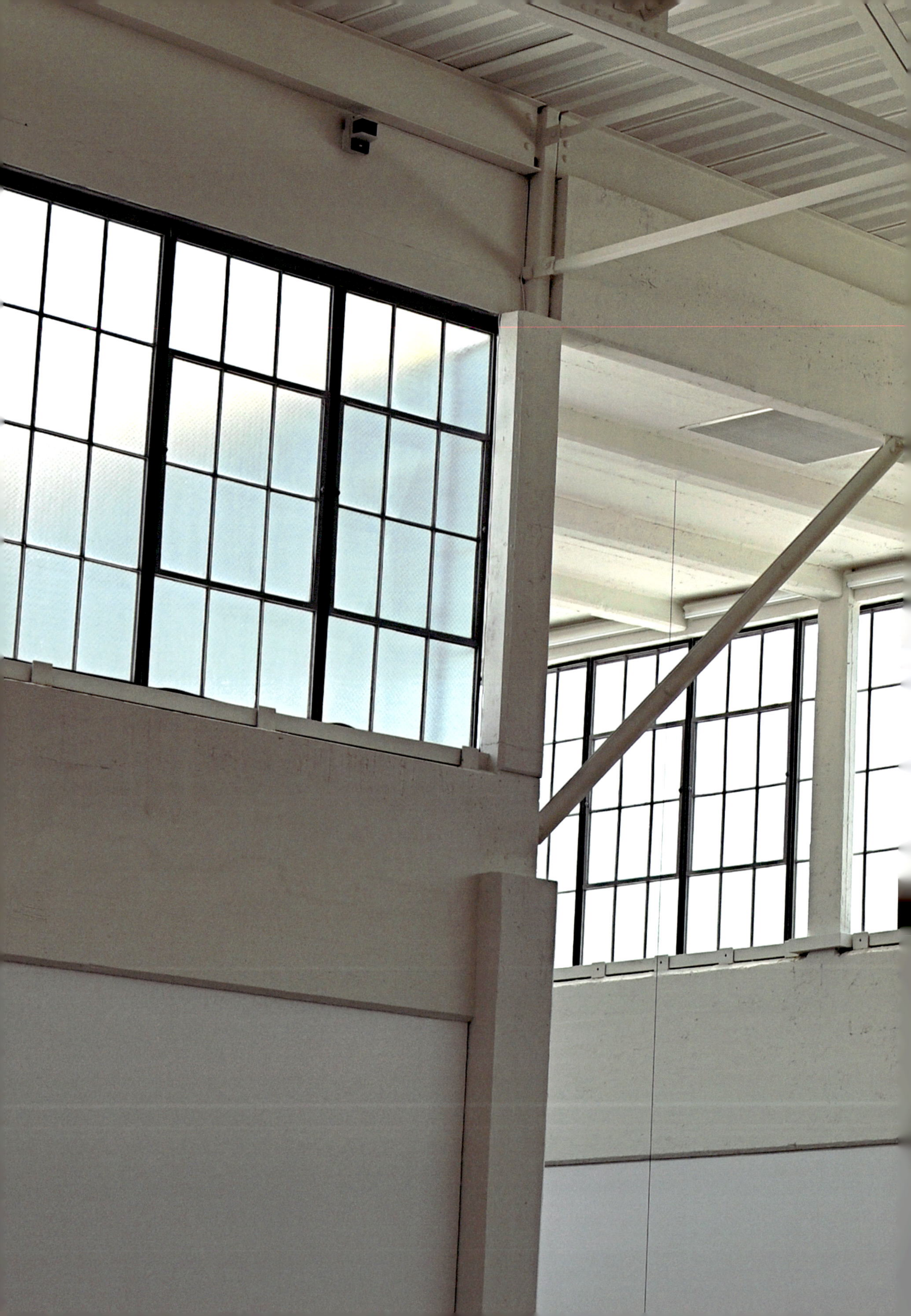

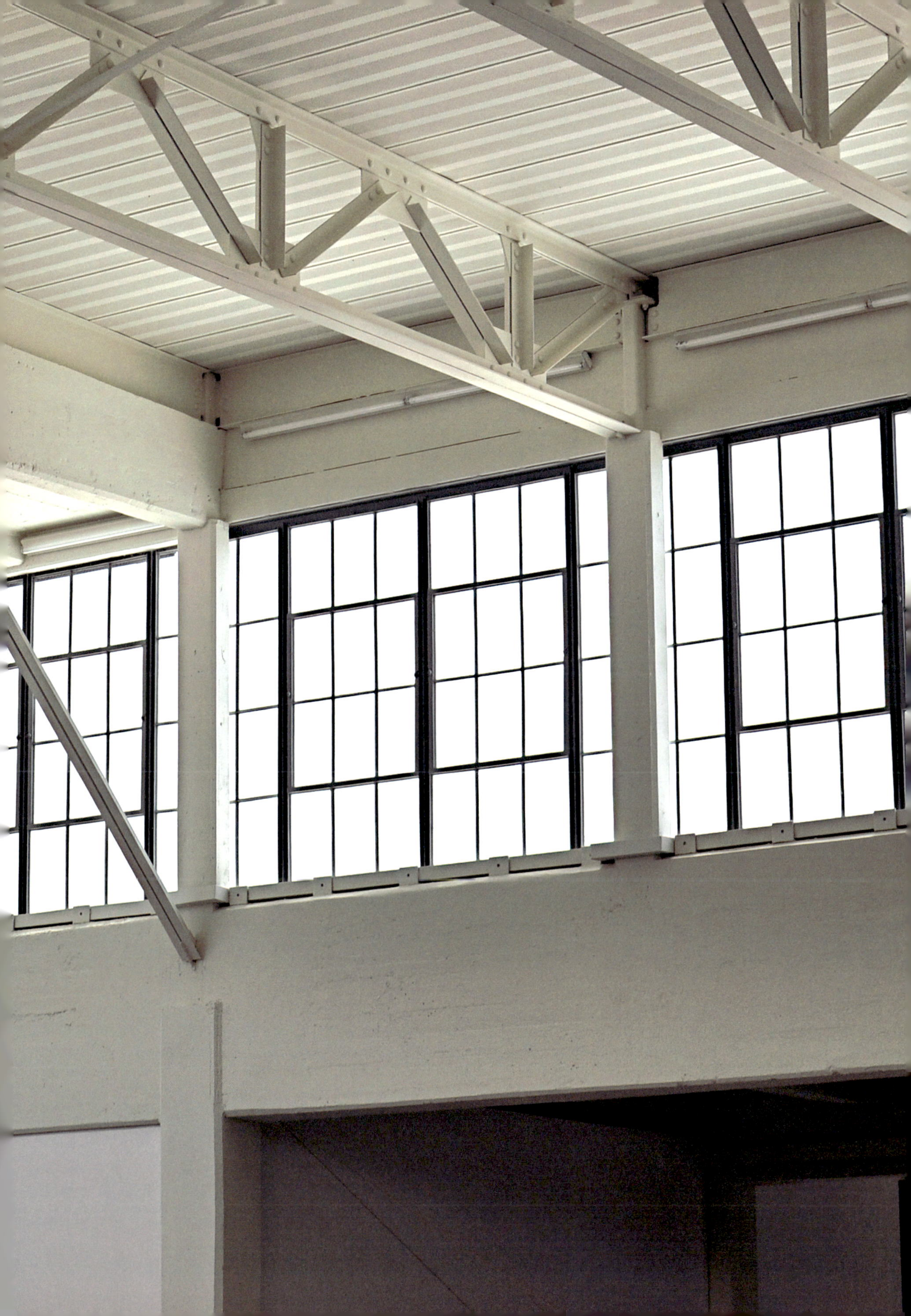

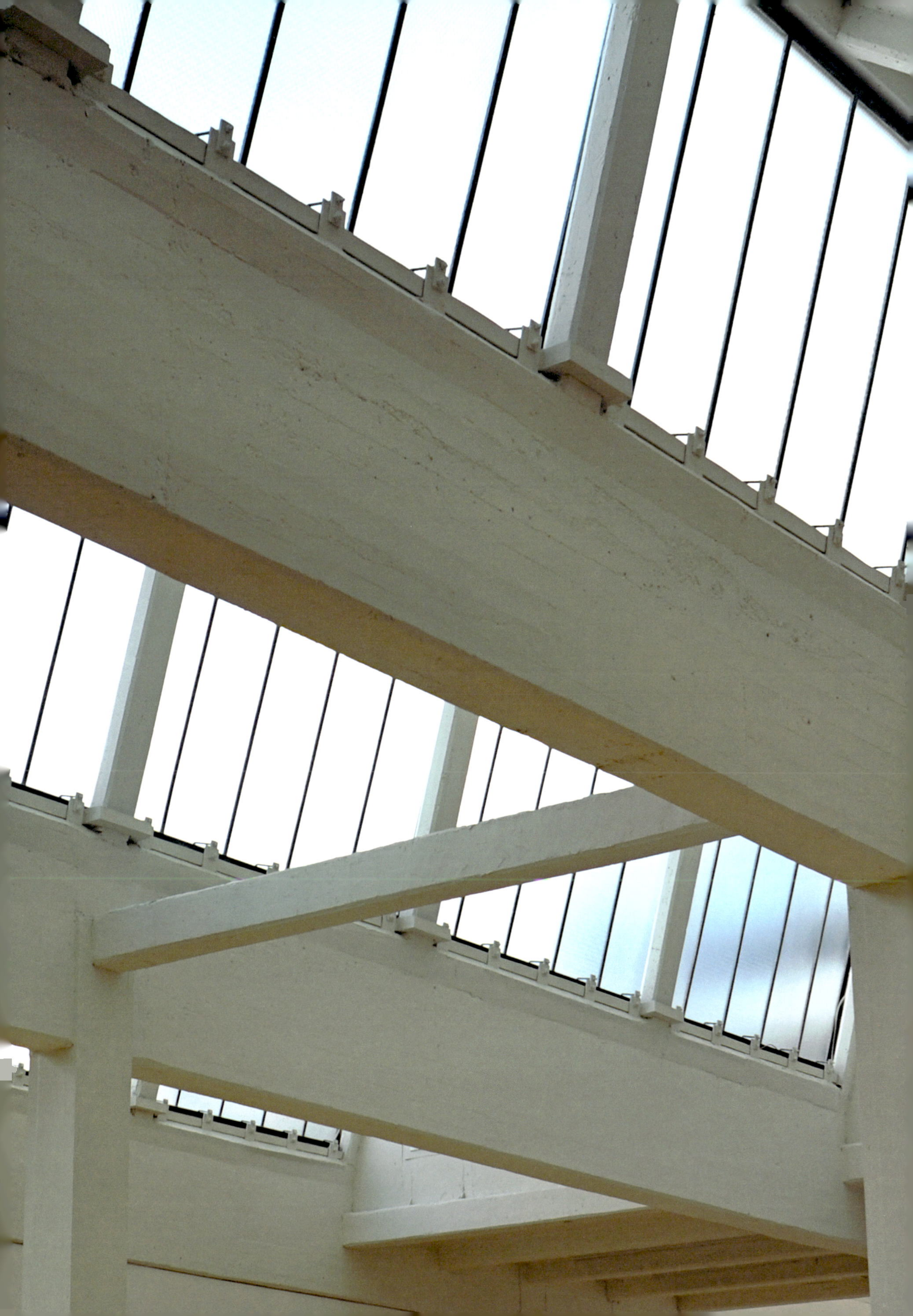

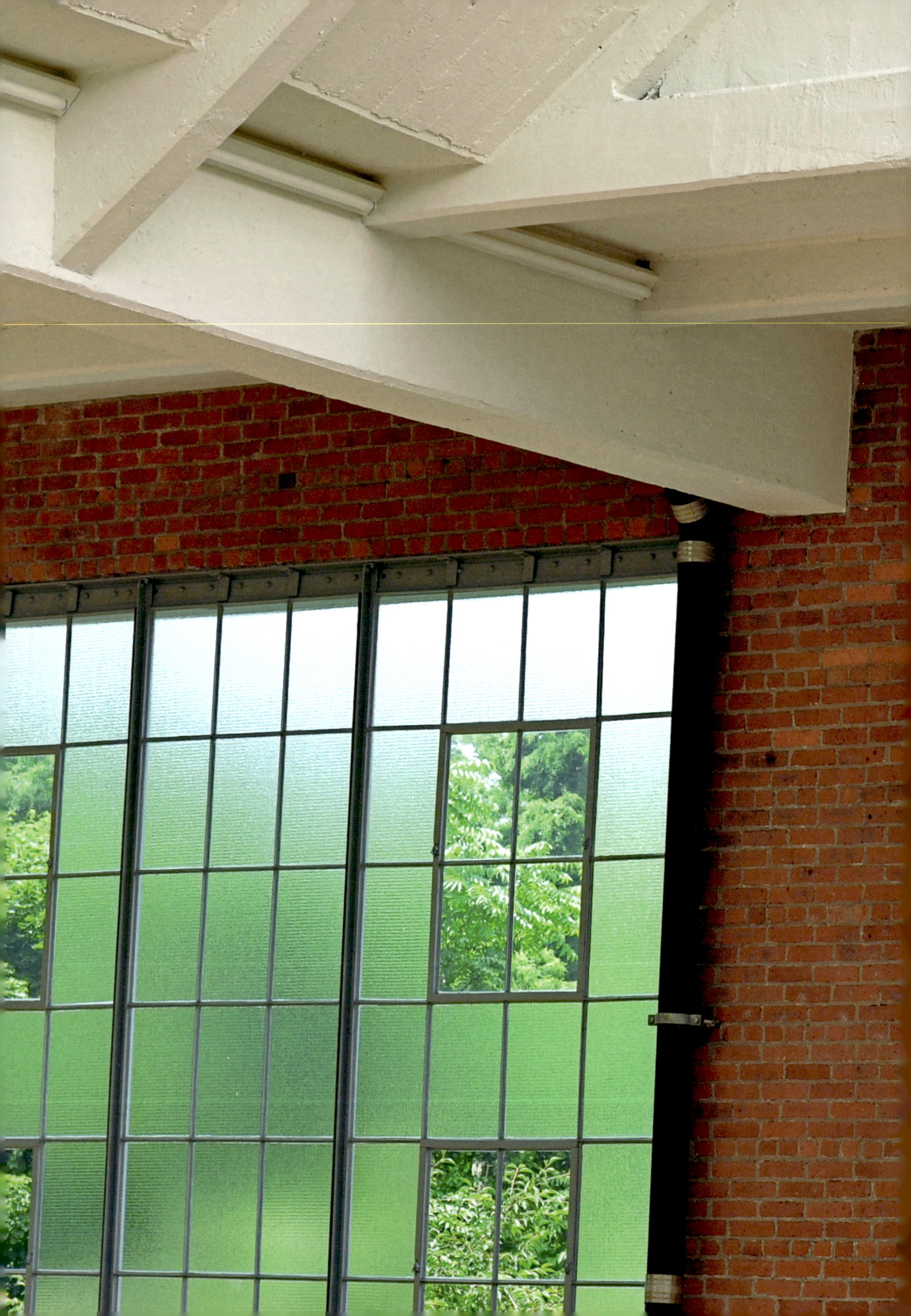

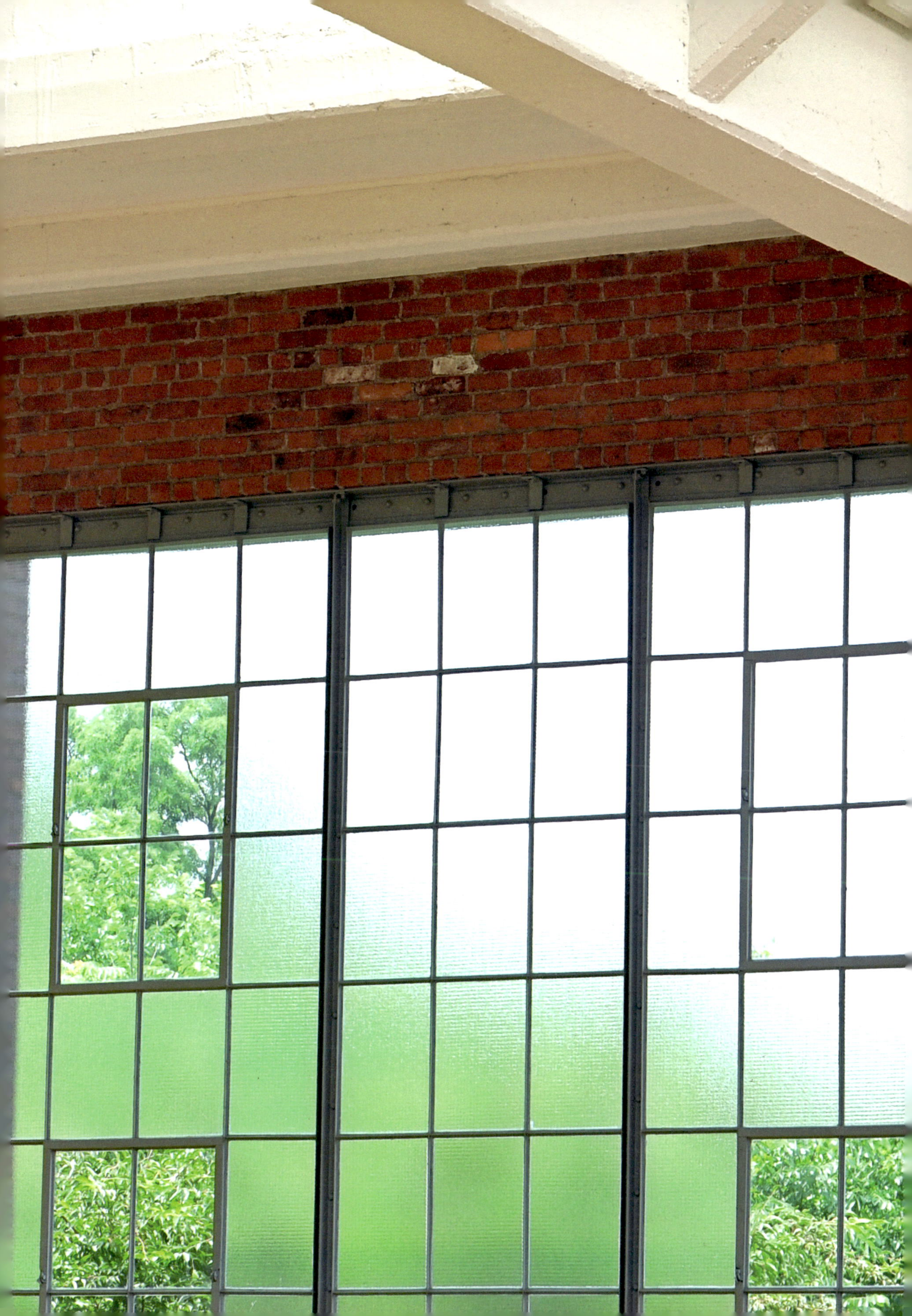

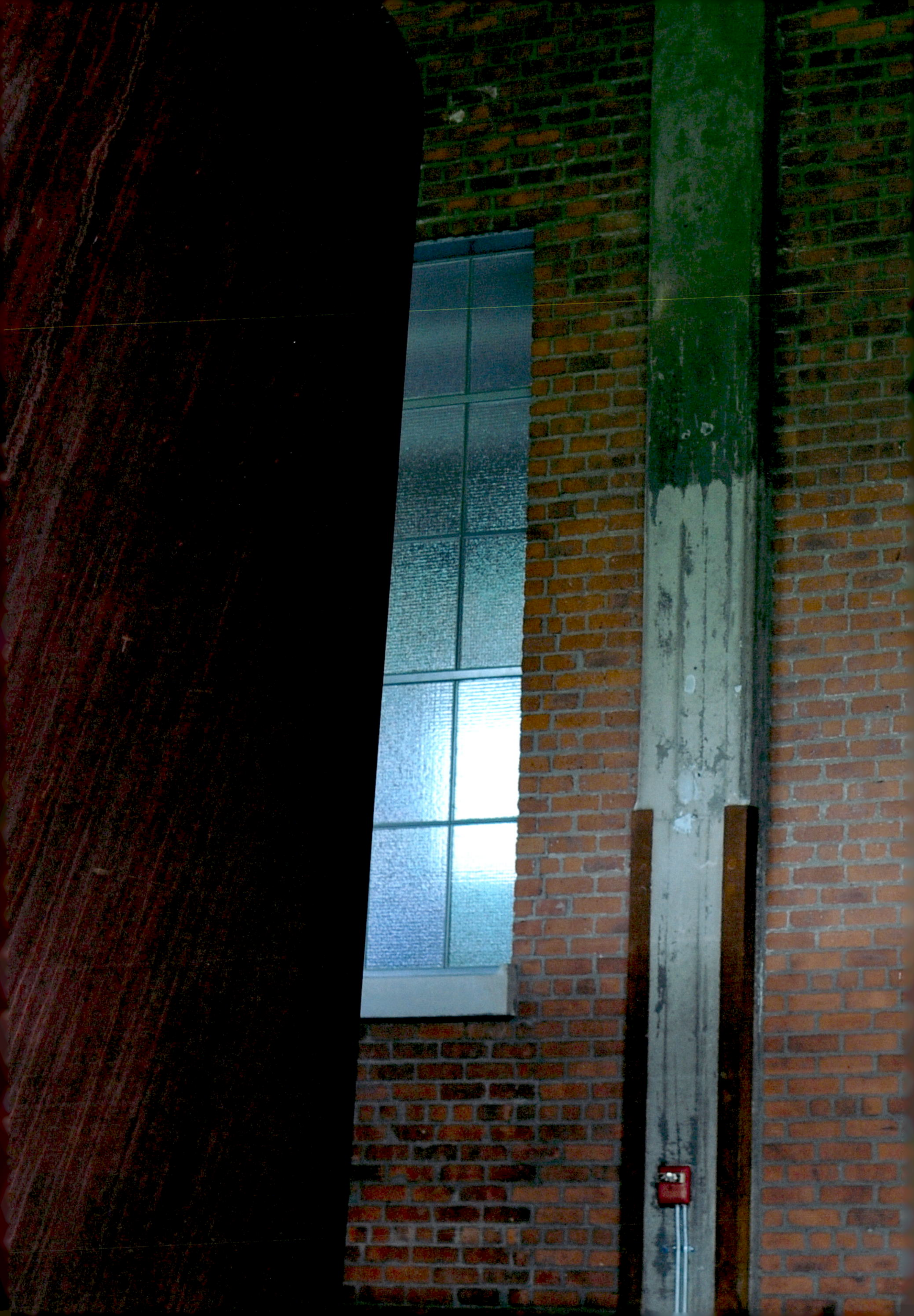

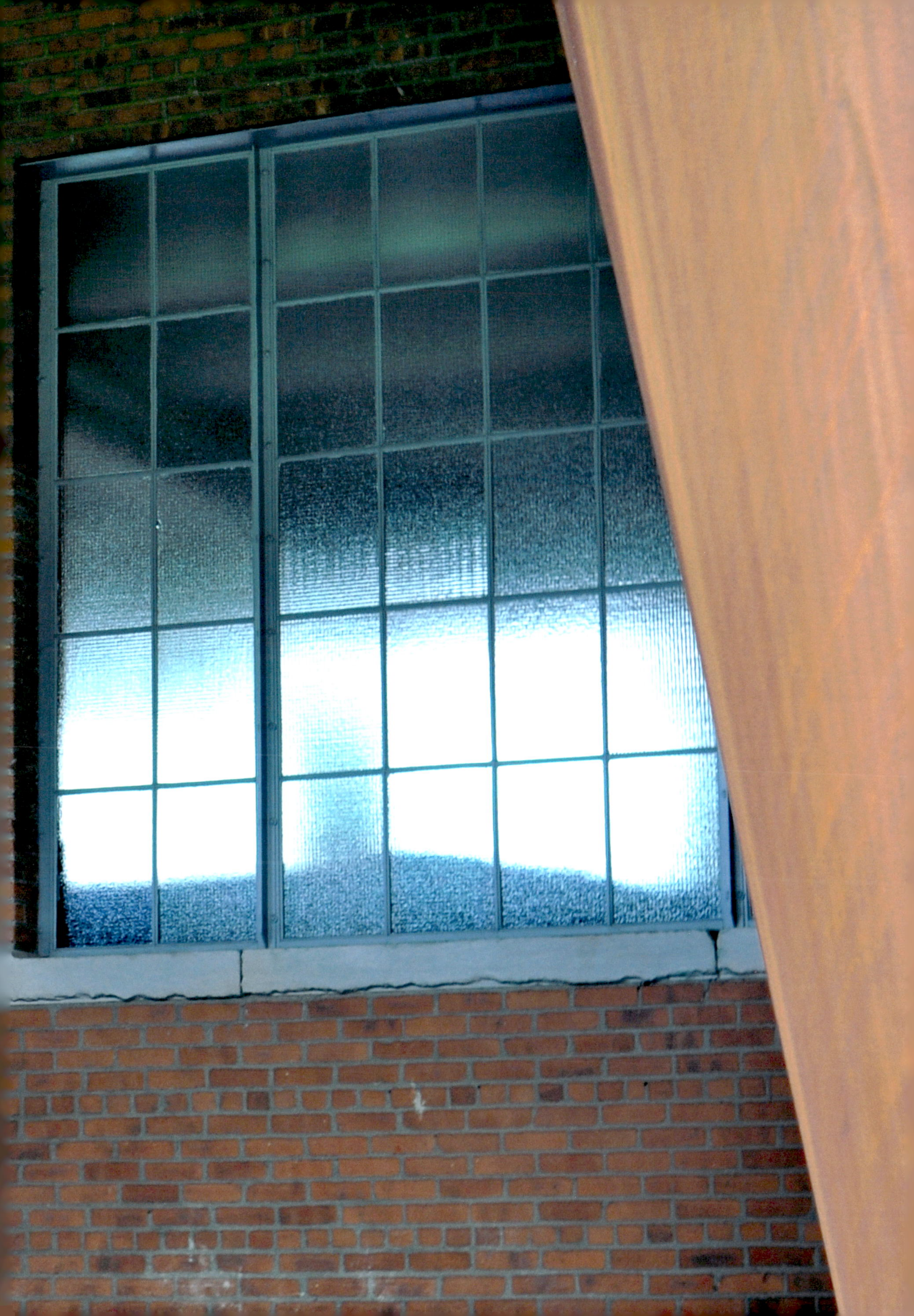

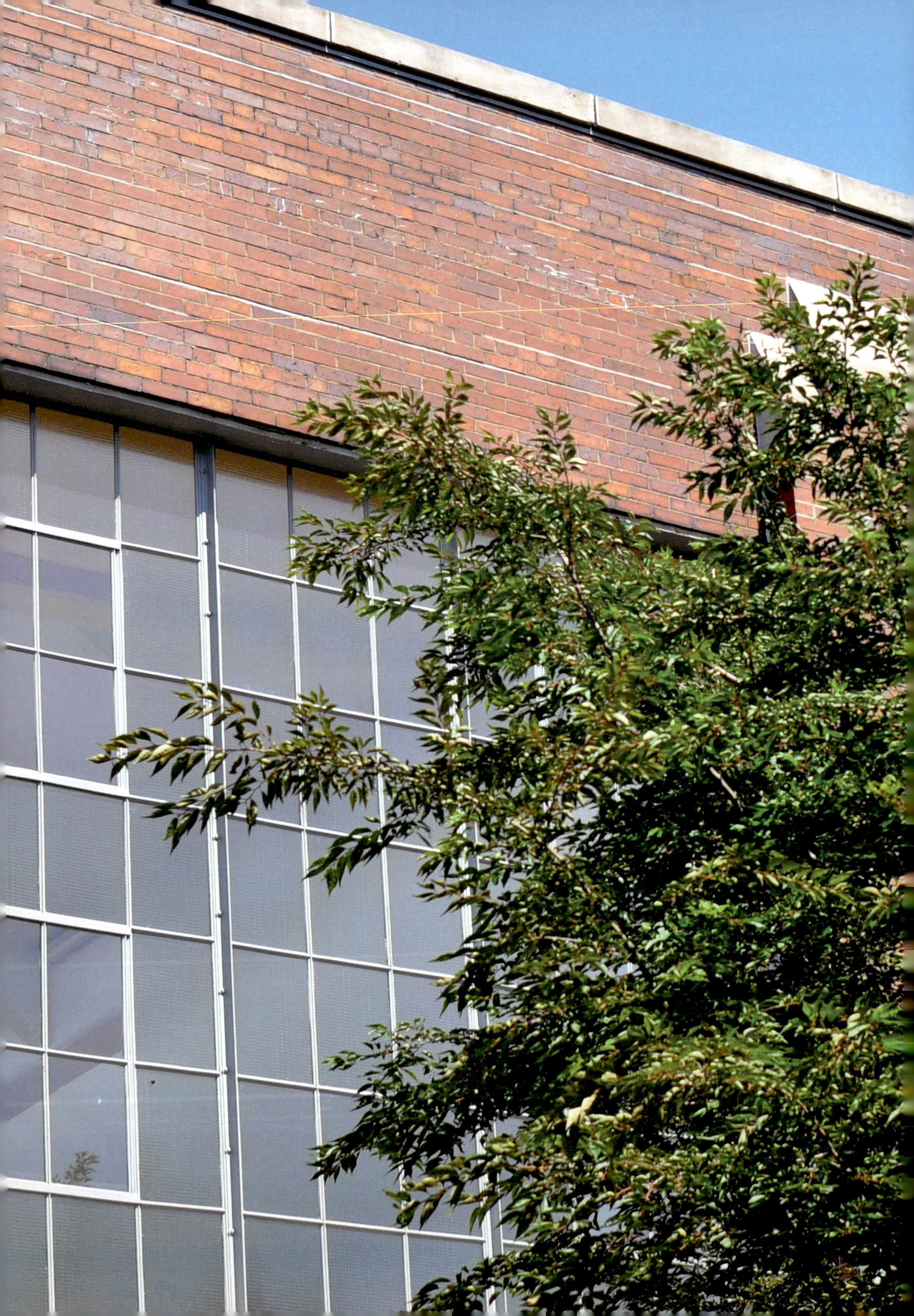

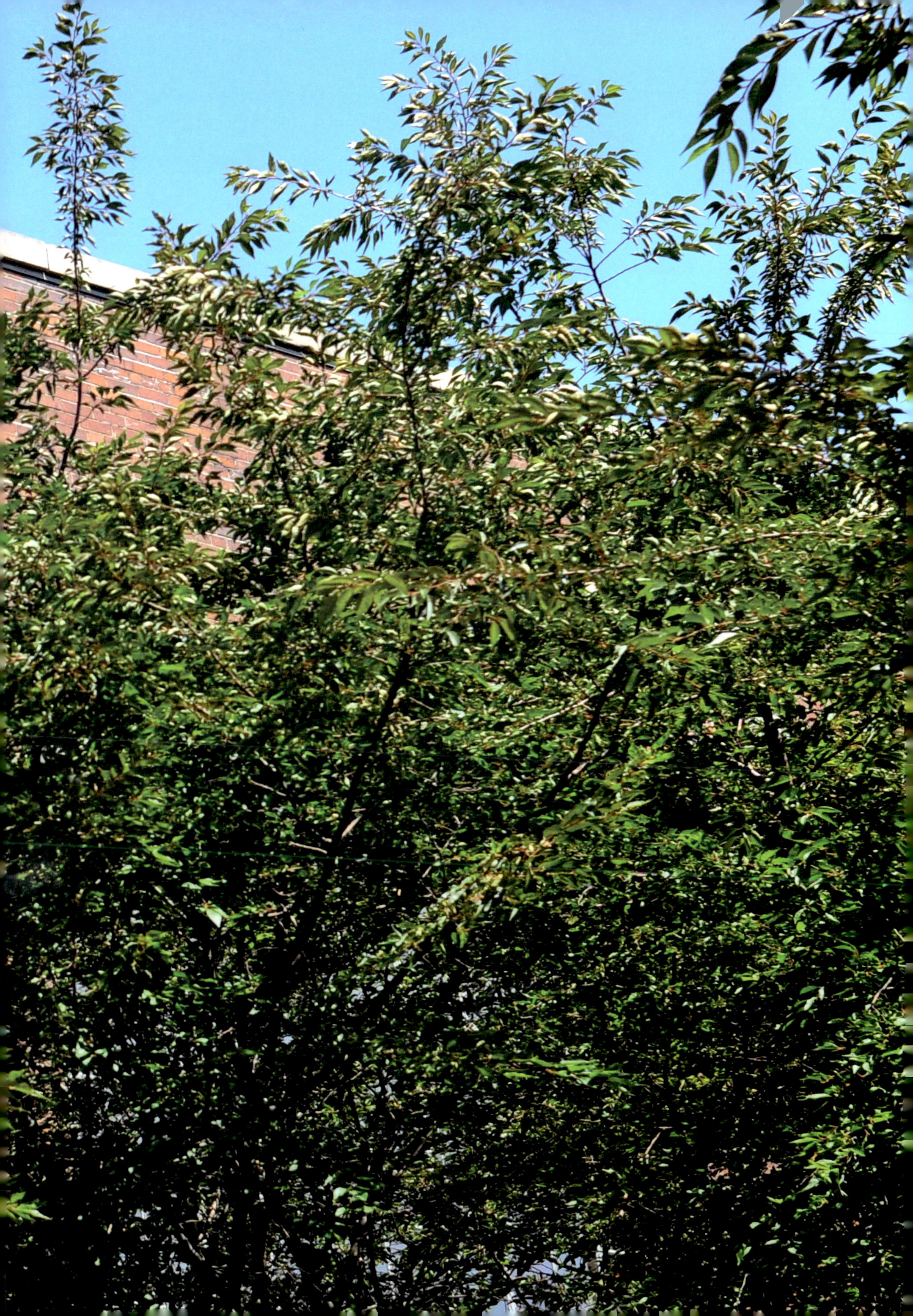

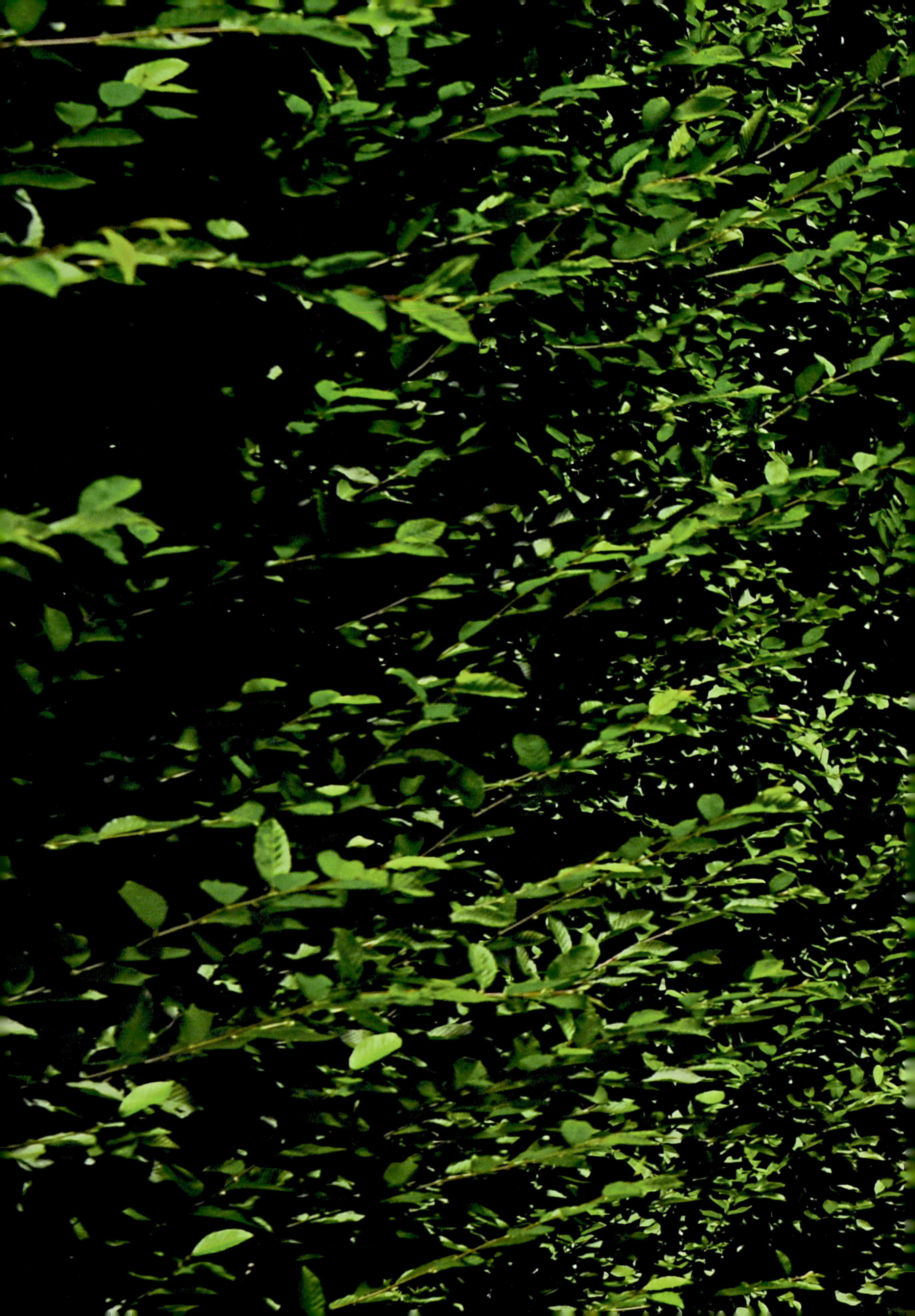

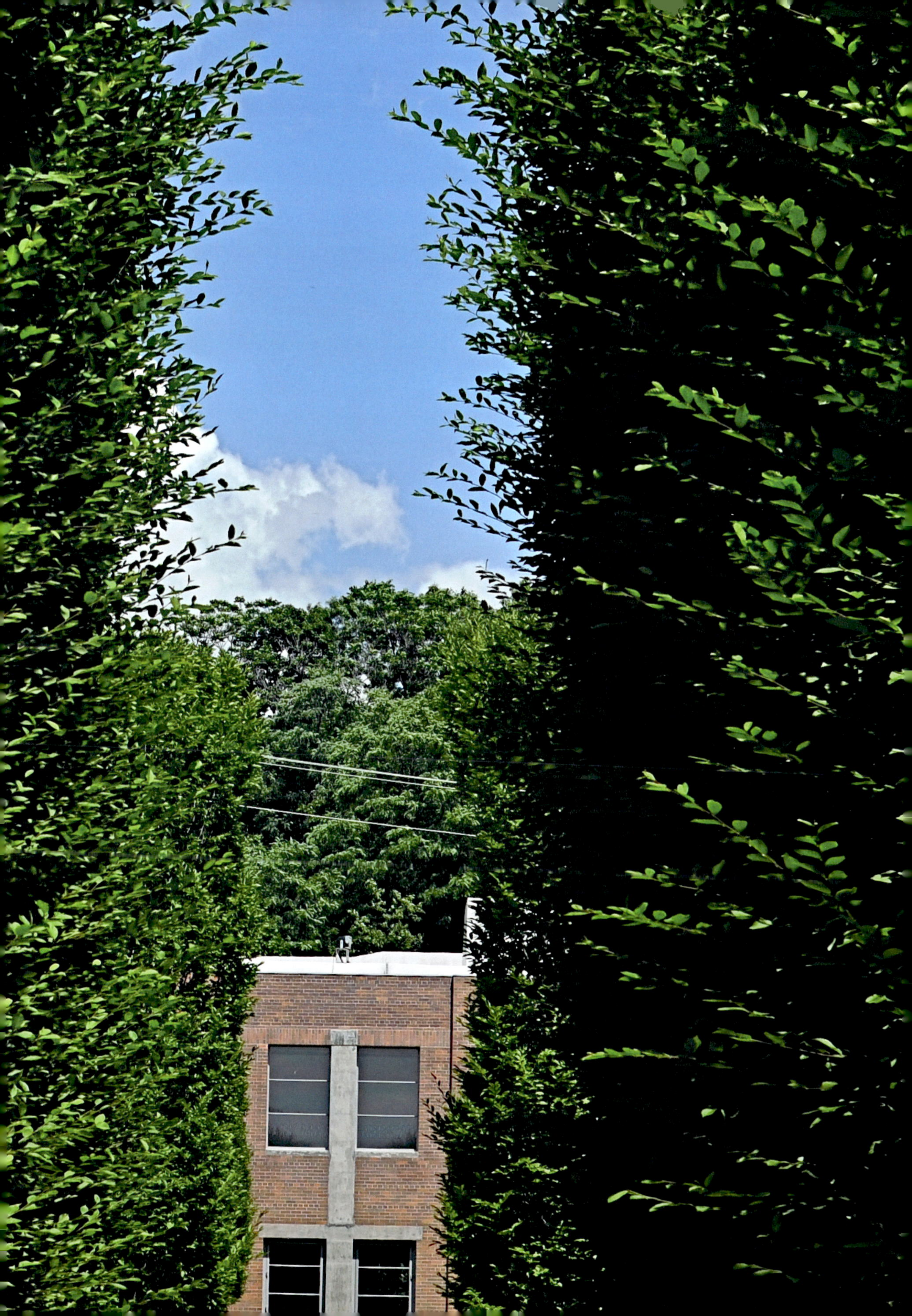

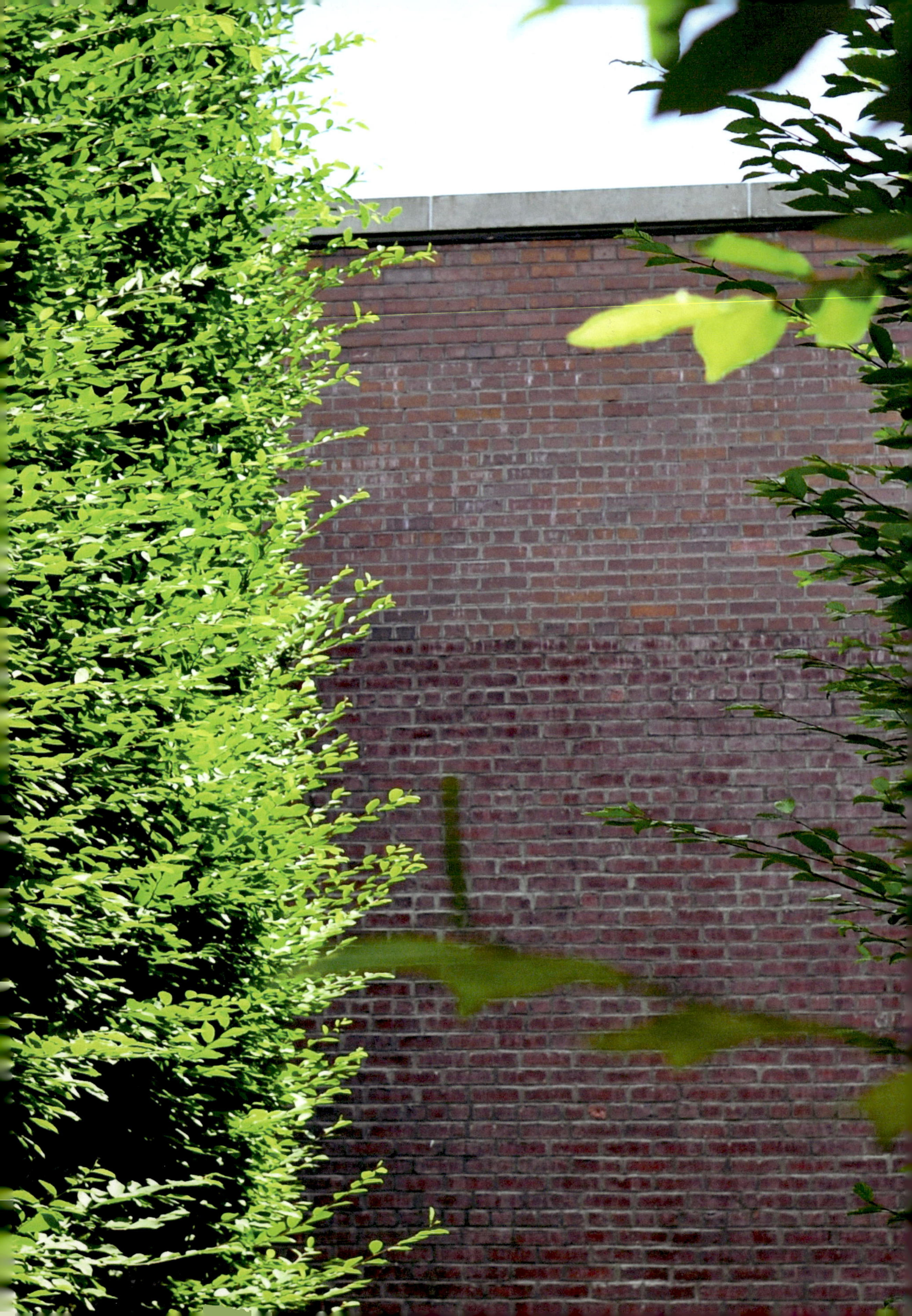

Time Piece Beacon

Extant: 2005–present
Location: Dia:Beacon, Beacon, New York
Collection Dia Art Foundation, New York

Time Piece Beacon creates a zone of subtle sound around the perimeter and in the galleries of Dia Art Foundation's museum in Beacon, New York. As each hour approaches, a low tone gradually emerges, almost imperceptibly increasing in volume; the hour is signaled by the sound's sudden cessation, creating what seems a silence in the ambient sonic environment.